MAKING INSTITUTIONS WORK IN PERU:

DEMOCRACY, DEVELOPMENT AND INEQUALITY SINCE 1980

Making Institutions Work in Peru:

Democracy, Development and Inequality since 1980

edited by

John Crabtree

British Library Cataloguing-in-Publication Data
A catalogue record for this book is available
from the British Library

ISBN   1 900039 70 2   (paperback)
         1 900039 64 8   (hardback)

INSTITUTE FOR THE STUDY OF THE
A M E R I C A S
UNIVERSITY OF LONDON · SCHOOL OF ADVANCED STUDY

Institute for the Study of the Americas
Senate House
Malet Street
London WC1E 7HU
Telephone: 020 7862 8870
Fax: 020 7862 8886
Email: americas@sas.ac.uk
Web: americas.sas.ac.uk

CONTENTS

ACKNOWLEDGEMENTS

The editor of this volume would like to thank the Warden and Fellows of St Antony's College, University of Oxford, for hosting the conference which was the basis for this book. In particular, thanks go to Rosemary Thorp, Director of the Latin American Centre at St Antony's, for her part in the conference and her suggestions with respect to the conclusions. In addition, the conference (and therefore the book) benefited from the helpful comments from Julio Faúndez (University of Warwick), Eduardo Posada-Carbó (St Antony's College, University of Oxford) and Laurence Whitehead (Nuffield College, University of Oxford). The conference and book owe much the financial support received from the Asociación Cultural Peruana-Británica, the Department for International Development (DFID), the British Embassy in Lima and the Foreign and Commonwealth Office (FCO) in London. Finally, thanks also go to Carolina Aguilera and Rose Marie Vargas for their help with translation.

CONTRIBUTORS

John Crabtree is a research associate at the Latin American Centre at Oxford University and senior member of Saint Antony's College. He is the author of numerous books on Peru and Bolivia, including *Peru under García: An Opportunity Lost* (Macmillan, 1992), *Fujimori's Peru: the Political Economy* (co-edited with Jim Thomas, ILAS, 1998), *Towards Democratic Viability: the Bolivian Experience* (co-edited with Laurence Whitehead, Palgrave, 2001) and *Patterns of Protest: Politics and Social Movements in Bolivia* (LAB, 2005).

Eduardo Dargent is a lawyer, and holds an MA in Political Philosophy from the University of York. Currently he is studying for a doctorate in the Department of Government at the University of Texas, Austin. He has worked as a researcher on justice issues at the Comisión Andina de Juristas, where he was involved in projects on judicial reform in the Andean region, due process and the Defensoría del Pueblo, and methods to reduce judicial corruption.

Paulo Drinot is a lecturer in history at the University of Manchester. He completed his doctorate at Oxford University in 2000, and has taught at both Oxford and Leeds Universities. He is co-editor (with Leo Garofalo) of a book *Mas allá de la dominación y la resistencia: estudios de historia peruana*, published in Lima by the Instituto de Estudios Peruanos. He has published articles on Peruvian social history in several journals. Currently he is researching the history of prostitution in Lima.

Francisco Durand is senior lecturer in the Politics Department at the University of Texas, San Antonio. He has a PhD from the University of California at Berkeley. He has published widely on business and politics in Peru, both within Peru and internationally. He has been a consultant for the IDB, CIAT and DAI. Between 1992 and 1994, he took part in the reform of the Peruvian tax authority (SUNAT).

Fernando Eguren is president of the Centro Peruano de Estudios Sociales (CEPES) and director of the journal Debate Agrario. He studied sociology at the University of Louvain and undertook postgraduate research at the Ecole Pratique des Hautes Etudes in Paris and at the San

Marcos University in Lima. He is a past president of the Seminario Permanente de Investigación Agraria (SEPIA), and is currently a member of its board of directors.

Pedro Francke is a researcher and consultant on poverty and social policy. He holds a masters in economics from the Catholic University, Lima, where he is currently a lecturer in the Economics Faculty. He was formerly executive director of the Fondo Nacional de Compensación y Desarrollo (Foncodes), technical secretary to the Comisión Interministerial de Asuntos Sociales and executive secretary of the Comité Interministerial de Cooperación Internacional. His published works include books on educational spending and the poor, individual targeting, geographic targeting, rural poverty, reasons for lack of educational attainment, targeting in health spending, growth and poverty, the measurement of poverty, strategies for fighting poverty and health policy.

Carlos Monge holds a PhD in history from the University of Miami. He has been a researcher at the Centro de Estudio Rurales Andinos Bartolomé de las Casas and at the Centro Peruano de Estudios Sociales (CEPES). He has also been a researcher at the North-South Center at the University of Miami and lecturer in anthropology at the Catholic University in Lima. Currently, he works as head of communications at the Grupo Propuesta Ciudadana.

Fernando Rospigliosi is a sociologist, journalist and political analyst. He works currently at the Instituto de Estudios Peruanos (IEP) where he published *El consumo tradicional de la hoja de coca en el Perú* (IEP, 2004). During the Toledo administration he was twice minister of the interior, and once head of the Consejo Nacional de Inteligencia. He has written widely on democratisation in Latin America.

José Tavara is senior lecturer and academic director of the economics faculty of the Catholic University, Lima. He holds a PhD from the University of Massachusetts, Amherst. He is a member of the managing council of OSIPTEL and the Consejo Consultivo de Radio y Televisión. He has been president of the Consorcio de Investigación Económica y Social, as well as vice-minister for communications. He has worked in the Defensoría del Pueblo and has been senior economist at Macroconsult. He has published on local development, competition policy and regulatory reform in Peru.

Richard Webb is an economist, international consultant and director of the centre for economics research at the Universidad San Martín de Porres, Lima. He holds a PhD from the University of Harvard. He has been president of the Peruvian Central Bank (BCRP) on two occasions (1980–86 and 2001–03) and professor at a number of US and Peruvian universities. He has authored several books, among them *Government Policy and the Distribution of Income in Peru (1963–1973)* (Harvard University Press, 1974) and *The World Bank: Its First Half Century* (Brookings Institution, 1997).

Coletta Youngers is an independent consultant and senior fellow at the Washington Office on Latin America (WOLA). She is the author of *Violencia política y sociedad civil en el Perú* (IEP, 2003). As an analyst of human rights, political development and US policy towards the Andean region, she has written and published widely. She is co-editor (with Eileen Rosin) of *Drugs and Democracy in Latin America: Their Impact on US Policy* (Lynne Rienner, 2004).

Introduction

The publication of this book on institutions and institutional weaknesses in Peru coincided with the election campaign to choose a successor to President Alejandro Toledo. It seemed an appropriate moment to stand back and reflect, not just on Toledo's term as president (which began in 2001) but on the broader agenda for building a polity at once more democratic and inclusive. In a country of such extreme social inequality, such an aspiration represents an enormous challenge. An election campaign provided a timely opportunity to analyse the process of institutional change and to look back at what had (or had not) been achieved in the past. Such reflections enrich the policy debate. However, looking to the future, the issues broached by the book will remain ones of key concern for years to come. This book, therefore, seeks to widen the time horizons over which such issues are normally discussed.

The sudden collapse of the Fujimori regime, which had dominated Peru throughout the 1990s, provided an important opportunity for institutional reform and rebuilding. The so-called 'Vladivideos' had laid bare to all those with access to television the way in which the country had been governed over the previous ten years, with power concentrated in the hands of two individuals — President Alberto Fujimori and his 'security advisor' Vladimiro Montesinos — who had used corruption and manipulation to accumulate and retain power at the expense of institutionalised practices of government. Fujimori's resignation and flight from Peru, the result of a sequence of events caused by the screening of the first of many such videos, helped generate a widespread consensus on the need not just to revert to a system whereby government is subject to rules but to improve those rules in ways that would enhance the quality of Peruvian democracy.

Fujimori's tempestuous resignation as president at the end of 2001 was therefore one of those rather rare moments in Peruvian history when a widespread consensus emerged on the need to move forward and to build anew. The interim administration of Valentín Paniagua, which lasted barely eight months, saw a flurry of new initiatives across a range of different areas of governance. It was a sort of Lima 'spring', a time of considerable creativity in public policy, oriented by a desire to create a more equitable and responsive relationship between the state and society, government and citizen, between the country's rulers and the ruled. This reforming momentum also infused the beginning of the government of Toledo, which took office in July 2001. It seemed that a new page had been turned.

The impetus proved short-lived. The political difficulties that ensnared the new government, many of them of its own making, undermined its capacity to act. The mood of optimism swiftly turned into one of cynicism, as the new president's popularity sank to levels previously unplumbed in the country's recent history. The reforming dynamic was thus swiftly lost, although in some spheres it lasted longer than in others, and the experience of these years was not altogether negative. The public support for Peru's democratic institutions continued to haemorrhage, calling into question once again their legitimacy. The enormous differences of economic power in a liberalised economy reflected themselves in the asymmetries of political influence.

The election of a new government in 2006, therefore, represented a fresh opportunity to take stock and to reflect on the way the lessons of the previous five-year period fitted into longer-term historical trends This book, it is hoped, will contribute to that process of learning and reflection. One of its guiding assumptions is that the challenges of institutional development run very deep, and are not peculiar to one government in particular. Another is that institutions need to be interpreted broadly, exploring the linkages between the actors on the stage of public policy at any one time and the legacy of norms, practices and assumptions which constitute the framework in which they operate.

This raises pertinent questions about how much can be achieved through institutional reform as opposed to deeper transformations, and the extent to which the former is a necessary precondition for the latter. Institutional change in Peru therefore has to be seen as part of a much wider process of transformation from an oligarchic society with relatively little public participation to one where the old order is progressively challenged by new participants demanding that their voices be heard and interests respected.

In many senses, the Velasco era in the 1970s saw old institutions and practices abolished or modified, but the period since then has yet to create a definitive new institutionality that reflects more democratic norms. In some respects, the new institutional architecture is more socially polarising than what existed previously. It is, therefore, perhaps unsurprising that attempts to engineer democratising political reforms have failed to resonate with public opinion. Reaching a degree of consensus in society over what needs to be done has proved elusive.

The challenges facing a new administration in the years after 2006 seemed great indeed. It was therefore with these in mind that the Latin American Centre of the University of Oxford decided in 2004 to convene a conference to discuss problems of institutional development. The conference took place over two days in February 2005 at St Antony's College in Oxford. Those invited to give papers were asked to consider the institutional record in various spheres, political and economic, underlining the importance of history. Rather than give a snapshot of the present, they were asked to analyse the underlying dynamics at work. We also wanted them to consider these problems both from an academic standpoint and a more practical perspective. Most of those who came to Oxford therefore combined proven academic prowess with ample experience in public policy. That everyone invited came all the way to Oxford, many from Peru itself, was testament to their belief in the importance of the subject. The conference helped to generate powerful synergies between the topics and approaches taken, which this book has endeavoured to capture. The world of institutions does not divide up into neat compartments that exist in isolation. The conference also provided an opportunity for frank and open discussion, both on the conference floor and on the sidelines. The book tries to reflect that spirit of reflection and openness.

The book opens with a historical overview from Paulo Drinot which seeks to define what we mean by institutions and how these fit into a wider compass of norms and value systems. The first section contains three chapters related mainly to political institutions. The first, by John Crabtree, takes up the topic of political parties and mediation, and seeks to explain some of the difficulties involved in establishing robust representative institutions. The second, by Carlos Monge, focuses on decentralisation and the difficulties in changing the centralised system of decision-making that has evolved in Peru. The third, by Fernando Rospigliosi, looks at the obstacles in the way of reform of the security apparatus: the military, the police and the intelligence services. The next section broaches issues of poverty, inequality and trends within agrarian society. Pedro Francke looks at the institutional developments of the Fujimori years as they related to social problems and the legacy of top-down clientelism that they engendered, while Fernando Eguren looks at institutions and actors in rural Peru, where poverty is most pronounced, from the agrarian reform onwards, focusing on new property rights. The third section takes up the problems of the justice system, both within the judiciary itself and in relation to human rights violation. Eduardo Dargent explains why it has proved so difficult to achieve a judicial system that serves the wider society, while Coletta Youngers examines the role of non-state institutions, like the Coordinadora Nacional de Derechos Humanos, in placing what was once a taboo subject at the centre of political debate. The last section shifts the focus towards the relationship between the public and private sectors in a liberalised economy. Francisco Durand looks at the inequalities of economic power and influence as a consequence of liberalisation and privatisation. José Távara examines the development of regulatory institutions, their strengths and shortcomings. Richard Webb considers some of the issues involved in the financing of institutional development. Finally, the book concludes with some reflections on future challenges and the obstacles in the way of building institutions that are at once solid, democratic and inclusive.

1

Nation-building, Racism and Inequality: Institutional Development in Peru in Historical Perspective

Paulo Drinot

This book focuses on institutional development in Peru over the past two decades. Such a focus is particularly timely given the dominant perception in Peru today that 'institutions' from the presidency and (*a fortiori*) the congress to the media, from the judiciary to the armed forces, and from the business community to the trade union sector, have lost practically all legitimacy in the eyes of the average Peruvian. Such a degree of illegitimacy is particularly worrying given that, as the other chapters in the book attest, most of these institutions have undergone profound (and in a few cases positive) changes in the last two decades. Illegitimacy therefore seems to be associated not only with the functioning of institutions but also with the institutions themselves. Peruvians, it would seem, have come to expect little from their institutions and this, in part, is reflected in the widespread privatisation of state functions from below, a phenomenon that may have had more or less auspicious results — such as the *clubes de madres* — and unquestionably tragic ones — as with the proliferation of vigilante justice and instances of lynching. It is especially significant that individuals of all social classes, and not only those who can afford private security, substitute private for deficient state services. Of course, the privatisation of state functions from below occurs in tandem, and probably in part as a consequence of, the widespread privatisation of state functions from above.

Nelson Manrique has written that such developments have led high-ranking officers in the US military to conclude that Peru, with Ecuador and Bolivia, is not a viable nation-state 'for having failed to solve its most basic economic problems or to integrate as a nation'. These US experts suggest that in the next 50 years Peru will be divided in two, with the southern part of the country being occupied by Chile and the rest by Brazil.[1] Are these analyses of Peru's lack of viability as a nation-state bunk, a by-product of hurried interpretations based on questionable scholarship and politically-motivated models of 'state failure', or should scholars and activists take such prognoses seriously? Are events in southern Peru such as the 2003 riots in Arequipa or the 2004 lynching of the mayor of Ilave (Puno) evidence of the absence of state legitimacy and of Peru's impending implosion, as some argue? We do not need military hawks in the Pentagon to tell us that Peru has largely failed either to address 'basic economic problems' or about its lack of national integration. There is nothing new, sadly, about such assessments of Peru's 'failure' as a nation-state, as those who have read Manuel González Prada's speeches or the report of the Truth and Reconciliation Commission will know (Comisión de la Verdad y Reconciliación, CVR). But such assessments do point to a growing sense, both within and outside Peru, of the volatile nature of the current situation and of the need to address it.

On Institutions: Defining what we Mean

It has become a commonplace, in the academic and in the policy worlds, that institutions 'matter'. The New Institutional Economics (NIE), consecrated by two Nobel prize-winners (Ronald Coase and Douglass North), has provided an important corrective to neoclassical economics. Economic historians, who had struggled to explain differences in economic development with the models of neoclassical economics, were quick to embrace the NIE. Institutions, many economic historians concluded, were at the root of economic divergence, and, above all, explain the 'rise of the West' and the relative stagnation of other parts of the world. But, although institutional explanations of economic divergence are a marked improvement on neoclassical economics, they are no panacea. As Kenneth Sokoloff and Stanley Engerman point out, 'ascribing differences in development to differences in institutions raises the challenge of explaining where the differences in institutions come from' (2000, p. 218).[2] Too often NIE approaches have resulted in somewhat simplistic 'culturalist' (and ahistorical) explanations that have focused, for example, on how 'British' institutions were more conducive to economic growth than 'Spanish' institutions, thus accounting for the divergence between the United States and

Latin America.[3] More recently, a number of studies of Asia have shown that the West was not as exceptional as once thought: similar institutional frameworks (governing property rights, say), existed elsewhere prior to the West's industrial take-off and, as such, cannot by themselves account for the divergence (Pomeranz, 2000).[4]

In the international policy world, the Washington Consensus is being replaced by 'post-Washington consensuses' and 'new meta-narratives' which emphasise 'the quality of institutions underpinning markets, and also voice and partnership in the governance of states' and 'a strong focus on social exclusion and human rights, to set alongside the commitment to poverty reduction' (Maxwell, 2005). This shift is a product of the growing acceptance that 'as Adam Smith knew and the new 'institutional' economics rightly stresses, economic activity does not take place within an ethical and cultural vacuum; the market is neither amoral nor anomic' (Knight, 1999, p. 125). However, the reasons for this shift probably have more to do with the poor record of neoliberal policies in promoting growth than with the influence of academic debate on policy-makers (Chang, 2003, pp. 5–6). Moreover, the growing attention to institutions does not necessarily represent a challenge to the politics of the Washington Consensus, since it is usually assumed that there are 'good' and 'bad' institutions and that 'the 'good' institutions are essentially those that are to be found in developed countries, especially the Anglo-American ones. The key institutions include democracy, 'good' bureaucracy, an independent judiciary, strongly protected private property rights (including intellectual property rights), transparent and market-oriented corporate governance and financial institutional, including a political independent central bank' (Chang, 2002).

Institutions matter, but by themselves they probably explain less than the NIE suggests and their trumpeting, like everything else in the policy world, is a product of a broader political agenda. Yet, the NIE does provide conceptual insights that can help us better to address the challenges that Peru faces vis-à-vis institutional development. For the purposes of this discussion about institutions, the distinction established by the NIE between institutions and organisations seems particularly useful. As Douglass North suggests:

> Institutions are the rules of the game — both formal rules and informal constraints (conventions, norms of behaviour and self-

imposed codes of conduct) — and their enforcement characteristics. Together they define the way the game is played.
Organizations are the players. They are made up of groups of
individuals held together by some common objectives. Economic
organizations are firms, trade unions, cooperatives, etc.; political
organizations are political parties, legislatures, regulatory bodies;
educational organizations are universities, schools, vocational
training centers (North, undated).

While North's definition of organisations is straightforward, his definition of institutions is more suggestive. Indeed, there are clear echoes in
this formulation of Gramsci's concept of hegemony, of Foucault's concept of biopower, of Bourdieu's concept of habitus, and indeed of
Philip Corrigan and Derek Sayers' concept of the 'cultural revolution',
'an enormous transformation of social identities, dispositions, and
meanings produced by the 'forms, routines, and rituals' of state-making'
(Silverblatt, 2004, p. 12). Closer to home, there are echoes of Aníbal
Quijano's concept of the coloniality of power, which proceeds through
'the "naturalisation" of institutions and categories which order power
relations imposed by the conquerors/dominators [on the
conquered/dominated]' (Quijano, 2000, p. 379). All these concepts
point to the importance of the 'normalisation' of ideas and behaviour
in explaining how societies are hierarchically structured.

    While not wildly original, the NIE's conceptualisation of institu-
tions and the distinction it introduces between institutions and organisations is useful for the purposes of this book. Naturally, both institutions and organisations are worthy of study in the Peruvian context.
But we should be alert to the distinction, and be careful not to restrict
our assessment of Peru's 'institutional development' in the last 20 years
simply to an examination of the development of 'organisations'. As
North notes, 'if the highest rate of return in an economy comes from
piracy we can expect that the organizations will invest in skills and
knowledge that will make them better pirates' (North, undated, p. 8).
This would suggest that if efforts at institutional development in Peru
are aimed at sinking pirate ships without addressing the institutional
structure that rewards piracy, then little progress will be made. In other
words, although we should pay attention to organisations such as political parties, the forces of order or the judiciary we must also pay atten-

tion to the institutions, hegemonic practices and normalised ideas and behaviour that shape these organisations.

The primacy of institutions does not mean that attempts to reform organisations, a task that a number of contributors to this book are or have been directly involved in, is futile in the absence of a transformation of the underlying institutional structure. As John Harris, Janet Hunter and Colin Lewis have suggested, 'while it may be argued that to a large extent growth is institutionally path determined, agents being conditioned by prevailing cultural norms and possibly deflected from behaviour that is optimal or maximising, this does not preclude individual organisations acting for institutional change' (Harris, Hunter and Lewis, 1995, p. 6). To focus on reforming organisations rather than institutions may therefore be inevitable. Trying to alter underlying institutions in the short to medium term may be hugely difficult, and it may even require the prior reform of organisations, such as the education system, for an institutional reform to succeed. Institutional reform may thus be impossible without prior organisational reform. But it is apparent that the successful pursuit of organisational reform would benefit from (indeed, requires) a better understanding of the institutional structure, of the normalised ideas and behaviour that shape Peruvian society, and of how that normalisation affects the functioning of organisations and Peruvians' perceptions of them.

The importance of addressing Peru's institutional structure is borne out by the conclusions of the Truth and Reconciliation Commission.[5] As the report of the commission indicates, although Sendero Luminoso and Peru's armed forces were directly responsible for the country's recent violent past, that violence was made possible and exacerbated by the underlying political, economic and social exclusion that shapes Peruvian society. The report laid bare the rotten pillars of Peruvian society like no other analysis, pointing to the 'normalised ideas and behaviour' that underpinned both the violent actions of Sendero Luminoso and of the armed forces and the indifference of Peru's 'included' few to the predicament of the 'excluded' many. This indifference, sometimes bordering on contempt, is shaped by and shapes the deep inequalities that characterise Peruvian society — inequalities that are themselves produced and perpetuated by racism. In this chapter, then, I suggest that in order to assess recent institutional development and the need for institutional reform in a society that largely fails to address the 'basic economic problems' of Peruvians or their lack of national integration, it is essential to take seriously the normalised ideas and behaviour that shape state and civil society organisations. In particular, I argue that we need to be attentive to how racism is embedded in Peruvian society, how it shapes policy (particularly development policy), how it is reproduced by a series of organisations, and, why, in light of this, many Peruvians feel that they can expect next to nothing from them.

Inequality and Patterns of Development: Peru and Latin America

Recent studies of Latin America stress that inequality has negative consequences not only for democratic consolidation but also for economic development. In a post-Washington Consensus context, the need to address inequality as an obstacle to development is again on the agenda and it is increasingly accepted that the reduction of income inequalities would have a positive impact on poverty reduction: one study suggests that if levels of inequality in Latin America were similar to those in OECD countries, poverty in the region would be reduced by two-thirds (Justino, Litchfield and Whitehead 2003, p. 9). The concentration of power in a few hands, these studies suggest, produces a vicious cycle, in which 'poverty and high levels of inequality impede growth, and growth rates are subsequently too low to adequately address the problems of poverty and inequality'. This cycle is 'perpetuated and exacerbated through the normal functioning (or non-functioning) of political institutions' (Karl, 2003, pp. 135–6). Interestingly, these studies of contemporary patterns by political scientists and development economists echo the findings of economic historians Stanley Engerman and Kenneth Sokoloff (2000), who have recently pointed to the importance of inequality in explaining long-run economic divergence between the United States and Latin America.[6]

According to Sokoloff and Engerman, the initial factor endowments that characterised Peru and Mexico — rich mineral resources and abundant labour — led, as in the Caribbean, to 'extremely unequal distributions of wealth and income', in contrast to the colonies north of the Chesapeake River, where natural and human factor endowments led to the development of a society based on relatively equal independent proprietors. Initial factor endowments, therefore, 'predisposed [each region] towards paths of development associated with different degrees of inequality in wealth, human capital and political power'. However, Sokoloff and Engerman go on to suggest, this ecological predisposition to inequality in Latin America was enhanced by 'government policies and other institutions': 'in those societies that began with extreme inequality, elites were better able to establish a legal framework that insured them disproportionate shares of political power, and to use that greater influence to establish rules, laws and other government policies that advantaged members of the elite relative to non-members — contributing to the persistence over time of the high degree of inequality' (2000, p. 223). By restricting broad access to economic opportunities, Sokoloff and Engerman conclude, 'this path of institutional development may in turn have affected growth' (2000, p. 228).

These studies point to the need to reassess Peruvian development strategies. The current economic orthodoxy in Peru holds that economic growth, fuelled by exports of raw materials and agricultural commodities, will produce economic benefits that will 'trickle down' to the poor. This has been the dominant, if not the only, 'development' model in Peru since the mid-nineteenth century.[7] It is especially striking that the current orthodoxy echoes Sokoloff and Engerman's characterisation of Peru's initial factor endowments, i.e. rich mineral resources and abundant labour. Because of technological change, abundant labour is no longer as important as it was when the Indian *mita* in the highlands of Arequipa, Cuzco and Puno provided much of the labour force for the Potosí and other mines. Nevertheless, the Washington Consensus policies introduced in the 1990s and continued by the Toledo administration have served to re-establish abundant and cheap labour as a characteristic of the Peruvian economy, by subduing the labour movement and rolling back the social and economic rights that workers had won from employers in the course of the twentieth century (Baer, 2002). To be fair, in the early years of the new millennium economic growth was fairly high. But it remains to be seen whether it is sustainable (driven as it is largely by high commodity prices that result from very specific conditions). Meanwhile, there is already plenty of evidence to show that hardly any 'trickle down' was taking place. As Pedro Francke has noted, 'employment grew by a mere 2.6 per cent in 2004 and wages and salaries on average did not rise at all (zero), while the caloric deficit (a measure of malnutrition) of urban families in Peru rose from 26 per cent to 29 per cent'.[8]

Peru's increasing dependence on mineral exports as the engine of economic growth and its failure to invest in human capital seem bound to make it repeat the mistakes of the past (Thorp and Zevallos, 2002). By not addressing problems of inequality, this development strategy was unlikely seriously to reduce poverty levels. Meanwhile, failure to reduce poverty further enhances inequality, thus starting anew a vicious cycle of heightened social and political tensions. The question that needs to be addressed, therefore, is why this model of development, which does so little to address Peru's poverty and inequality, has been so dominant in Peruvian history. To put it another way, why is it so diffi-cult to imagine and implement development strategies that are more equitable? As I suggest below, institutions are an important part of the answer. Initial factor endowments, as Sokoloff and Engerman suggest, may have predisposed Peru to a path of development that was based on unequal access to power, but inequality has thereafter been reproduced and justified via institutional means, i.e. via the deployment of normal-ising ideas and behaviour that, through various organisations (such as the judiciary or the education system), make inequality appear not only inevitable but, in some cases, desirable.

Explanations of Poverty and Inequality in Peru

As every Peruvian knows, Peru is a beggar sitting on a bench of gold. This characterisation, coined by the Italian 'savant' Antonio Raimondi in the nineteenth century, continues to shape many Peruvians' under-standing of their country. First imagined as a land of gold by the Spanish Conquistadors, for much of its history Peru has been imagined and represented by both Peruvians and non-Peruvians as a land of plen-ty whose abundant resources, whether gold or silver, guano or rubber, fishmeal, copper or gas, have time after time rekindled the image of Peru as El Dorado. There is little doubt that the country has been sin-gularly blessed (some would say cursed) in the commodity lottery: although principally a mining economy, its export quantum has always been varied.[9] More recently, Peru's cultural riches have been added to images of the country's wealth (witness Toledo's participation in a

Discovery Channel documentary).[10] In particular, the country's ecological and archaeological attributes are routinely exalted: Peru is a land of extreme biodiversity and cultural significance. Go to any tourism website and you will probably be told that more than 80 per cent of the world's recognised ecological zones can be found in Peru. As the cradle of both the Inca civilisation and, as recent archaeological findings seem to suggest, as the site of one of the oldest city-states in the world, Caral, Peru's cultural wealth and worth is immense.

This supposed ecological, cultural and resource-based wealth seems at odds with the fact that today of every two Peruvians one lives in poverty.[11] Indeed, although officially Peru is a 'middle income country' and boasts an 'average' Human Development Index as calculated by the United Nations Development Program (UNDP), poverty is widespread, and in some parts levels of poverty are comparable to Sub-Saharan Africa. Accordingly, international images of Peru, particularly those produced by aid agencies, tend to focus on its poverty. In a television documentary highlighting the work of Sports Relief, a British charity, broadcast by the BBC in 2004, Lima's slums were chosen alongside the AIDS ravaged villages of Zambia and the railway children of Calcutta, as an example of extreme poverty and deprivation. Victoria Beckham, ex-Spice Girl, celebrity footballer's wife and cultural ambassador in the making, spent an afternoon wading through mountains of rubbish in a poor neighbourhood of Lima with a young girl called Dina, who spends most of her day looking for bits of metal or glass to be sold to recycling plants. Mrs Beckham was moved to remark that Dina's poverty had forced her to reconsider her own wealth, to 'put things into perspective', perhaps in order to reassure the viewers that at least one person's life would be changed by the experience.[12]

These contrasting images of Peru, a land of natural and cultural wealth and of human poverty, have underscored numerous attempts since the late nineteenth century at forming a coherent interpretation of Peru's history and of Peruvian society. The question at the heart of such attempts has remained the same: how is it possible that such a potentially rich country is so poor? Although there have been many attempts to provide an answer, two interpretations have prevailed until recently. On the one hand, Peru's failure to realise its potential has been blamed on the country's mainly indigenous and mestizo population. For some, such as early twentieth-century positivists and racists like Alejandro Deustua and Clemente Palma or modern-day novelists and former presidential hopefuls like Mario Vargas Llosa, Peru has been held back by a population that is either racially degenerate or irrationally wedded to tradition (or an 'archaic utopia' based in the Andes) and averse to capitalism.[13] For others, Peru's underdevelopment is the handiwork of treacherous elites and their foreign masters. If Peru is poor it is because its natural wealth has been plundered by an oligarchy that has put its interests before those of the nation, and by an assortment of foreign exploiters, including Spanish colonial administrators, British merchants, US oil and mining companies, and more recently Spanish and Chilean multinationals, not forgetting, of course, 'el pirata' Francis Drake.

Although these interpretations have tended to be produced by scholars who stand at opposite ends of the political spectrum, they share what has been called a common 'uchronic' vision of Peruvian history, as it could have been and not as it was, which has produced an interpretation of that history as one of failure, of defeat and unrealised potential: the beggar sitting on the bench of gold (Chocano, 1987; Flores Galindo, 1988). In this sense, although the right and the left pointed to different factors to explain Peru's economic 'backwardness' and the causes of the wretchedness of Peru's population, they tended to reproduce acritically the idea that Peru's (potential) wealth resided in its natural resources while locating Peru's poverty in its indigenous population (although, naturally, the right and left blamed the poverty of the indigenous population on different factors). These days, historians of Peru, both Peruvian and foreign, have moved on from such interpretations. But the contrasting images of wealth and poverty at the centre of such interpretations remain very much present within non-academic discussions in Peru (to the extent that 'indio' and poor have become synonymous; or, to put it another way, an affluent 'indio' is inconceivable), and, I suggest, inform policy in various ways.

The image of Peru as a beggar sitting on a bench of gold has proved enduring because it alludes to Peru's potential riches: the bench of gold represents Peru's natural wealth, its varied natural resource endowment, its El Dorado, and more recently it has come to mean also other forms of wealth, including Peru's potential as a tourist destination thanks to its ecological and archaeological/historical attributes. In this sense, the image is a source of national pride. But the image has also endured (although this is less often recognised) because it illustrates Peru's predicament as formulated by Peru's elites at various moments in the country's history. According to this view, Peru sits on a bench of gold but is incapable of using that gold in order to transform itself from a beggar into a king.[14] The beggar, which represents a Peru that is handicapped by the nature of its population, cannot properly exploit the country's riches because, like Peru's indigenous masses, he is dirty, ignorant, dependent on others, as well as devious and untrustworthy. In this sense, the image is a source of national disgrace. In sum, the image locates Peru's wealth in its natural resources and its poverty in its people while at the same time representing Peru's population as incapable of using that wealth to raise itself out of poverty.

The image of the beggar sitting on the bench of gold points to how ideas about the sources of wealth and poverty in Peru are intimately linked to ideas about the character of Peru's predominantly indigenous and mestizo population. It illustrates the highly racialised character of development thinking in Peru. In brief, I am suggesting that ideas about the location and sources of wealth and poverty in Peru, shaped by the deep racism that pervades Peruvian society, rather than, say, changing commodity prices, account for the character of the development strategies pursued by Peruvian governments since the mid-nineteenth century, strategies that have focused almost exclusively on the exploitation of natural resources (and, more recently, cultural resources) with minimal investment in developing the capabilities and freedoms, to draw on Amartya Sen's terminology, of Peru's population. These ideas point to the difficulties in imagining and formulating development strategies that centre on the development of human capital since, in its most extreme but not unusual formulation, racism in Peru questions the very humanity of the indigenous population. In a sense, then, Peru's dominant 'development' model, much like — as the Truth and Reconciliation Commission's report suggests — the violence that engulfed Peru during the 1980s and early 1990s, can be seen as an expression of the inequalities structured by racism that have characterised Peruvian history.[15]

Racism and National Identity

Ideas about racial difference have been central to nation-building throughout Latin America and not least in Peru (Appelbaum,

Macpherson and Rosemblatt, 2003). Racism in Peru must be traced back to the sixteenth century and to the Spanish Conquest of the Inca Empire, which produced a colonial society based on a system of *castas*, both 'ethnic' and legal entities.[16] The system of *castas* placed Peru's indigenous and Afro-Peruvian populations at the bottom of the social/racial ladder, although it implicitly recognised them as constituent if subordinate members of the Spanish Empire and subjects of the Crown. This system of *castas* can itself be traced further back to the Spanish *Reconquista*, which introduced the concept of 'purity of blood' and shaped the 'mental universe' of Francisco Pizarro and his successors (Manrique, 1993; Silverblatt, 2004). The inequalities enshrined by the colonial caste system were reproduced in the republican period by other means. The process of independence in Peru, marked by a general reluctance to embrace the patriot cause among Peruvian creoles, was shaped by the fears of race war produced by the very local Tupac Amaru rebellion and the not so local Haitian Revolution (Walker, 1999; Chambers, 1999). Subsequently, republican Peru devised legal, political and socio-economic forms of exclusion that denied full citizenship to indigenous and Afro-Peruvians.

In the mid- to late nineteenth century, the scientific racism emanating from Europe helped Peruvian elites reach the conclusion that their country's largely indigenous population was unsuitable for emulating the progress achieved by European nations. This led to varied proposals put forward throughout the nineteenth and early twentieth centuries aimed at transforming the local population in order to make it suitable for 'progress'. Such proposals ranged from the systematic genocide of Peru's indigenous population to the promotion of European immigration (in order to favour the biological and cultural whitening of the population) to, in the 1930s, the development of a eugenic programme that would combine sterilisation with social engineering.[17] Echoes of such proposals can be found in Fujimori's forced sterilisation programmes of the 1990s, which targeted poor indigenous and mestizo women, and, as Nelson Manrique has noted, in the fact that even today, in some upper-class private universities, one can find the following message etched in classroom tables: '*Haga Patria, mate a un cholo*' (Be patriotic, kill a *cholo*).[18] Arguably, for some (although, clearly, not all) Peruvians, Peru's non-white populations, and particularly the indigenous population, belong, like European Jews, 'to the species of what Ancient Romans called *Homo sacer* — those who, although they were human, were excluded from the human community, which is why one can kill them with impunity' (Zizek, 2002, p. 141).[19]

However, in contrast to the United States or Argentina, in the nineteenth century the elites in Peru were not able to carry out 'nation-forming' genocidal campaigns against the indigenous population. As in Mexico, the indigenous population in Peru was simply too large for such a project to be undertaken. But in contrast to Mexico, where a syncretic mestizo identity began to form in the nineteenth century and was consolidated in the twentieth, in Peru biological *mestizaje* did not produce a cultural *mestizaje* that could form the basis for national identity.[20] Whereas *indigenismo* in early twentieth-century Mexico fed into Vasconcelos' 'cosmic race', in Peru by 1930 *indigenismo* had become a marginal movement, whose intellectual thrust in any case was too often limited to a chauvinistic exaltation of a romanticised Inca past coupled with lamentations regarding contemporary indigenous people, whose wretchedness was attributed to, if not racial degeneration, then certainly cultural backwardness (Méndez, 1996; de la Cadena, 2000). Although voices, such as that of José Carlos Mariátegui, were raised in opposition to such racist/culturalist assumptions, even Mariátegui agreed that little could be expected from Peru's indigenous masses in terms of national development. Even for radical thinkers like Mariátegui, the 'Indian problem' could only be solved through the integration of Peru's indigenous masses into a 'modern' national project, in his case a socialist one (de la Cadena, 2000; Manrique, 1999).

In the twentieth and early twenty-first centuries, these issues have been only partially overcome. Whereas most processes of nation-state formation have involved a degree of nationalisation of local populations, the classic 'peasants into Frenchmen' model, in Peru nationalisation was limited until the mid-twentieth century, when a concerted effort at extending access to education was undertaken (Contreras, 2004b). Indeed, as a number of historians suggest, what pressure for nationalisation existed prior to the mid-twentieth century tended to come from below rather than from above, as various groups including indigenous communities and women used the rhetoric of liberalism that had dominated the political lexicon since independence to negotiate and redefine their positions in Peruvian society (Thurner, 1997; Hunefeldt, 2000). Since the 1950s Peru's 'popular overflow' has created a new con-stituency of *cholo* migrants, whose increasingly important political voice largely has been expressed through non-traditional channels (Matos Mar, 1984; Stokes, 1995; Dietz, 1998) but whose demographic (and electoral) presence has had a profound impact on electoral politics to the extent that it is now impossible (as Vargas Llosa discovered in 1990) for candidates to ignore the *cholo* vote. Indeed, as Toledo demonstrated, a positive affirma-tion of *choledad* has become a key electoral asset (Quijano, 2003).

However, despite these important challenges, the political and social structure has remained largely exclusionary. If in Mexico the revolution-ary state played a key role in fostering a sense of shared nationality, in Peru the oligarchic governments of the first half of the twentieth cen-tury did precisely the opposite, reaffirming and indeed enhancing class and race divisions — divisions which were only minimally addressed by post-oligarchic governments (whether military or civilian). Until 1980 a large section of Peru's population was legally excluded from full citizen-ship through a literacy requirement in national elections, but that polit-ical exclusion was the expression of a deeper socio-economic exclusion that, in many ways, continues unabated until today. Although today the *cholo* vote is crucial, as the Toledo administration demonstrates, it is a *cholo* vote in-itself rather than for-itself, an expression of multiple indi-vidualities rather a collective vote with a *cholo* agenda. As Quijano sug-gests, 'these groups are today attracted, susceptible to be attracted, to participate not so much as citizens aiming for the democratisation of social relations and the nationalisation of the state, but rather as con-sumers and merchants in the political market'. As a consequence, 'even if *choledad* is [politically] successful, it does not free [*cholos*] from 'racial' classification in Peruvian society' (2003, p. 58).

Arguably, the Velasco 'experiment' was an attempt at a 'cultural rev-olution' from above based on the inclusion of previously excluded sec-tors of the population into a new nation-state (Portocarrero, 2003). It included a broad range of far-reaching reforms, including an agrarian reform which wiped out the traditional *sierra hacienda*, an industrial reform that produced Yugoslavian-type industrial cooperatives, an edu-cational reform and the expropriation of key foreign enterprises in oil, mining, fisheries, the print media and export agriculture. As has now been well documented, this 'experiment' was a resounding failure and by the return to democracy in 1980 the positive reforms of the 'first phase' of the military revolution had been largely scaled back thanks to an orthodox and debilitating structural adjustment (Lowenthal, 1975; McClintock and Lowenthal, 1983; Booth and Sorj, 1983). But the Peruvian experiment was a failure also in terms of political and social goals that the military reformers had set themselves. In attempting to channel the popular mobilisation that had originally prompted the generals to intervene, the revolutionary armed forces reproduced the traditional top-down vertical structures of domination of the oligarchic period. In particular, by failing to acknowledge the central role that racism played in shaping the structures of domination which they sought to remove (and — like the insurgent left-wing movements — by reducing all antagonisms to class antagonisms: witness the replacement of '*indio*' by '*campesino*' in official rhetoric), the generals did little to alter the exclusionary character of the oligarchic period (de la Cadena, 2000).

Racism, then, as a normalised idea and behaviour, is central to the exclusionary character of nation-building in Peru. As Gonzalo Portocarrero notes, racism hinders the capacity of Peruvians to 'construct a memory, a narrative that creates a national *we*, a common history through which Peruvians can recognise themselves as equal while diverse' (Portocarrero, 2003, p. 252). It is a 'discreet' or 'silent' racism (de la Cadena, 1998) precisely because it is institutional, hegemonic, legitimising, normalised. As Romeo Grompone suggests, racism in Peru 'is strengthened by what is silenced, veiled, not said and yet, at the same time, known by everyone' (2001, p. 508).[21] In sum, racism in Peru structures social hierarchies and shapes development policies because, by racialising culture and culturalising race (by making ideas of racial and cultural superiority/inferiority mutually reinforcing), it constructs the non-white 'other' (the indigenous, the mestizo, the Afro-Peruvian, the *chino*) as the depository and agent of poverty, cultural backwardness and national failure. Racism leads Peruvians to perceive socio-economic and political inequalities as both inevitable and, in some cases, desirable because, perversely, by putting everyone in his or her place, racism constructs a 'normalised' order that, given the racial and cultural aptitudes of every Peruvian, is optimal. The colonial roots of this form of racism should be evident. But this normalised order, as I have suggested, impacts negatively on both 'growth' and national integration.

Conclusions

In this chapter, I have suggested that racism, and the inequalities that racism underpins, is central to understanding the character of both nation-building and the economic development strategies pursued by successive governments since the mid nineteenth century in Peru. In this sense, I have been concerned essentially with how racism, in Douglass North's terms, helps define how the game is played. But at the same time, and here I want to recall the distinction established by the NIE between institutions and organisations, it is clear that racism is central to the ways that many organisations, both of the state and of civil society, operate in Peru. Non-state organisations, such as — to name only a couple — discotheques and employment agencies that discriminate on the grounds of *'buena presencia'* have gained some degree of notoriety and, at least in some quarters, opprobrium. But, as a number of recent sociological and anthropological studies have shown, state organisations, such as the armed forces, the education system and the public health service, also discriminate on racial grounds and, in so doing, contribute to the reproduction of racial hierarchies (as well as, it must be stressed, gender hierarchies) in Peruvian society.[22] It is therefore not surprising that most Peruvians engage in these organisations with a fair amount of suspicion and caution.

Organisations, the NIE suggests, play the game according to the rules established by the institutions. To the extent that the rules seem to be set in order to systematically discriminate against large sectors of the population, it is not surprising that many Peruvians have come to expect little from the organisations that play according to those rules. As Deborah Poole suggests:

> as anyone who has perused the legal archives of highland Peru can well imagine, many peasants would be surprised to find that legal cases can, in fact, be resolved — rather than simply archived (or closed) for reasons having to do with either private 'influence' or some seemingly arbitrary judicial time limit. Indeed, in one study conducted in the late 1980s, a vast majority of highland peasants who were or had been involved in legal cases declared that they simply did not know whether their cases had been resolved (Poole, 2004, p. 60).

In this sense, the challenge of institutional reform is great. Many Peruvians, I would suggest, perceive organisations such as the judiciary or the political parties to be illegitimate because they are inefficient and corrupt, but also, and perhaps more importantly, because they are seen to be the expression of an institutional system that they have to come understand, and for good reason, as responsible for, and dependent on, their exclusion from full citizenship. This, of course, does not mean that all attempts at institutional reform are futile. It does suggest that policies that do not address these issues are unlikely to succeed.

Notes

1 See *Peru 21*, 16 October 2004.

2 Or, as Jeremy Adelman (2001, p. 28) argues 'institutions may provide proximate explanations for economic advance or retardation. As such they are important, but they are not ultimate causes for development or retardation. These lie in the social, political and cultural fabrics in which institutions are embedded.'

3 As Sokoloff and Engerman suggest 'the case for the superiority of British institutions is usually based on the records of the United States and Canada, but the majority of the New World societies established by the British — including Barbados, Jamaica, Belize, Guyana, and the lesser-known Puritan colony on Providence Island — were like their other neighbours in not beginning to industrialise until much later' (Sokoloff and Engerman, 2000, p. 219).

4 See, however, Parthasarathi (2002) for a critique of such studies.

5 In addition to revising the number of victims from the armed conflict up to almost 70,000, the Report noted that the conflict 'reproduced in large measure the ethnic and social rifts that affect the whole of Peruvian society' (vol. VIII, p. 159). The violence of the 1980s and 1990s, the Commission concluded, superimposed itself on, and reproduced, deep class, ethnic and gender inequalities that separate those who are included from those who are excluded in the nation-state. As Salomon Lerner noted in his speech of 28 August 2003, the Commission's report reveals that Peru is 'a country where exclusion is so absolute that tens of thousands

of citizens can disappear without anyone in integrated society, in the society of the non-excluded, noticing a thing'. See http://www.cverdad.org.pe/informacion/discursos/en_ceremonias05.php.

6   This study is part of a growing literature that uses cliometric methods to attempt to isolate initial factors that may account for divergence in the Americas.

7   Peru stands out in Latin America as one of the few larger countries to have emphasised export-led growth for much of the nineteenth and twentieth centuries. There have existed alternative projects, but few of these prospered (Gootenberg, 1993). For an economist's analysis of Peru's short inward-oriented focus in the 1950s–1970s period, see Jiménez (2002).

8   Pedro Francke, 'Política económica: una reevaluación,' in *La República*, 13 February 2005.

9   On Peru's economic history, the key reference remains Thorp and Bertram (1978) but see also Sheahan (1999).

10   On the political use and misuse of Peru's tourist destinations, see López Lenci (2005).

11   For an excellent critique of how the current celebration of Peru's cultural and biological 'megadiversity' does little to address, and in some ways reinforces, the exclusion and marginalisation of large sectors of the Peruvian population, see Oliart (2004).

12   See http://www.bbc.co.uk/pressoffice/pressreleases/stories/2004/06_june/14/sport_relief.shtml.

13   For a recent analysis of the echoes in Vargas Llosa's narrative of nineteenth-century racist thought, see Denegri (2003), López Maguina (2003) and Vich (2002). See also Mayer (1991). For how such views have 'real life' consequences, see del Pino (2003).

14   For varying formulations of this view, see, among others, Marcone (1995) and Contreras (2004b).

15   The need to take seriously the role that racism plays in development, or underdevelopment, is increasingly acknowledged by development economists. See Stewart (2002). Observers of Latin America will not be surprised to discover that countries in the region with large ethnic groups, such as Peru, are the most unequal (Justino, Litchfield and Whitehead, 2003, p. 11).

16   On racism in Peru, see among others, Callirgos (1993); Portocarrero (1993); Poole (1997); Manrique (1999); de la Cadena (2000).

17   The calls for European immigration coincided with the belief that Peru
      was an 'empty country'. See Kristal (1991) and Contreras (2004a). On the
      eugenic movement in Latin America and its various national institutions,
      now largely forgotten but in the 1930s and 1940s perceived as both legit-
      imate and progressive, see Stepan (1991).

18   On this point, see Boesten and Drinot (2004). Quote taken from
      Manrique (1999, pp. 126–7).

19   Of course, Zizek is referring to the work of Giorgio Agamben.

20   On the relative strength of national identity in Mexico and its relative
      weakness in Peru, see Mallon (1994) and Henríquez (2000).

21   Witness a recent survey of 320 students in four high schools and four uni-
      versities in Lima, where 'about half of the students in the survey admit-
      ted either to being 'somewhat racist' or to actually practising 'racial' dis-
      crimination' (Drzewieniecki, 2004, p. 22). Admittedly, a fair number of
      students rejected racism and racial prejudice, indicating that there is
      potential for change.

22   See, among others, Gonzalez Cueva (2000); Oliart (1999); and Boesten
      (2004).

2

Political Parties and Intermediation in Peru

John Crabtree

Introduction

The role to be played by political parties in modern democracies remains a central issue in political science. Since Sartori's now classic formulation (Sartori, 1976), there has been much discussion over the functions that parties play, but most agree that — like them or not — they have an essential role in a democracy in mediating between society and the state, and that it is difficult to think of a stable democracy without them. In Peru, since the attempts of President Alberto Fujimori to establish a regime that banished discredited parties to the side-lines of the political system, their role has been a central issue of debate. Fujimori's sudden fall from power at the end of 2000 and the subsequent attempt to return to a system of party-based government has therefore raised important issues about how to promote and improve the functioning of the party system in the interests of creating a more stable and legitimate political system. Although the experience of the last few years has compounded a degree of pessimism about the prospects for Peruvian democracy, it has included some important initiatives in institutional design that seek to make the country's parties, and the party system more generally, work better. This chapter therefore seeks to examine these initiatives and to initiate a preliminary discussion as to the possible beneficial effects that such initiatives may have over the longer run.

The way in which political parties undertake their mediating role will vary according to time and place, and trends across the world in recent decades have seen it change (Angell, 2004). Yet parties still need to fulfil some basic requirements with respect to representation and governance, roles that cannot be assumed by other sorts of institution.

Parties alone can represent the views of ordinary people, relaying and aggregating these at the level of the state. Parties provide choices for electors and provide catalysts for electoral mobilisation. They also play a central role in government, recruiting people into government, legislating and directing processes of decision making. These twin responsibilities, one 'bottom up' the other more 'top down', are frequently difficult to reconcile, not least in countries like those of Latin America where the sheer distance between the state and society is very great and where party organisation at the local level is often tenuous and inconsistent. Parties that begin life representing social interests often end up overly entangled with the affairs of state, estranging themselves from their initial roots and those who elect them (or only occasionally reconnecting themselves at times of election or re-election). Clustered around the nuclei of centralised political power, they can easily become vehicles for cooptation and/or clientelism. Parties that meanwhile remain faithful to their supporters, successfully articulating their demands and grievances, may contribute little to the sort of pact-building that helps to underpin government stability, exacerbating rather than resolving problems of governance. Combining these two functions is difficult in most countries, but in countries like Peru — where the gap between state and society is particularly wide and where social, geographic and racial divides are extreme — it can be a tall order.

Peruvian parties do not command much respect among the voting public, and their lack of legitimacy makes them one of the weakest links in the country's political system. All the available polling evidence suggests that they are rated unfavourably and that they are distant from the concerns of ordinary people. Most voters do not consider that parties represent their interests, especially those living in poverty or far from the centres of political power. Many believe that parties are part and parcel of a system of domination and exclusion. The small amount of public esteem they once may have had dropped precipitously at the end of the 1980s. The ten years of the Fujimori government (1990–2000) further reduced their relevance, closing off avenues of representative democracy in favour of a top-down system of clientelism and control. The sudden and somewhat unexpected return to more open, democratic government at the end of 2000 created a fresh opportunity to reconstruct representative institutions, but raised serious questions about how first to revive and then rebuild the parties. Yet, how much can be achieved by institutional architecture in shifting patterns of political behaviour? How long does it take for institutional practices to be made solid and permanent? To what extent do political institutions need to 'fit in' with an existing political culture, and to what extent are they able to transform that culture? The architecture establishes the blueprint to construct an edifice; this may affect the behaviour of those living in it — architects at least would like to think so — but ultimately what the people do in a building depends on a range of factors other than the walls or the physical lay-out. As we shall see, the objectives of the institutional designers in the period after 2001 were primarily to rescue and then to strengthen a multi-party system around fewer and stronger parties or party blocs, whilst seeking to make these more responsive to those they purport to represent and more responsible in carrying out their allotted functions of government.

Given Peru's recent, and not-so-recent, history, this is no easy task. As we shall also see, there are deeper reasons why political parties command so little respect. This chapter therefore begins with a historical survey that underlines the elitist and exclusive nature of the political system and the lack of a representative tradition in Peruvian politics; factors that have made it harder to build a democratic culture. It then identifies some of the advances made in the 1980s and the retreats of the 1990s, before going on to evaluate the institutional weaknesses of the post-Fujimori period. It then focuses on some of the institutional changes that were contemplated during the Toledo administration, in particular the 2003 Law on Political Parties. The chapter concludes with some thoughts about the prospects for further institutionalisation and the difficulties that this may encounter, both in the short and, more speculatively, the longer term.

Democratic Deficit

Peru stands out among the countries of Latin America for the weakness of its democratic institutions and the absence of a strong democratic culture. This is clear from a range of comparative studies, as well as the annually published figures from Latinobarómetro.[1] It is not one of those republics — like Chile, Uruguay, Costa Rica, Colombia or even Venezuela — that can look back to a tradition of party-based government. Nor is it one of those countries — like Mexico, Brazil or Argentina

— in which the mass of the population became integrated into the political system over the twentieth century, albeit imperfectly. In Peru, the mass of the population remained at the margins of the political system until much later than most other countries. For most of the twentieth century, Peru was governed by authoritarian, centralist and often military regimes that resisted democratic participation and privileged the development of the capital over that of the rest of the country. These had been interspersed by fleeting interludes of constitutional government, elected on a very narrow franchise and without a popular mandate. In both cases state structures were elitist and exclusive. Only with the Constitution of 1979, when illiterates won the vote for the first time, was universal suffrage achieved,[2] and even this was but a formal statement of rights that would only translate into practice with the passage of time.[3]

There was therefore no period in the past to which people could look back and discern the existence of an open political system based on stable party government.[4] This is, of course, not to say that there were not political parties that enjoyed mass support or that these did not exist over substantial periods of time. The American Popular Revolutionary Alliance (Alianza Popular Revolucionaria Americana APRA) was established as long ago as 1924.[5] Under the leadership of Víctor Raúl Haya de la Torre, APRA became Peru's first mass-based party with a strong insertion among lower-income earners. The Peruvian Socialist Party (Partido Socialista), which turned into the Communist Party (Partido Comunista del Perú) in 1930, also developed a real presence, although the formal working class it sought to organise was necessarily small. The 1950s saw the emergence of two other parties with a claim to be mass parties, Popular Action (Acción Popular, AP) and the Peruvian Christian Democrat Party (Partido Demócrata Cristiano, PDC) which eventually turned into the Popular Christian Party (Partido Popular Cristiano, PPC).[6] These are therefore parties that can claim some longevity and a degree of popular support; and they are still live political forces today.

However, none of those parties — not even APRA — became national parties in the sense that they permeated all levels of society or all parts of the country. All were, to varying degrees, hierarchical and undemocratic in their internal workings, reflecting the social, regional and ethnic prejudices of the society from which they emerged. Peru also lacked a 'party system', understood as a relatively stable set of political rules and practices, in which parties could compete in electoral contests and thus provide the basis of government. Elections were irregular, frequently manipulated and organised on a narrow franchise. Politics was also conducted within narrow ideological limits. For example, the traditional elite was ill-disposed to acknowledge the electoral ambitions of APRA, yet it lacked a convincing or durable conservative party to protect its interests. Perhaps the closest Peru came to establishing something approaching a party system was in the 1960s, when APRA and AP vied with one another for political office. Nevertheless, their failure to agree on the basic rules of the political game led to the 1968 coup and 12 years of military government during which party activity was outlawed and electoral competition abolished.

The first time that a party system emerged based on democratic rules was in the 1980s, when parties competed for the support of a mass electorate in elections that were frequent, regular and reasonably clean. The parties that emerged from the military dictatorship offered ideological diversity (if not polarisation), ranging from the Marxist left through to the conservative PPC. They also offered a degree of social penetration, although many Peruvians still remained at the margins of the political system. The parties of the left in particular sought to organise previously excluded sectors, both in rural areas and in urban *pueblos jóvenes*. However, party loyalties did not run deep, as the volatility of electoral outcomes in the 1980s shows. Given the incipient nature of the party system, this is perhaps unsurprising.

The system also had to encounter a series of unforeseen challenges that was to shake it to its (weakly constituted) foundations. The debt crisis of the 1980s led to economic policies that shattered expectations that democracy would bring with it improved living standards; the 1980s saw per capita incomes plummet and poverty rates rise. At the same time, the emergence and seemingly unstoppable growth of Shining Path (Sendero Luminoso) compounded these doubts about the efficacy of democracy. The combination of economic and political insecurity nurtured a profound questioning of the capacities of the political class, and especially the parties and their leaders; they were widely seen as irresponsible, incompetent and corrupt. The 1980s, therefore, did not commend itself as a decade when a nascent party-based democracy brought positive results.

Such questioning of the parties and their leaders was clearly in evidence well before Alberto Fujimori, the quintessential outsider, came from nowhere to win the 1990 presidential elections.[7] All the main parties suffered, not just AP and APRA which had governed the country respectively during the early and late 1980s. Left-wing parties were tarred with the same brush, even though they had taken no part in government except at the local level. The public questioning of the political class provided a propitious context for the Fujimori phenomenon in 1990 and after. Politically isolated at the outset, Fujimori was quick to realise how the climate of 'anti-party' sentiment could be turned to his advantage. The 1992 palace coup (*autogolpe*) was a carefully premeditated attempt to use the unpopularity of what Fujimori called the *'partidocracia'* to strengthen his position and weaken the opposition. Fujimori's system of 'direct democracy' was designed to cut out the parties as intermediaries between state and society.[8] At the same time, the economic crisis of the 1980s plus Fujimori's policies of privatisation and state shrinking reduced the relevance of parties as access points to the state.[9]

The *autogolpe* sought to perpetuate Fujimori in office well beyond his initial electoral remit by means of constitutional innovation, the manipulation of judicial institutions and the media, as well as through the adoption of clientelistic political practices to use state resources to build support at the local level (de Belaunde, 1998). Parties were excluded from decision making and became largely irrelevant, even at election times. The media helped fan anti-party sentiments. The traditional parties combined managed to score a mere 6.3 per cent of the vote in the 1995 presidential elections, compared with 64.4 per cent for the Fujimori re-election bandwagon. Politicians, keen to maintain a presence in national politics, dropped their previous party affiliations, becoming 'independents' of different types. The consequence was the fragmentation of politics into small personalist groupings, each trying to survive by dealing directly with the president. Fujimori's aversion to organised party politics even extended to resisting the temptation to establish his own political party, even though this brought problems at election time.[10] In the official discourse, then, parties were responsible for all the ills that Peru had undergone in the late 1980s, and Fujimori's personal popularity, which held up well until the end of the 1990s, was a mirror image of the bitterness felt by ordinary people towards the parties and their leaders. But, as the 2000 elections showed, the maintenance of an electoral system brought a continued need for parties to field candidates and structure their campaigns; pure personalism was not enough.

The Task of Institutionalisation

The collapse of Fujimori in 2000 was to lead to a return to a more open, democratic government. The 2001 elections were widely credited as being free and fair, in striking contrast to those of the previous year which Fujimori had used to secure a constitutionally-dubious third term. However, Fujimori's fall from power, amid scandals over how the intelligence community had sought to manipulate politics, was not in itself a validation of Peru's parties nor a public endorsement of their role in a more democratic, rules-based political system. Notwithstanding this, the 2001 elections gave them an important role to play and how to improve their public profile suddenly became a major preoccupation. Denigrated for the best part of a decade, how were they going to resuscitate themselves and their public credibility? How were they going to insert themselves as more effective and legitimate intermediaries between state and society than those in the past? What institutional structures would help the parties develop such capacities? The return to a more open and democratic government, first under the interim presidency of Valentín Paniagua and then after the 2001 elections under the new government of Alejandro Toledo, suddenly saw a good deal of thought being given to such questions.

Before going on to look at the steps taken to reform the workings of the political system post-Fujimori, it is worth first pausing a moment to assess the status of the Peruvian parties and the party system at the beginning of the new millennium. In order to do so (and thus to judge the size of the hill they had to climb), it is worth looking at these in the light of four well-established criteria for the institutionalisation of party systems (Mainwaring and Scully, 1995).[11]

The first of these is stability and respect for the rules of party competition. As we have seen, the 1990s saw the attempt to ostracise political parties by institutional manipulation and by working on anti-party attitudes through, among other things, the media. The return of party competition in 2001 brought with it a degree of consensus about the need to rebuild the party system and the changes that would be required to achieve this. The scale of manipulation and fraud during the previous years, made manifest by the 'Vladivideos', brought condemnation of unbridled executive discretion and demands for a more rules-based approach. Appalled by the scandals of the previous period, political actors and commentators argued that the time had come to re-balance the division of powers and restore basic democratic norms. As in other respects, this situation provided an (unexpected) opportunity for change to take place. Characteristic of this new climate was the establishment of the National Accord (Acuerdo Nacional). An attempt to construct an area for dialogue between political parties, civil society and business organisations, the Accord was able to establish some agreed principles for reform.[12] There was less agreement, however, over whether Fujimori's 1993 Constitution should remain in place or whether there should be a return to the 1979 Constitution. Some argued plausibly that the 1993 Constitution was in itself the direct consequence of an illegal act, namely Fujimori's April 1992 *autogolpe*.

A second condition is whether political parties have stable roots in society. This is a much more difficult condition to fulfil in Peru. We have seen how in the past Peruvian parties failed to become truly national or popular institutions. The experience of the late 1980s and 1990s had weakened social insertion still further. Not only did the Fujimori decade reduce the relevance of parties as intermediaries, but the period prior to his election had seen the weakening of those collective identities (such as trade unions or peasant confederations) that previously had provided them with some sort of social base. It was also a time when the collapse of the Berlin Wall rendered largely obsolete many of the pre-existing ideological divisions that had distinguished Peru's political parties. In their place came ad hoc parties, such as We Are Peru (Somos Perú, SP), Union for Peru (Unión por el Perú, UPP), the Independent Moralizing Front (Frente Independiente Moralizador, FIM) and Possible Country (País Posible, PP), parties defined far more by personalities than by any ideology or organised presence in society. The various Fujimori parties — Change 90 (Cambio 90), Let's Go Neighbour (Vamos Vecino), Peru 2000 — conspicuously came and went according to the electoral calendar, refusing to institutionalise themselves. Of Peru's traditional parties in the 2001 elections only APRA was able to draw on some sort of national organisation, but even APRA's real presence in society had become far weaker than it had been ten or twenty years earlier.[13] Much of APRA's surprising electoral revival in 2001 appears to have been the result of the charisma and political acumen of Alan García. For its part, AP declined to participate in the 2001 elections, while the PPC, which had entered into a broader alliance known as the National Unity (Unidad Nacional, UN), had once again shown that its organised presence outside middle- or upper-class districts of Lima was limited. Many of the social conflicts that developed during the Toledo years — riots in Arequipa, protests by coca farmers and strikes in any number of sectors — took place beyond the reach of any national parties, demonstrating their almost total absence at the grass roots and therefore an inability to mediate. By contrast, some regional parties had more success in putting down roots. A notable example was Yehude Simon's Movimiento Humanista in the department of Lambayeque.[14] However, as we shall see, to expand a regional movement beyond its base to exert influence at the national level remained a challenge for *provinciano* politicians.

A third criterion is whether political elites put their faith in parties as mechanisms for achieving power. During the Fujimori period, parties had little or no relevance for decision making and therefore had little role to play. The debacle of the Fujimori government, however, effectively reasserted the party system (or what was left of it) as a means of influencing policy. In spite of their poor reputation, they seemed better as channels than the methods employed by Fujimori and Montesinos. Their new acceptance therefore reflected more the collapse of the Fujimori system rather than any great faith in their intrinsic worth. The weakness and venality of the PP, the ruling party after 2001, did little to convince a sceptical public. It was widely perceived as little more than a grouping of political opportunists that had jumped onto the Toledo bandwagon to take advantage of the access provided by the 2001 elections. The reputation for corruption and sleaze surrounding PP and the FIM, its coalition partner, contributed little to building the stability of the new political system. Their main saving grace, and one which became evident early on in the Toledo administration, was that the opposition parties, particularly APRA, had every interest in Toledo lasting out his term of office for fear that his early demise would damage their own longer-term interests.

A fourth condition is that parties should have their own autonomous organisation and be internally democratic and transparent in the way they manage their affairs. Latin American political parties have tradition-ally been run in a top-down, vertical fashion, and Peru's parties are certain-ly no exception to this rule. The history of APRA is particularly sympto-matic of this trait, both under Haya de la Torre and more recently under Alan García. Peru's left-wing parties grew up on Leninist principles that afforded little scope for internal democracy, with dissent usually ending in party splits. Nor have centre-right parties, AP and the PPC, been run in a particularly open or democratic manner. Personalist styles of lead-ership thus run deep across the board, preventing renovation and the emergence of new generations of party leaders, and local party organi-sation tends (at best) to be both weak and patchy as well as subservient to centralised control. Party finances have been particularly opaque, giv-ing rise to suspicions that donor pay-back leads directly to corruption. However, as we shall see in the next section, there have been moves towards fostering more open and participative styles of party manage-ment; it remains to be seen though how successful these will be in changing established patterns of control and in the opening of parties up towards a more democratic, 'bottom-up' systems of management. The initial signs are not auspicious.

Reforms to the Party and Electoral Systems

A law was promulgated on 1 October 2003 that aimed to regulate polit-ical parties and party competition, the first law of its kind in Peru. At the time of its passage Peru was one of the few countries in Latin America not to have a law governing the activities of political parties. The importance of such a law had been identified early on by the elec-toral authorities, in particular by Fernando Tuesta, the head of the National Office for Electoral Processes (Oficina Nacional de Procesos Electorales, ONPE) and a pre-eminent political scientist. Discussion over the new law took over 20 months, and involved a wide range of actors, including the political parties themselves, ONPE, specialist for-eign agencies, NGOs, civil society organisations and members of the international donor community.[15] At the outset, politicians were scep-tical about the chances of enlisting the support of the parties.[16] However, in the end, the law was approved — most unusually — by unanimous acclaim on the floor of Congress, a positive sign of the degree of consensus forged among political elites over the need for reform.

The genesis of the legislation reflected a genuine concern among all the main political parties about their predicament and the need for institutional incentives to help them more adequately 'bridge the gap' between state and society. According to Jorge del Castillo, the general secretary of APRA and a key force behind the scenes, 'it is quite clear that we are all of us going to sink if we fail to build this (an inclusive party system)'.[17] In common with other party leaders, he blamed the media for constantly stirring up anti-party feelings. The consensus achieved around the Law on Political Parties also reflected the involvement of the National Accord, a key agency in helping to build a consensus between Peru's fractious parties. The way in which the law was negotiated is worth noting. The draft legislation was fully discussed in the Congress's Commission of Constitutional Affairs, which had set up a sub-group that worked with specialist agencies like Transparencia, IDEA and the National Democratic Institute (NDI) on a text that met both party concerns and international best practice. The sub-group involved many sessions and worked in a politically neutral setting, well away from Congress. Among the congressmen that took the lead here were del Castillo from APRA and Henry Pease from the PP. In the words of Lourdes Flores, leader of UN, building a consensus over party reform was of crucial importance but an objective that was difficult to achieve: 'you have to depoliticise something that is inherently highly politicised (...) each party tends to look at it through the lens of their own self interest'.[18]

The legislation had two main objectives. The first was to reverse the trend towards political fragmentation that had become so evident during the Fujimori period, if not before. The second was to promote transparency and internal democracy within the parties.

To limit further fragmentation, the party law established barriers to entry that were designed to lead to fewer but stronger political parties. To qualify for recognition by the electoral authorities, parties needed to show that they had an active presence (local committees) in at least 65 provinces (out of a total of 194). They would also need to present to the electoral authorities 125,000 signatures; this figure was, in fact, lower than the threshold under Fujimori, but was considered more realistic to avoid parties setting up the sort of 'factories' that came into being in 2000 to forge them.[19] Some of those involved in framing the new legislation argued that the barriers to entry needed to be higher.[20] The idea of those involved was that the system would in any case be further tightened by subsequent changes to the electoral code; parties which failed to achieve five per cent of the vote in national elections would be obliged to re-register if they wished to enter future contests. The established parties naturally supported the idea of using barriers to entry to encourage the development of fewer parties, since they would probably be the main beneficiaries. In del Castillo's view, 'the ideal' would be to achieve a multi-party system with only four or five parties, although he admitted that this would take time to achieve.[21]

The second objective of the law was to encourage greater accountability, both to party members and to society more generally. As we have seen, Peru's parties developed in a culture of secrecy and vertical control, in particular with respect to sources of funding. Because of the abeyance of political parties during the 1990s, Peru did not experience the innovations carried out in some other Latin American countries. The new law established for the first time that registered parties would have to supply the electoral authorities with detailed accounts of their income and spending. Such disclosure would, it was thought, help reduce corruption and clientelism. The law also included new norms about internal organisation, requiring that registered parties hold regular internal elections and that candidates for election should be selected in an open and democratic manner. Though commonplace in other countries, such innovations were quite contentious in Peru, and the original requirements governing party financing and internal democracy had to be whittled down when the proposals came to be debated on the floor of Congress. Finally, the law established new norms for state funding of parties. This proved to be one of the most difficult areas and one which nearly derailed the whole agreement. It raised awkward questions about state control and influence over parties and their activities. In the end, it was agreed that official funding would be limited to training and election expenses, and would not come in before 2007 (i.e. after the 2006 elections).[22]

The discussions within Congress and outside it over reforms to the political system were premised on the idea that the Law on Political Parties would be followed up by a package of reforms to the electoral system. The success in striking a consensus over the former led to a similar approach being adopted for the latter. With the help of outside agencies (again, including IDEA and Transparencia), a draft bill (*dictamen*) was produced, although without the same degree of party input as before. At the time of writing, these proposed changes had yet to be adopted, and the approach of the 2006 elections meant that the chances of this happening had dwindled. A number of the suggested changes involved amendments to the 1993 Constitution, and these require majority votes in Congress in two separate but successive legislatures. The suggested changes included: replacement of a single-chamber Congress with a bicameral system (i.e. bringing back the Senate abolished in the 1993 Constitution); giving the vote to members of the military on active service; scrapping obligatory voting; eliminating the use of the preferential vote; separating out the election of congressmen from the first round of presidential voting; and reforming the system of electoral administration.

From the point of view of strengthening the party system, the last three were of particular importance. The abolition of the system of preferential voting would encourage party unity and therefore help enhance discipline.[23] Under the current system, voters in congressional elections choose a party and then a candidate on that party's slate. The system tends to encourage party infighting, as individual candidates on a slate vie with one another for public support. A particularly conspicuous instance of this was the 1990 elections, when individual candidates on Mario Vargas Llosa's Fredemo (Democratic Front) ticket spent large sums conducting their own campaigns to attract voter support at the expense of others on the same ticket. Changing the timing of congressional elections would also have important implications. The current system encourages dispersion in elections for Congress, as parties field their own candidates in the knowledge that an almost certain second round of presidential voting necessarily involves the forging of alliances, but without any of the political costs of doing so. There is therefore little incentive for parties to enter pacts for congressional elections, and the fact that each fields their own presidential candidate militates against the formation of pacts. The third reform concerns the system of electoral administration and oversight. Since the 1993 Constitution, there have been three agencies involved in elections rather than a single one, the National Electoral Jury (Jurado Nacional de Elecciones, JNE) as previously. As well as the JNE there is the ONPE, which is in charge of administering elections, and the National Registry for Identity and Civic Status (Registro Nacional de Identidad y Estatus Civil, RENIEC), with responsibility for the electoral roll. These agencies (particularly the JNE and ONPE) have been working at loggerheads in recent years, often sowing confusion.[24] However, since the new systems of party registration and financial oversight give important new powers to the electoral authorities, the return to a single agency would probably concentrate power. In view of recent experience of electoral malpractice, this may not be the optimal solution.

Rebuilding Faith in Political Parties

It is early days to judge the extent to which these institutional changes will affect the performance of political parties and how they are perceived by the wider society. Even if eventually the reforms to the electoral system become law, it is likely to be only over the next decade or more that the effects of these and the Law on Political Parties become clear. Generally, the proposals adopted conform to the sort of reform packages adopted in other Latin American countries and reflect a shift within multilateral lenders towards encouraging political reform.[25] They enjoy a good deal of support among the existing parties, and this in itself is an important first step. The interviews conducted for this study with political leaders from a range of different parties made it clear that they see that parties either become more open and responsive to the voting public or their future is in doubt — and with it that of representative democracy in Peru.[26]

So far as the two main objectives of the Law on Political Parties are concerned — to reduce fragmentation and increase party openness — first impressions are mixed. In terms of party registration, 29 parties had qualified by late 2005 to take part in the 2006 elections. This does not suggest that fragmentation is being reduced or that Del Castillo's aim of 'four or five' major parties will be achieved any time soon. In the build-up to the 2006 elections, there was a good deal of discussion as to the formation of coalitions and fronts and most party leaders were aware of the need to reach out beyond their own very limited worlds to bring the non-committed voter into the fold; APRA probably went further than most in seeking to build what García called '*un frente social*'. Given the collapse in party militancy, this was an attempt to appeal to a wider range of voters and create some sort of loose organisation among *simpatizantes*. But given the weakness of collective identities beyond those sectors of the population that still have a modicum of organisation, such a strategy seemed likely to have only limited chances of success.[27]

So far as the second goal is concerned, there were some signs of the parties beginning to organise themselves in a more democratic and accountable manner. Again, their leaders recognised the need for change, whilst acknowledging the difficulties of 'changing their ways'. Several parties had held internal elections to choose or ratify their leaders, although as yet there were few signs that this was leading to a renewal of political leadership.[28] At the time of writing, parties were also making preparations to elect their presidential and congressional slates rather than simply designate these behind closed doors. If such institutional practices become permanent, they may have significant effects in changing the culture of internal party management; so too will the insistence on parties coming clean on where they receive their funds. But the extent and the speed at which such changes would be brought about was by no means clear, and the temptation would be strong simply to adapt old practices to the new requirements without fundamentally changing that culture.

In the longer term, political parties need to insert themselves within the electorate and build an organised presence in the country as a whole. The advent of elections, such as those of 2006, provided a catalyst for them to extend their roots into society, reaching out for public support. But it is hard to understate the size of the task of insertion, especially among the poorest and most marginalised. Voters are likely to remain sceptical until parties prove their worth in fighting their battles and opening up to participation in an inclusive and democratic manner. Such inclusiveness would probably be harder to achieve, for instance, among marginalised peoples of the highlands and jungle than among more traditional areas of party support. Large numbers remain effectively outside the ambit of the franchise, in spite of universal suffrage.[29] Most parties lack any sort of organisation at the regional/departmental or provincial levels, let alone at the district level or beneath. Many of those elected for political parties in the 2002 regional and municipal elections were not genuine party militants. It is not easy for parties to move in from outside and create such a presence. The practice now known as 'electoral franchising', whereby a party extends its logo to a local candidate of some stature in turn for his or her support, is widespread. Even many of those elected as regional presidents for better-organised parties, like APRA, were elected in 2002 as a consequence of such 'franchising' arrangements.

The process of decentralisation should, in theory, work to the advantage of parties that seek to build up local organisations, since they increase the significance of local politics, long a backwater in Peruvian political life. As regions increase both their functions and their budgets, political competition to control them should increase. A new municipal law seeks to increase levels of public participation in local government, providing openings for the parties as well. However, decentralisation also lends itself to the multiplication of local parties, a tendency that the Law on Political Parties aimed to check. A few local parties have managed to turn themselves into dynamic organisations that seek to take advantage of local pride to push 'bottom-up' regional agendas at the national level. Simon's Humanist Movement (Movimiento Humanista) in Lambayeque is a good example, having built up a strong local organisation in a region traditionally an APRA stronghold. It may be the case that regional parties form coalitions in order to meet the new requirements of the law. The issue of decentralisation and democracy at the local level is taken up by Carlos Monge in the next chapter. So far, the efforts of political parties to take advantage of the opportunities provided by decentralisation have been limited. As in the past, there appears to be an absence of linkage between politics at the local level and politics on the national stage, even within party structures. There seems to be a 'ceiling' above which local-level politics fail to shape national politics in any decisive way.[30]

Perhaps more important is the ability of parties to reflect adequately the 'cleavages' in society, the areas of tension that challenge political systems. As we noted at the outset, it is not easy for parties at once to represent discontent in a highly divided society while at the same time underpinning the work of government. Protest in Peru is not hard to find, but none of the conflicts that have erupted in recent years have been channelled through party structures or have been resolved by party mediation. For the most part, political parties are disengaged from the politics of disenchantment or even irrelevant to them. The new parties are, as we have noted, defined more by personalities than policies, and have no roots in the real world of ordinary people. Social cleavages are perhaps slightly better reflected by the more traditional parties which retain some links to collective identities, such as trade unions or business organisations. However, the differences that distinguish them are no longer as sharp as they used to be, especially in areas like economic policy. The clustering of political parties in the centre-ground means inevitably that they cease to offer electors clear alternatives in the resolution of their problems. Parties, therefore, need to articulate alternatives and organise their support base to that end; but in weakly-constituted polities like that of Peru, it is often difficult to combine this within the confines of agreed rules of the game in such a way that such rules are not placed in constant jeopardy.[31]

Conclusions

Institutional design is an important element in shaping political outcomes, but alone it is not enough. Whilst it sets the parameters within which politics are conducted, these parameters are in themselves liable to be breached and constantly subject to change and to re-interpretation. In a country like Peru, where the rule of law has traditionally been weak, it is to be expected that the outcomes may not be those that the policy-makers had in mind. It may take much more than a Law of Political Parties, an inherently 'top-down' measure, or reforms to the electoral machinery to create a real and vibrant party system in Peru, where such a thing has been absent for most of its history. Whether or not it can be achieved will only become clear in the long term. Still, institutions do have a role in formulating political conduct so long as they command a strong degree of consensus, conform to local practices and are able to make themselves self-sustaining over time. That the 2003 Law of Political Parties passed Congress unanimously is an encouraging sign, as is the verdict of many of those consulted in the course of this study who regarded this legislation as one of the more significant fruits to come out of the Congress elected in 2001.

But it cannot be taken for granted that such legislation will achieve its intended objectives. The number of parties requesting registration under the new law is not an encouraging sign. Whether or not party political life will become more responsible and responsive will depend a great deal on whether political actors adapt their behaviour not just to the letter but to the spirit of the law. Once again, the political leaders consulted gave the impression that they had come to the conclusion that their parties had no option but to change, but in practice there may be strong incentives to continue with time-honoured political practices, particularly in difficult areas like financial transparency. As Lourdes Flores wryly commented, '*Hecha la ley, hecha la trampa*'.[32] And in a situation of political competition, the behaviour of one actor colours that of all the others. A system of electoral oversight will therefore play a crucial role in establishing and defending new standards of conduct among parties.

To regain public confidence, parties need not just to clean up their act in the electoral sphere; they need to prove themselves competent in the field of government (or opposition) and in their ability to represent divergent social interests. Their record in the 1980s with regard to the former was a fairly lamentable precedent, though arguably the problems they confronted at the time were unusually severe. With respect to representation, a huge amount has yet to be done in building (or rebuilding) channels of effective intermediation, whether at the level of the region, the province or the district. So long as parties are widely regarded as more part of the problem than of the solution, this will not happen. Social tensions — ever-present throughout Peru — will flare up entirely at the margins of the party system. A huge amount needs to be done to build a party presence at the regional and local levels, a task that can only be accomplished when parties are seen as valid intermediaries by those who elect them. Even if politics can be stabilised nationally by lowering the number of parties to four or five, this will mean little unless these parties command legitimacy among ordinary people. Electoral contests may help in building party organisation in society, but they are not enough.

Notes

1   Latinobarómetro (Latinobarómetro, 2005) provides a useful source for comparing political attitudes between different countries and over time. In the case of Peru, it shows that politicians and political parties are held in extremely low public esteem.

2   This was, for example, nearly 30 years after it had been established in Bolivia, where the 1952 revolution brought (at least nominally) universal rights of citizenship.

3   As Drinot notes in the first chapter of this volume, the Truth and Reconciliation Commission would uncover a world in which formal political rights meant little or nothing.

4   Eduardo Morón and Cynthia Sanborn underscore this institutional fragility when they remind us that 'Since gaining independence in 1821, the
country has had 13 constitutions, at least 26 successful coups, and 108 different governments, only 19 of which were elected and only nine of
which completed their terms' (Morón and Sanborn, 2004, p. 1).

5   APRA was established in Mexico City; it was in 1930 that the Partido
Aprista Peruano (PAP) was founded in Peru.

6   AP dates from 1956. The PDC was established a year earlier, although the
PPC was founded in 1966 as a right-wing splinter of the PDC.

7   The electoral success of Ricardo Belmont, a media personality, as candidate for the mayor of Lima in 1989 was, to some extent, a premonition
of the Fujimori phenomenon of the following year.

8   For an account of the various measures taken to this end by the Fujimori
government in its first few years in government, see Crabtree (1994).

9   Tanaka (2002) shows how the mechanisms binding the state and society, not
just political parties but also social movements, gave way to a new sort of
mediation in which the media played a key role.

10   Among these was the need to re-register as Fujimori substituted one official
party for another. One of the first signs of electoral manipulation to emerge
in the 2000 presidential elections was the use of 'factories' to produce the
requisite number of signatures for the official party to achieve registration
for the elections. As it turned out, this was also a practice used by others too.

11   Mainwaring and Scully establish these as ways of gauging institutionalisation. Though it is possible to think of others, these four provide a useful
starting point for our discussion.

12   A forerunner of the National Accord had been the Accord for
Governability (Acuerdo para la Gobernabilidad), set up in 1999 among the
opposition parties to the Fujimori government. The vitiated 2000 elections
led to the establishment of a 'round table for dialogue' (*mesa de diálogo*) under
the auspices of the Organization of American States (OAS) to negotiate
with Fujimori. It brought together opposition parties, government and representatives of civil society. After Fujimori's fall this round table became a
place to discuss the transition, privileging discussion of longer-term goals. In
March 2003, President Toledo gave it a more institutionalised presence.
Members of the National Accord included leaders of political parties and
representatives from civil society, including business lobbies, the Churches,
regional groupings etc. Its remit was to come up with long term policies in

four key areas: (i) democratic governance; (ii) promotion of a competitive economy; (iii) equity and social justice; and (iv) the building of a transparent and efficient state. According to Rafael Roncagliolo, technical president of the National Accord until 2005, it constituted 'a learning process' in which 'it was hard to maintain the balance and neutrality required'. He says that 'the keys were negotiation and deliberation', but that the Accord had to avoid becoming an area of government (*instancia de gobierno*)'. Interview with the author, October 2004.

13 In 1994, on a visit to Trujillo, the author sought to evaluate how APRA's grass-roots organisation had been hit by the changes of the previous two or three years in this, a traditional bastion of party strength. Although there were some remnants of party activity in the central core area of the city, the party was almost non-existent in the *pueblos jovenes* in surrounding areas, where support for Fujimori was overwhelming.

14 This was a party that was elected to the regional presidency in 2002, but which managed to build a substantial local following on the basis of honest and effective local government.

15 It is worthwhile at this point to recognise the role played by donor agencies, particularly the UK's DFID and Sweden's SIDA, in conjunction with local NGOs and ONPE in seeking to open up the political system in an attempt to make it more representative of Peru's poor majority. As local DFID officials admit, this was an unorthodox application of foreign assistance funds but nonetheless an important one in trying to give poor people more of a political voice. For an account of this approach and DFID's role in Peru, see DFID (2005).

16 Interview with Percy Medina (November 2004) of the NGO Transparencia, one of the prime-movers of the initiative. He says that at the outset most of the party leaders were of the opinion that the initiative was doomed to fail.

17 Interview with the author, November 2004.

18 *Ibid.*

19 As well as Fujimori's Peru 2000 party, two other parties — Renovación and Toledo's País Posible (the forerunner of Perú Posible) — have been accused of falsifying signatures.

20 According to del Castillo, the 'barriers to entry' would need to be 'raised further'. Interview with the author, November 2004. This is also a line of argument adopted by Tanaka (2004).

21   Interview with the author, November 2004.

22   It took the casting vote of the president of Congress to achieve inclusion of the principle of state funding for parties.

23   The inclusion of a clause to discourage congressmen from changing parties (*transfuguismo*) between elections, a move that would have also helped boost party discipline, was dropped from the final version of the Law on Political Parties at the insistence of members of Congress.

24   Interview with Fernando Tuesta, November 2004. According to Tuesta, the JNE had been working hard to close down the ONPE. Shortly after the interview, Tuesta was removed from his post. Appointed in December 2000, Tuesta played a key role in the April 2001 presidential elections, helping to rebuild ONPE almost from scratch in a very short period of time, whilst organising presidential and congressional elections that were generally deemed to have been free and fair.

25   The IDB's publication 'Democracies in Development' (Payne et al., 2002) was an important step in that institution becoming more involved in the explicitly political terrain. The IDB recognised that politics 'matter' for development.

26   According to veteran left-winger Javier Diez Canseco 'There is a search for new forms of political organisation. People are tired of old forms of political leadership and their methods. Parties have been unable to separate out what is public and what is private. People no longer accept the old style.' Interview with the author, October 2004.

27   APRA, conspicuously, did not enter into any coalition or *frente* with other parties.

28   The legislation does not stipulate the introduction of open or closed primaries.

28   It has been estimated, for instance, that up to five per cent of the adult population are disenfranchised because they lack the identity documents required to vote (DFID, 2005). Lack of identity documentation is most common in rural parts of the highlands and jungle and among women.

29   I am grateful to Carlos Santiso for this point.

30   The emergence of Ollanta Humala as an 'anti-system' candidate in the 2006 elections reflects this difficulty. As Fujimori found out in 1990, the 'anti-system' dynamic, especially among the poor and marginalised, can be a powerful force in Peruvian politics.

32   Interview with the author, November 2004.

3

Decentralisation:
An Opportunity for Democratic Governance

Carlos Monge Salgado

P eru is a country of many exclusions. More than half of the population lives in poverty and over a quarter in extreme poverty, without the possibility of gaining access to employment, a decent income, quality public services (such as education and health), positions in the state or political representation. Exclusion is more marked in the case of those living in rural areas, women and indigenous people (PNUD, 2004). This systematic exclusion, with its counterparts — the concentration of wealth and the privatisation of the state by economic, social and political elites — has contributed to a profound crisis in the legitimacy of state institutions, of democracy as a system of government and of politics in general (Latinobarómetro, 2004; PNUD, 2004).

Decentralisation can offer citizens in different localities and regions the possibility of participating on a daily basis in decision-making on key issues. It affords them a possibility to become involved in crucial areas such as developmental plans, annual budgets or strategies for local-level health and education. Where truly participative decentralisation can make an important contribution to restoring citizens' belief that the state can be of service to them, that democracy can be effective on a daily basis and that politics is worthwhile.

This chapter seeks to develop several related ideas. First, that decentralisation is the culmination of a medium-term cycle of institutional destruction and reconstruction which began in the 1950s and 1960s with social mobilisations and reforms that led to the collapse of the 'oligarchic' state. Secondly, that decentralisation forms part of a short-term democratic transition, which explains the emphasis placed on citizen participation. Third, that support for decentralisation is based on the hypothesis that the impetus behind economic, social and political modernisation no longer emanates from the centre against conservative regional elites (which has always been the case since Independence), but from the regions and localities themselves. Fourth, that the way in which the mechanisms of participation currently work has good points that need to be developed further, but also defects that need to be tackled as a matter of urgency. Finally, that these workings, alongside other aspects of decentralisation, raise deeper issues about the relations between representative and participative democracy and between politics and society.

From the Oligarchic State to Participatory Decentralisation: A New Chance to Build a Democratic State

Until the 1940s and 1950s Peru was an oligarchic state. A small elite controlled the land, finance, industry and commerce. This elite also controlled the state, monopolising access to quality education and health; it also enjoyed a monopoly over political representation. The majority of the population found itself excluded from access to property, employment, decent incomes, basic public services and political representation. Between the 1950s and 1970s, mobilisation from below along with the reforms undertaken by military governments to pre-empt a possible repeat of the Cuban revolution, brought the oligarchic state to an end. As part of this transformation, the majority of rural people won access to land and water resources; urban workers won labour rights; poor urban dwellers were able to access basic services; and generally gained the social rights they previously lacked.

However, the fall of the oligarchic state and the extension of social rights to the majority of people did not lead to a democratic state. On the contrary, between the 1970s (when the reforms that brought the oligarchic state to an end were implemented) and the end of the 1990s (with the fall of the Mafia-like Fujimori-Montesinos regime), at least three opportunities were lost to construct a democratic state to fill the space left by the demise of the oligarchic one.

1. *The military government*. This pushed through the reforms of the 1970s, giving millions of Peruvians access to social and economic citizenship

previously denied them. However, it sought to establish a corporative social and political order that denied them the exercise of the political rights of citizenship. The military authorities abolished municipal elections (only introduced in 1964), returning to the system whereby local authorities were appointed arbitrarily from the centre. They sought to establish (without much success) corporative channels to link social organisations with the state, repressing free expression, autonomous mobilisation and social organisation, and independent citizenship.

2. *The return to democracy.* At the beginning of the 1980s elections to choose national and local authorities were re-established. However, the reluctance of the Belaunde and García administrations to abandon the elitist and exclusive state and the existence of a system of representative democracy that lacked any real meaning for the majority was the second wasted opportunity. Additionally, this period saw the development of internal war which brought with it the militarisation of a large part of the country and the predominance of violence among individuals and groups. This led to the aborting of the second opportunity to build a democratic state. At the same time, new economic policies were put into effect, geared to the development of the market economy and the promotion of private investment. These reversed many of the advances made in the 1970s in the economic and social rights won by most rural and urban populations.

3. *The authoritarian period post-1990.* With Shining Path (Sendero Luminoso) and the Revolutionary Tupac Amaru Movement (Movimiento Revolucionario Túpac Amaru, MRTA) defeated in the early 1990s, a Mafioso-style dictatorship established itself, sustained by the military and police and supported by those sectors of the elite which had gained from the aggressive neoliberal reforms it enacted and by the extreme poor being dependent on centrally managed social programmes. So far as national institutions were concerned, this involved a strategy of total control involving the corrupting of Congress and the judiciary as well as the electoral authorities. In terms of state-society relations, the regime sought to manipulate the needs of the poor to build a system of top-down clientelism. This worked through a system of social programmes orchestrated from the very apex of the power structure, bypassing institutions and democratic local authorities.

The Democratic Transition and Citizen Participation in Decentralisation

Inspired by the important role played by civil society in the downfall of Fujimori, the interim administration of Valentín Paniagua sought to make civil society participation and the quest for consensus between state and society central policies. The establishment in 2001 of a forum for dialogue over combating poverty (Mesa de Concertación de Lucha contra la Pobreza MCLP) was a clear sign of this disposition.

With civil society participation a key criterion of public policy, decentralisation turned into a core issue in the 2001 election campaign. For this reason, it came as no surprise that in his inauguration speech on 28 July 2001, the recently-elected President Alejandro Toledo announced that this would be one of his main policies, and that November 2002 would see the election of regional presidents to replace authorities hitherto appointed by Lima. The announcement was welcomed by all social and political sectors. In the months that followed, as part of the design for the new legal framework for regional and local government, Congress introduced a series of participatory mechanisms.

So, two or three decades after the oligarchic regime had collapsed under pressure of mobilisation from below, decentralisation and citizen participation came together as part of a comprehensive democratic reform of the state. However, this new convergence took place under a government that had neither a coherent view regarding the problem of centralisation or a clear proposal or agenda for decentralisation and participation. Indeed, this very lack of clarity and political will explains why the process came to be dogged by so much uncertainty, and why policy ended up being so inconsistent. At the time of writing, it seemed that bureaucratic resistance to decentralisation, both within ministries and social programmes, was stronger than the will to proceed. This was particularly the case in the Ministry of Economy and Finance (MEF). It helps to explain the paralysis on decentralising budgetary matters and transferring responsibility for social programmes to the local level, as well as the lack of significant advances in transferring responsibilities to regional and local governments.[1]

In sum, the central government supported decentralisation and greater public participation in general terms, but it lacked a clear notion where to take the process, and seemed to be unable to overcome the bureaucratic resistance in centralised ministries which saw a 'danger' of loss of power and resources to the regional and local echelons of government.

Decentralisation as Local-led Modernisation

A strong presupposition in the pledge to decentralise is that today the impetus in modernising the state and political life comes not from the centre but from the local level. From the time of the foundation of the republic up until the military reforms of the 1970s, the central state posed as the force of modernity against the retrograde nature of economic, social and political life in the mainly rural regions. This was the core element of debates between *centralistas* and *decentralistas* or between liberals and conservatives throughout much of the nineteenth century (Contreras, 2005; Zas Fritz, 2001, 2004). It was also the perception of distinguished thinkers in the early twentieth century, who saw regionalism as a defensive response from local landowning interests to the modernising instincts of the middle classes and central government (Mariátegui, 1928; Belaunde, 1930; Basadre, 1931).

This enduring debate between the modernising *centralistas* and reactionary *regionalistas* from the time of Independence was, of course, not something that was peculiar to Peru. It seems to have been a common trait, at least in Brazil, Argentina and Mexico, up until the first two decades of the twentieth century, with oligarchic regional landowners resisting the growing power of middle-class urban sectors and specific economic and social policies that ran counter to their interests (Skidmore and Smith, 2000). In the Peruvian case, the reforms undertaken by the military in the 1970s were profoundly modernising in the sphere of economic and social rights, and in this area the military took on any resistance from the oligarchy or business sectors opposed to the widening of such rights. Yet at the same time, the reforms were profoundly centralist and undemocratic, as might be expected of a military regime (Stein and Monge, 1988).

By the 1990s, however, the central government was no longer an agent of modernisation in any sense. Neoliberal reforms and macroeconomic policies involved major reverses in the area of basic social and economic rights. There were also reverses in the relationship between citizens (especially the poorest) and the state, as these became ones of clientelism based on the needs of an impoverished population desperate for stability and security. Furthermore, political power became ever more centralised as elected regional authorities were replaced by government appointees and as the functions of local government were reduced and its legitimacy undermined by the direct local involvement of the executive through social programmes.

In opposition to this concentration of power and the erosion of political, economic and social rights, new experiences in local public management took place in the *provincias* and *distritos*. These were rooted in ideas about citizen participation and the need for inclusive development. Thus, there is reason to believe that the impetus for widening political, economic, social and cultural rights for the majority now emanates from the localities and the regions, and no longer from the centre.

Citizen Participation: Accumulating Experience

The Authoritarian Context with Restricted Participation

As a result of the 2002 *autogolpe* an authoritarian regime came into being in Peru, backed by the military and the intelligence service and supported by top businessmen and sections of the political elite.[2] The regime of Fujimori and Montesinos was extremely vertical, centralising and opaque in its use of state resources. The regional governments elected in 1987 were dissolved. The Association of Peruvian Municipalities (Asociación de Municipalidades del Perú) was destroyed as an entity representing local government. District authorities were set against provincial ones, with the former given resources and decision-making powers over investment projects previously run by the latter. And the status and legitimacy of all municipalities were weakened as centrally-run social programmes (with greater resources and discretionary powers) sought to legitimise central government at the local level.

Within this overall framework, restricted areas for limited grass-roots participation in decision-making were encouraged through the social programmes, as well as in spheres like education and health. The most noteworthy were:

- The executive nuclei (*núcleos ejecutores*) encouraged by the Fund for Development and Social Compensation (Fondo de Desarrollo y Compensación Social) Foncodes. These had the responsibility for identifying small investment projects presented to Foncodes and managing the resources provided for executing them.

- The conservation committees (*comités conservacionistas*) promoted by the National Programme for Watershed Management and Soil Conservation (Programa Nacional de Manejo de Cuencas y Conservación de Suelos, Pronamachcs) to coordinate and participate in the way in which projects were carried out by technical teams from this agency in the areas of soil management, irrigation and forestation.

- The soup kitchens (*comedores populares*) backed by The National Food Assistance Programme (Programa Nacional de Asistencia Alimentaria, Pronaa), with the task of organising the beneficiaries and of receiving, distributing and preparing food for distribution.

- The local communities for health administration (Comunidades Locales de Administración de Salud — Clas), promoted by the health ministry to manage the finances and human resources of local health centres.

- Parents' Associations (Asociaciones de Padres de Familia), pro-moted by the education ministry to oversee the activities of teachers and local officials in the sector, and to provide resources for local schools.

There were also some other experiences in limited participation in man-agement and decision-making at the local level, including:

- The rural community self-defence brigades (Rondas de Autodefensa). These grew up in the south-central highlands and the central jungle to defend peasant communities from attacks and harassment by Sendero Luminoso. They ended up being trained and coordinated by military authorities in those areas under states of emergency from the mid-1980s onwards.[3]

- Organisations involved in irrigation. Although these had existed from the beginning of the twentieth century, they were reorgan-ised in the 1970s as part of the agrarian reform. From the end of the 1980s onwards, they became increasingly involved in the local management of irrigation waters, in coordination with local offi-cials from the Ministry of Agriculture.

- Committees managing protected natural areas. These came into being under Law 26834 of the Sistema Nacional de Areas Protegidas passed in June 1997.

- Citizen participation in the selection of local justices of the peace (*jueces de paz*) and governors (*tenientes gobernadores*), where citizens propose lists of names from which the authorities (the judiciary or *sub prefectos* in each case) choose.

These experiences in participation, in some cases dating from previous decades and in others from the 1980s and 1990s, were restricted to local decisions and took place within clientelistic and manipulative networks. In no case did they empower local communities by giving them a role in defining policy at the local, regional or national levels. Perhaps the most flagrant example of the manipulative use of these networks was the conditioning of food aid to political support for Fujimori's re-election campaign.

In view of the crisis of legitimacy both in the party system and the public administration (from their incapacity to get to grips with poverty, violence, insecurity and corruption), these clientelistic mechanisms sought to build legitimacy at the local level for a central government that sought to do away with parties and democratic institutions. Notwithstanding the intentions behind it, the success of clientelism depended a great deal on the local or regional circumstances and the specific sectors concerned. In many instances, those who took part in these various clientelistic nexuses managed to maintain a degree of independence and thus affirm their own citizenship. This is the case, for example, of a number of the women running the *comedores populares* or the committees involved in distributing milk rations (*comités de vaso de leche*). Whatever the clientelistic intent, they maintained their independent stance, and indeed some became political leaders in the opposition.

Probably the best-known case is that of María Elena Moyano, whose experience in the *vaso de leche* programme in Villa El Salvador developed into the local women's federation (Federación de Mujeres Populares de Villa El Salvador). She became a local, and then national, left-wing leader, murdered by Sendero Luminoso. A collective expression of this ability to overcome state clientelism was an organisation of women that brought together those working in the *comedores* (the Federación de Mujeres Organizadas en Centrales de Comedores Populares Autogestionarios y Afines de Lima y Callao —Femoccpaalc), established in 1990.

The Authoritarian Context and Local Democratic Management

During the 1980s and 1990s, there were also a number of experiences in democratic management in local government. In most cases, these involved mayors who had a background in unions or left-wing parties, or who had worked in projects associated with NGOs or international donor programmes. They helped develop participatory mechanisms for local decision-making. The modalities and names they adopted were varied (Comités de Desarrollo Distrital, Mesas de Concertación, Comités de Gestión Local, Consejos de Desarrollo Comunal, etc.). Still, they had a number of things in common:

- The primacy given to local political will in the face of the lack of any participatory national regulations. None operated on the basis of obligatory norms or procedures, rather on their own drive and creativity.

- The incorporation of usually excluded sectors (women, peasant communities, grass-roots organisations) in local decision-making. They therefore challenged the domination of local power groups, whether traditional or new (ex-*hacendados*, local traders, owners of transport, medium-sized producers, etc.).

- The binding nature of the agreements reached. These were not so much consultative gatherings as ones for taking decisions on the basis of public participation.

- The combining of notions of participation and oversight.

- The importance of local mayors in driving the process forward. Paradoxically, the widening of the scope of participation of those previously excluded depended in the last analysis on the will of the authorities involved.

- The central role played by NGOs, foreign donors and the Church in both backing the local will to push ahead with these new practices and in providing financial help and technical assistance.

New Mechanisms for Participation under Decentralisation

As a result of the democratic transition and the process of decentralisation, a number of new sectoral mechanisms (national, regional and local) came into being, as well as territorial ones (regional and local) for participation, consensus-building and oversight.

National, Regional and Local Spaces for Consensus-building

As part of the democratic transition, a number of steps were taken to create national mechanisms to build consensus between the state and society. The National Labour Council (Consejo Nacional del Trabajo, CNT) was resuscitated, while a number of new institutions came into being, notably the National Council for Consensus-building in Agriculture (Consejo Nacional de Concertación Agraria, Conaca), the National Education Council (Consejo Nacional de Educación, CNE) and the National Health Council (Consejo Nacional de Salud, CNS). The CNT is designed to be a space for consensus-building between the state, organised labour and employers. It has played a very important role as a place where potentially conflictive laws and policies can be discussed. The CNS and Conaca both involve representation from civil society; in the case of the CNS representatives are mostly private entities like NGOs, while in Conaca they are mostly producer organisations. In the case of the CNE, those involved are mostly experts in education, but without a representative function (Del Aguila and Monge, 2005).

As decentralisation of health and education got under way, spaces for consensus-building have been established at the regional and local levels. In the case of education, Participatory Regional Councils for Education (Consejos Participativos Regionales en Educación, Copares) have been constituted in the 15 regions surveyed to involve representatives from society in developing regional educational policies. Some 55 such councils have been established in eight of these 15 regions. On the health side, these 15 regions also have their Regional Health Councils (Consejos Regionales de Salud), created between February 2003 and September 2004. Their job is to work out regional health plans. More has been accomplished at the local level in health than in education; there are 67 provincial councils in twelve of the 15 regions surveyed.[4]

This dynamic in creating regional spaces for consensus-building around plans and strategies for education and health — which may in the future involve policy and co-management — has brought with it the challenge of how to fit in with the structures that already exist. What will be the relationship, for instance, between the development blueprint (Plan Concertado de Desarrollo) of a region and its respective regional plans for health and education? And what of the relations between the regional and local sectoral councils and their respective Regional or Local Coordination Councils (Consejos de Coordinación Regional/Local, CCRs and CCLs)?

Regional and Local Territorial Spaces for Consensus-building

There are three different territorial spaces for participation and consensus-building that have arisen from the democratic transition and decentralisation.

1. *The Mesas de Concertación de la Lucha Contra la Pobreza* (MCLPs). A national *'mesa'* was established during the Paniagua transition government in 2001. In that and the following year, departmental *mesas* came into being (now known as regional *mesas*) as well as district *mesas*.[5] According to the national *mesa*, by late 2003 there were 1,283 *mesas* in every region of the country, most of the provinces and a large number of districts.[6]

The objective of the *mesas* is to reach consensus solutions between the state and civil society regarding the design and implementation of anti-poverty strategies, and to provide oversight as to how these are carried out. However, in practice the MCLP has constantly been redefining its own agenda. At the time of writing, its main concerns included the Plan for Agreed Development and Participatory Budgets (Plan Concertado de Desarrollo y Presupuesto Participativo); the monitoring and oversight of social policy; the monitoring of implementation of the Truth and Reconciliation Commission (Comisión de la Verdad y Reconciliación, CVR) recommendations; decentralisation; regional educational and health policies; and encouraging the strategy known as Working for Childhood (Tabajando por la Infancia).[7]

The national MCLP has had, and still has, an undeniable influence over the definition of a number of national level public policies. It played a central role in the design and implementation of Participatory Budgeting (Presupuestos Participativos). At the time of writing, it was influential in the design of reparations policies as part of the follow-up to the CVR and of a national campaign centred on children's rights.[8]

The situation was more complicated at the regional and local levels.

The *mesas* enjoyed a great deal of legitimacy at the outset in giving rise to the Planes Concertados de Desarrollo and with the initial experience in Participatory Budgeting. Since 2003, it would seem, the situation of the *mesas* has become very variable between different provinces and districts. In some regions, they seem to have lost ground because of the protagonism of the newly-elected regional and local authorities, and the difficulties in setting clear and precise agendas of their own. However, in other regions, the *mesas* continue to work vigorously, especially where there is a strong Church presence (Piura) or favourable conditions for linking up and working with civil society (Cuzco and San Martín). In all cases, they enjoy greater legitimacy and capacity for action in regional capitals than at the level of provinces and districts.

2. *Consejos de Coordinación Regional/Local.* The Regional and Local Coordination Councils (Consejos de Coordinación Regionales, CCRs and Locales, CCLs) have been established as consultative organisations for regional governments to enable elected authorities and the representatives of society to reach agreements on regional/local development plans and on annual investment budgets.[9] The law establishes that 40 per cent of those on the CCRs and CCLs come from civil society and 60 per cent from locally elected authorities. They meet twice a year, and their agreements are consultative and not binding. The CCRs came into being between January and July 2003, since Congress placed a limit on the time period for their constitution.

The CCLs continued to be established until mid-2004 as one of the requirements for accreditation for having social programmes transferred and for presenting annual budgets for 2005 to the MEF. The National Decentralisation Council (Consejo Nacional de Descentralización, CND) calculated that up to 2005, there were CCLs in 600 municipalities. The MCLP reckoned that CCLs had been set up in nearly 800 districts (around 60 per cent of the total), and at the provincial level there were 159 (82 per cent of the total) (Arroyo and Irigoyen 2004).

Despite their short history, some preliminary conclusions can be reached about the role played by the CCRs and CCLs as spaces for achieving consensus. For example, their design reveals three fundamental problems:

- They meet only twice a year, which makes it impossible for them to become a framework for any real consensus-building

- They limit civil society participation both because of the 40 per cent limit on membership, and because the organisation from which people come has to be registered in the Public Registry. In view of the very high rate of informality in Peruvian society, especially at the popular level, this requirement means that many grass-roots social organisations are in effect precluded.

- Their agreements are not binding, which means that the regional or local authorities can decide on their own what a development plan or annual budget should be, ignoring 'agreements' reached in the CCRs or CCLs. This lack of any guarantee that agreements reached or efforts expended will be respected inhibits participation. Where the authorities ignore agreements, it generates a climate of frustration that casts a pall over the legitimacy of consensus-building and even the idea of participation as such (López Ricci and Elisa Wiener 2004).

- In addition to these design problems, the CCRs and CCLs run into problems caused by the authorities' lack of respect for democracy and participation. Since the convening of CCR and CCL meetings is in the hands of these authorities, their level of dynamism and their projection depend a good deal on whether the authorities want them or not. In addition, civil society often fails to take the initiative in making sure that they are constituted and work properly.

The great diversity of experience is worth highlighting. There are examples (a minority) of CCRs and CCLs where regional or local authorities have taken the initiative in ensuring that representatives from civil society are chosen in ways that are open and participatory and that they also work in this way. Particularly outstanding are the CCRs in Piura and Lambayeque, where members of civil society meet permanently with the organisations that choose them both to report back on their activities and to gather their ideas.

3. *Participatory budgets.* Peru's experience with participatory budgeting began with a pilot project coordinated by the MCLCP, the MEF and the prime minister's office. During 2003 and 2004 all regional and local governments produced development plans and their budgets for 2004 and

2005 respectively. In 2005 the process was under way to produce a budget for 2006 for all regions and municipalities. While in 2002 and 2003 these were based only on directives from the MEF, in the following year the directives were supported by the 2003 Framework Law for Participatory Budgeting (Ley Marco del Presupuesto Participativo) and its detailed regulations.[10]

As with the CCRs and CCLs, the effect of Participatory Budgeting is limited by the fact that these procedures are consultative and not binding. In this case, there are no requirements about the involvement of social organisations, and the rules even allow for individual participation. From this point of view it is less restrictive and the conditions for participation are better. However, a number of design problems have become evident:

- The small proportion of investment spending that is subject to participatory budgeting makes it less important for many.

- The lack of time for making decisions. There have been cases in which the eight stages specified in the law have been rushed through in just a week.

- The lack of time spent in discussing the development plan, which should provide the framework for the annual budget.

- The lack of linkage between district, province and region. Often plans and proposals do not form part of a comprehensive view that brings together different levels of sub-national government.

- The reduction in the levels of involvement of the *mesas* and the CCR/CCLs vis-à-vis other actors, which weakens levels of public confidence.

- The lack of information and interest on the part of large sectors of citizens.

However, it is important to stress that the instructions prepared by the MEF for the preparation of participative budgets for 2006 sought to tackle some of these problems. These gave CCLs and CCRs a coordinating role over civil society participation and also called for coordinating planning and participatory budgeting at the three different levels (regional, provincial and district). It remains to be seen whether these resolve the various initial problems.

A common problem of the CCLs, CCRs and procedures for participatory budgeting is the lack of participation on the part of at least three different types of groups:

1   Women, indigenous people and the very poor, whose non-participation can be explained by material difficulties and/or exclusion by the state (through the use of Spanish in meetings, for example) or by civil society itself (non-election of women, indigenous people or very poor people as representatives).

2   Business sectors which prefer not to carry out their negotiations with the authorities in public on budget allocations and such matters.

3   Organised sectors that opt for mobilisation or direct bilateral negotiation with the authorities.

The three mechanisms we have discussed have a mandate to promote consensus-building by means of development planning and annual budgeting. There is considerable overlap here that generates confusion — if not conflict — within civil society. In view of this it is worth drawing attention to how some municipalities have sought to overcome such problems, often through quite creative institutional practices.

In the case of the municipal district of Pichirgua (Abancay province in Apurímac region) there is a Community Coordination Committee (Comité de Coordinación Comunal) made up of the presidents of six peasant communities. This takes part in the District Coordination Committee (Comité de Coordinación Distrital, Cocodi) to which all private and public institutions in the district belong. In 2004, under the leadership of the mayor, the Cocodi and the CCL were merged. This brought into being a mechanism for participation where the members were 70 per cent representatives of civil society and 30 per cent those of the district municipality (Pisconte and Villavicencio, 2005).

In the case of San Marcos province in Cajamarca, there existed from the late 1990s an Institutional Committee for the Development of San Marcos (Comité Institucional para el Desarrollo de San Marcos, Cindesam). When the *mesas* got going, Cindesam absorbed the *mesa* within its own structure. In Santo Domingo (Morropón province in Piura) a District Development Committee (Comité de Desarrollo Distrital, Codedi) was set up towards the end of 1999 as a meeting place between the authorities and both social organisations and local producers. In 2001, the Codedi adopted the design of the *mesas* and renamed itself as Committee for Development and the Fight against Poverty (Comité de Desarrollo y Lucha contra la Pobreza (CDLCP). In tandem, nine Zonal Development Committees (Comités de Desarrollo Zonal, Codezos) were set up and 40 Village Development Committees (Comités de Desarrollo de Caserío, Codecas). Finally, they have established a CCL in order to comply with the law, but have widened the ambit of civil society participation (using municipal directives) to 32 members, and have integrated it with the Cocodi, the Codezos and the Codecas to form a District General Assembly (Asemblea General Distrital) with a total of 382 members.[11]

As indicated above, many of the best examples of successful participation in local management involve those who were previously left-wing militants or in peasant union organisations. It is for this reason that a central aim has been to give greater voice to rural peasant sectors, traditionally excluded from the municipalities previously controlled by old or new local elites. As might be expected, such elites have resisted the changes that reforms in local government have brought about in democratising decision-making and prioritising rural sectors in local development strategies and budget allocations. An extreme example of this sort of reaction was the successive denunciations made by local power groups against the provincial mayor of Anta (Cuzco), Wilbur Rozas, for his nine-year period as mayor of Limatambo district (which is in the province of Anta).

It is not always the case, then, that these are situations of consensus-building in which all local interest groups are harmoniously represented. On the contrary, the participatory and transparent management of local municipalities presupposes a loss of power on the part of those who were previously the beneficiaries of exclusion and opacity. This produces in a good many cases situations of conflict arising from resistance to change. Conflict, after all, is an aspect that is inherent in any process of democratisation based on participation and inclusion.

Comités de Vigilancia

The norms of participatory budgeting provide for the existence of Oversight Committees (Comités de Vigilancia) whose role is to ensure that agreements reached through participatory processes are put into practice. Unfortunately, at the time of writing, these Committees had only very recently been created and the information available was insufficient to evaluate their activities. However, it was possible to draw attention, once again, to the danger of overlapping responsibilities. This was particularly the case because, according to their relative dynamics, the *mesas*, the CCRs and CCLs geared themselves increasingly towards functions of oversight in many regions and localities.

In sum, the democratic transition from 2001 onwards and the experience in decentralisation had strong participatory components. There has been a proliferation of different sorts of mechanisms, often involving overlapping functions, activities and actors. At the same time, one of the limitations of the sorts of mechanisms was the restrictions on civil society involvement. For reasons of design, lack of information or public interest, discrimination or exclusion arising from civil society itself, participation still involves the few, not the many. The challenge is to ensure that the majority (especially those traditionally excluded) can really assume a participatory role.

Having said this, we have to bear in mind that the whole process is still fairly recent. It is therefore perhaps unrealistic to expect too much, too fast. The conditions are being created for future democratisation of state-society relations. It has also to be borne in mind that the *mesas*, the CCR/Ls and the participatory budgets will exert their effect in the short-to-medium term on larger budgets and more important areas of governance as decentralisation advances and greater powers and resources are transferred to the regional and local levels. It is to be expected that public interest will increase along with the importance of the decisions reached.

Inclusion, Negotiation and Participation in Representative Democracy: The Areas of Debate

Without seeking to minimise the importance of the necessary debate over norms and procedures or the decisions made and resources allocated, Peru's experiences in the area of participation highlight three deeper issues, namely:

1. *The continuing presence of exclusion within civil society.* A common feature of these mechanisms of participation and oversight is the fact that the

poorest sectors, women and indigenous groups are under-represented. The way these mechanisms are designed contributes to exclusion. However, the key problem resides in the attitudes and practices of discrimination within civil society. How is it that society reproduces such attitudes and practices? What can be done from the point of view of institutional design to overcome this? What can be done from within society itself in this direction?

It is not the purpose of this text to explore the possible answers to these questions, but it is important to take proper note that implementing citizen participation from the state confronts a citizenry with its own limitations in the struggle for inclusion. The main challenge that Peruvian civil society faces in response to these opportunities for participation and oversight is to overcome its own practices of exclusion. Participation needs to bring in those sectors — like women, rural populations and the very poorest — which have traditionally been excluded from decision-making and the exercise of oversight over those in government.

2. *Negotiation and conflict in state-society relations.* We have seen how there are sectors that do not take part in these mechanisms of participation because they opt for other approaches to the state, like mobilisation, confrontation and negotiation.

On the one hand, there is the business community, which is not accustomed to negotiating its interests explicitly or openly with the public sector since many such negotiations have sought unwarranted favours. Consequently, although there is a degree of business involvement in national-level politics around policy issues and general orientation (the National Accord, the CNT, the MCLP), this is much less common at the regional level (some Chambers of Commerce and CCRs) and almost non-existent at the local level. Consequently, at the provincial and district levels, the contacts are between the authorities and 'the poor' around the use of limited municipal and regional resources, in which 'successful actors' do not usually become involved, even those with an interest in commerce or transport or outside business people, like those who own hotels in poor districts.

On the other hand, many organised popular organisations work within a logic of mobilisation, confrontation and negotiation. These, like the business community, tend not to involve themselves in mechanisms of

participation and consensus building. The presence of trade union organisations — involving teachers, peasants, other agricultural producers and
those involved in urban-based employment — is very weak in the CCLs,
CCRs and in participatory budgeting. One reason for this is that such
mechanisms are territorial in nature and local authorities do not exercise
much sway over issues of interest to such actors. It is possible that the
transfer of sectoral responsibilities to sub-national tiers of government
will change these attitudes of disengagement on the part of union organisations. A second reason is that the ideology of these organisations is
often confrontational, feeding on the notion, based on a good deal of tangible evidence, that confrontation is the only way to draw the authorities'
attention to their demands and obtain solutions.

Within Peruvian society there is a mixture of attitudes, ideologies
and practices that seek open and consensual outcomes, negotiations
behind closed doors, and conflict in state-society relations. As decentralisation advances and as citizens find in participation ways to take
advantage of capacities, resources and commitment, it is possible that
more and more people will become involved. And as they become more
powerful and legitimate, they will be better placed to insist that business
interests and sector based unions negotiate their interests within them.
Otherwise, negotiation through confrontation or behind the backs of
citizens will remain the main means of engaging with the state.

3. *Representation and participation in designing and practising democracy in Peru.*
As in other Latin American countries, representative democracy in Peru
is fragile and has to contend with one crisis of governability after another. This stems from the chronic incapacity of democratic governments
to deal with the growing problems of unemployment and poverty
which afflict the majority of Peruvians. A contributory factor is the tendency to strike deals with the powerful — the so-called *poderes fácticos*
(large investors, the media, the military, etc.) — that ignore electoral
promises and about which the citizenry and voters have no information
or forms of exercising control.

Participatory democracy aims radically to change the terms of the
relationship between the state and citizens, and in so doing to create the
conditions for enhancing the legitimacy of representative democracy

and the democratic regime as such. It is not a proposal to substitute representative democracy by a system of participatory democracy. Rather, it seeks to increase the elements for participation to enable the traditionally excluded to exercise their voice in public affairs, thereby balancing the influence of the *poderes fácticos*. In spite of all the limitations that I have discussed, a system of participatory decentralisation offers the chance substantively to change the old pattern of state-society relations. It provides an opportunity to leave behind a tradition of exclusion, opacity and top-down rules that has been part of the colonial heritage but which representative democracy has been unable to replace.

But for this to happen, political elites need to know that participation is not the enemy of representation; rather it provides it with new legitimacy. Those elites need to understand that in a democratic system representation is not giving a blank cheque for the management of public affairs; on the contrary, it is the means of permanently negotiating public decisions with the whole range of social actors.

This, then, is the opportunity that participatory decentralisation offers us. But it is vital to emphasise the fact that it is an opportunity, not a given. Efforts at decentralisation have been frustrated before, but never before has participatory democracy been called for as a policy of state. It has potential, but is far from consolidated. The challenge now is to consolidate and make it irreversible. This requires a profound change in the understanding of the political class about what Peruvian democracy needs to make it legitimate and (on that basis) governable.

Notes

1   For an appreciation of the state of decentralisation see Participa Perú 24 May 2005, a monthly supplement published by Grupo Propuesta Ciudadana in the daily *La República* newspaper.

2   This section of the chapter is based on Ballón (2003) and Monge (2003).

3   It is important not to confuse these 'rondas' (or Committees for Self-Defence — Comités de Autodefensa) with the *rondas campesinas* of the northern sierra (Cajamarca, Piura and La Libertad). The latter were a response to the problem of cattle-rustling and delinquent behaviour in

general. They managed to maintain a large measure of autonomy. They were officially recognised by the Rondas Campesinas Law (Ley 27908) and its regulations (DS-025-2003-JUS). They were also afforded a role in local citizen security under the Internal Security System Law (Ley 27933).

4   See *Vigila Perú*, no. 6, February 2005, a report by Sistema Vigila Perú managed by the Grupo Propuesta Ciudadana.

5   The national *mesa* was created by D.S. 01-2001-Promudeh. In July 2001, D.S. 014-2001-Promudeh was enacted, modifying and complementing the original decree.

6   See www.mesadeconcertacion.org.pe.

7   See the VII National Encounter of the Mesa de Concertación para la Lucha contra la Pobreza, Lima 2005, at www.mesadeconcertacion.org.pe.

8   Interview with Federico Arnillas, executive secretary of the Asociación Nacional de Centros (ANC) and representative of the NGOs on the Mesa de Concertación, Lima, April 2005.

9   Law 27867 on Regional Governments (2002); Law 27092 (which modifies Law 27867) and Law 27972 (Organic Law on Municipalities, 2003).

10   Law 28056 and DS 071-2003-EF.

11   See López (2005). This includes presentations that highlight other similar cases.

4

The Blocking of Reform in the Security Services

Fernando Rospigliosi

Reform of the armed forces, the police and the intelligence services was one of the essential priorities following the collapse of the Alberto Fujimori and Vladimiro Montesinos regime in November 2000. The context for achieving this was ideal; not only was there a broad national consensus on the necessity for doing so, but there was no possibility of resistance from those who would otherwise oppose such changes. Changes were initiated, first in the police then in the armed forces. However, in both cases, the reform dynamic was frustrated and then reversed, and by the beginning of 2005 the chances of renewing the process of reform during what was left of the Toledo government looked slim indeed. Why did reform fail?

Reform of the Armed Forces

1. Before the Fall of Fujimori

Prior to the fall of Alberto Fujimori and Vladimiro Montesinos and their dictatorial regime, an unprecedented situation had occurred in Peru. It had become clear that the military leadership had been at the centre of power politics during the 1990s; that they had been guilty of illicit enrichment; that they had been involved in horrendous violations of human rights; and that jobs and promotions had been distributed not on the basis of merit but of political and personal loyalty. It had also become clear that the National Intelligence Service (Servicio de Inteligencia Nacional, SIN), run by Montesinos, had been the real centre of decision-making — controlling the government, the armed forces and the police. Montesinos's predilection for recording videos of his dealings with other actors and the screening of these made clear to millions of Peruvians just how power and wealth had been deployed under Fujimori.

The creation by the transitional Paniagua government (November 2000 to July 2001) of a system for rooting out corruption[1] had been instrumental in creating a situation unprecedented in the history of Peru: the commanders-in-chief of the armed forces and a substantial number of senior military officers were tried and sentenced to lengthy terms in civilian jails. They included Montesinos, other former heads of the SIN and senior police officers. Almost all senior military officers, even those who replaced the corrupt leadership that fell with Fujimori, were involved in one way or another with the previous regime, even though they may not have been directly involved in criminal activities. In short, the infamy of the Fujimori and Montesinos regime was shared by both the armed forces and the SIN, the dual sources of power in the 1990s.

The context for a thoroughgoing reform in the armed forces, therefore, and a radical shift in military-civilian relations could hardly have been more propitious. However, the Paniagua administration did not initiate any major reforms. In line with standard practice, the ministers of defence and interior were respectively retired army and police generals.[2] The interim government limited itself to forcing into retirement a number of Montesinos's best-known collaborators. In Paniagua's defence, it should be said that his period in office was short, that his government was unelected, that its composition was very mixed, its mandate limited and the tasks it confronted enormous.

2. Winds of Change at the Beginning of the Toledo Government

One of Alejandro Toledo's promises in the 2001 election campaign had been to nominate a civilian defence minister for the first time.[3] Symbolism apart, the purpose of this change was to establish civilian control over the armed forces. Toledo only partially met this promise. He named a civilian as minister, but one poorly qualified for the job: David Waisman, the second vice-president and a congressman. He lasted as defence minister only from July 2001 to February 2002.[4]

At the end of 2001, the government set up the Commission for Comprehensive Restructuring of the Armed Forces (Comisión para la Reestructuración Integral de las Fuerzas Armadas), presided over by Prime Minister Roberto Dañino.[5] The Commission had the invaluable support of Narcís Serra, Spain's defence minister for a number of years during the transition there. The Commission undertook an evaluation and came up with proposals for far-reaching reform. Among these was the creation of a defence ministry whose central objective would be to bring the armed forces under democratic control. The final report of the Commission pointed out that:

> *The restructuring of the armed forces forms part of a process of modernisation of the Peruvian state.* It should be considered as a key element in the consolidation of *democracy* in our country. The enhancement of democratic institutions, the reform of the judiciary, the strengthening of political parties, the modernisation of the public administration, amongst other things, should complement the restructuring of the armed forces.

> Following the reversal of democracy and the way the country has been governed over the past decade, which also affected the armed forces, it is essential that the democratically-elected government, charged by the nation to rebuild democracy, should undertake reforms in the armed forces that are at once far-reaching and irreversible. It is not just a question of reorganising each branch of the armed forces, reducing their size and making them more operational, important and necessary as such aims may be. *It is a matter of placing the armed forces within the framework of the rule of law and bringing them under the authority of the legitimately elected government.*

> Military-civilian relations should be the norm in a modern democracy. *In a democracy, the armed forces neither intervene nor seek to influence policy; rather they execute the defence and military policies decided upon by a freely-elected government.*

> In a democracy, military-civilian relations are such that they uphold civilian control of the armed forces. This is measurable not just by professionalism and rationalisation, but in establishing clearly that decisions on military matters are an attribute of civilian government, and that it is up to the government and the Congress to verify whether such decisions are carried out.

> Civilian control over the armed forces obviously implies their subordination to constitutional authority, but it also implies the

normalisation of civil-military relations within a democratic context and the adoption of axioms that reconcile and integrate the values of the armed forces and those of civil society. *This is a complex process that demands time* both with regard to elaboration and implementation.

As can be seen from this, the Commission defined the issue broadly, placing emphasis on the need to ensure civilian control over the armed forces. The Commission, furthermore, was clear in its diagnosis of the predicament facing the armed forces and the reasons for it:

> In addition to the foregoing, there was a serious process of *de-institutionalisation* that began at the beginning of the 1990s. Through its own command structure and in connivance with a dictatorship disguised as a democracy, and complicit with a military leadership wedded to Montesinos [currently in jail], the military deliberately and consciously involved itself in political activity, annulled the rule of law, and created a criminal apparatus that made the public Treasury its own. Never before had the reputation of our armed forces been so sullied in the eyes of public opinion both at home and abroad. [This situation] made it vitally urgent to extricate them from this situation and begin their immediate *re-institutionalisation*. This should begin with their radical *de-politicisation* and moralisation within their ranks, alongside their *professionalisation*. Both of these [aims] should be carried out within a transparent system of *oversight* in order to improve and harmonise *military-civilian relations*. In sum, the situation briefly outlined had seriously damaged the *image and prestige* of our armed forces, undermining the *professionalism and moral values* that have always characterised them and made them the moral backbone of the nation.

Finally, among the proposals and recommendations, the main instrument for reform is clearly identified:

> In restructuring the armed forces, the starting point should be *the creation of a new defence ministry*. This ministry should be equivalent to those of mature democracies. It would therefore work as *an organ for the design, implementation and oversight of defence policy, the basic tool for ensuring civil control over the armed forces.*

Although the creation of the Ministry of Defence represented a step towards modernisation of the system of national security, the situation that exists within the ministry is still unsatisfactory and urgent restructuring is needed. Today there is a *civilian minister* who lacks the organisation *to define defence policy and direct and oversee its application by the armed forces* (...)

The Ministry of Defence should fulfil two key roles: to act as a mechanism to ensure democratic control over the armed forces, and guarantee their military capacity. Equally, its function is to lead the process of restructuring. To this end, it is essential to modify Legislative Decree 434, the Framework Law for the Ministry of Defence to provide the ministry with a modern and efficient organisation. In view of the nature of the armed forces, this structure should conform to that of other ministries in the executive branch.

The Ministry of Defence should be *responsible for the formulation, management, coordination and implementation of overall state strategy in the area of defence policy.* The existing National Defence System Law defines it as the 'representative organ of the armed forces' and as the 'nexus between the executive and the system of military justice'. Such definitions are unacceptable from a constitutional and democratic point of view. They tacitly deny that they (the armed forces) form part of the executive branch and that the relationship is one of subordination.

It is worth repeating the point that the positions adopted by Narcís Serra were of utmost importance. His experience over almost a decade of the democratic transition in Spain helped the Commission establish the need for a proper ministry as precondition for carrying out the reforms required.

3. Applying the Reforms

In February 2002 Aurelio Loret de Mola, a member of the Restructuring Commission, replaced Waisman as defence minister. Having assimilated the overall orientation of the Commission's work, he sought to begin the task of implementing its recommendations, beginning with the creation of a proper ministry of defence. To this end, he prepared a bill for Congress and managed to achieve its passage. However, the process proved slow.

As well as the time taken up in congressional debate, there were delays due to the political turbulence that affected Peru from the very beginning of the Toledo administration.[6] Between congressional approval and implementation there was a further delay of several months. One of the reasons for this was the lack of any civilians with knowledge of military matters willing to take up public office at a time when the government's standing was in rapid decline. Another reason was the ploys adopted by the palace to seek jobs for specific people.

Loret de Mola found himself during 2003 involved in ever more bitter disputes with successive economy ministers over budgetary matters. The defence ministry managed to extract some budget concessions. For instance, it increased the budget for meals for troops from US$0.85 a day to US$1.80. It also managed to raise pay levels for officers. A key problem was the difficulty of attracting people into the army, following the scrapping of compulsory military service under Fujimori. The new system of voluntary recruitment did not involve any increase in the armed forces' miserable pay levels, with the result that many battalions had only a quarter or a fifth of the troops they required. Then, with the fall of Fujimori, the transition government ordered a cut in military spending that was never made up later.

At the beginning, at least, the military was reluctant to raise its voice on economic matters; the scale of corrupt military acquisitions under Fujimori had become clear after 2000,[7] as well as the huge sums paid to Montesinos, General Nicolás Hermoza (the commander-in-chief of the army for most of the 1990s) and General Víctor Malca (former minister of defence), amongst others. However, as time passed and the weakness of the new government became evident, the military became more assertive, although there was no real attempt to put a stop to military waste. Loret de Mola started to echo demands by the military for equipment, including those of the navy for new frigates, which the economy ministry opposed.[8] Loret de Mola finally resigned over budgetary issues. He argued that to push ahead with reform against the will of the military, something had to be offered in return. He also believed that a larger budget allocation was needed if operational capabilities of the armed forces were to be improved. He was replaced by Roberto Chiabra, a retired army general who had hitherto been army commander-in-chief.[9] His appointment saw a return to the old negative tradition of having military officers run the Ministry of Defence. Although a competent soldier, it was clear that Chiabra did not agree with the principles of the reforms whose key objective had been to establish democratic control over the armed forces. Under Chiabra, the ministry returned to its function as the representative of the armed forces in the council of ministers.

4. Toledo's About-Turn

Toledo's motives for this decision to appoint Chiabra were various. Firstly, he was interested in turning the armed forces into an instrument to defend his government. Early on his popularity began to plummet, whilst his government found itself increasingly under pressure over social demands. His inchoate parliamentary support also began to show signs of falling apart. The threat of being overturned by a wave of public protest and opposition manoeuvres in Congress became something of an obsession. Toledo believed, wrongly, that giving in to military pressure and appointing a military man as defence minister would be sufficient for the military to come to his rescue should the need arise. However, it was an illusion to think that this would commit the military to the defence of his government if it was on the point of being overturned. In practice, the military simply took advantage of this weakness to rebuild its own institutional autonomy and to lay claim to a larger budget allocation.

Still, from the very beginning Toledo sought to involve the military to protect himself. During his first weeks in office when protest broke out in Cuzco, there was a rumour (later shown to be false) that peasants had taken control of the airport. He convened his generals and demanded of them intelligence reports and what they would do to resolve the situation. It was clear that this was a problem of internal politics, in which the military had no part to play. Such situations recurred repeatedly. In June 2002, faced by a widespread protest movement in Arequipa which the police could not control properly, Toledo decreed a state of emergency and handed control of the situation to the military, ignoring the advice of both the interior and defence ministers. It was clear that military participation would do nothing to quell the disturbances. The Arequipa riots ended in a defeat for the government and the resignation of the interior minister.

The same sort of response was made to the kidnapping of pipeline workers in the central jungle in June 2003, when another state of emergency was declared and the military once again brought in. In the end, the kidnappers simply fled. The state of emergency was then widened to cover the whole country when, at much the same time, there was a series of marches and protests that resulted in the blocking of highways. In Puno a protest by university students over local problems (which normally would have passed virtually unnoticed) ended up in a confrontation between troops and students in which one person was killed and several wounded. As a result, several soldiers were put on trial, a further signal to the military not to become involved in problems of maintaining law and order. This sort of problem was repeated several times elsewhere, leading to military authorities refusing to respond to entreaties by the president and other authorities to intervene. Even on matters that properly concerned them — like the resurgence of terrorist activities in the jungle regions of Amazonia — the military tried to avoid becoming involved, arguing that it lacked the budget resources to do so.

A further reason for Toledo resorting to the traditional practice of placing military personnel in the Ministry of Defence was his fear of a coup. Such a possibility seemed most implausible, especially in Peru. The last successful coup in Latin America had been as long ago as 1982 in Bolivia.[10] From the end of 1980s it had been clear that the United States and other members of the international community had imposed a veto on *golpismo*. Given the changes in the international context, the sorts of pressure that could be exerted — both commercial and economic — were so strong that it would be almost impossible for a military government to survive an international blockade. Irrespective of this, neither Toledo nor many Peruvian politicians have perceived this, continuing to fear the possibility of a military coup. This has led them to make unnecessary concessions to the military, including putting trusted commanders in key posts.[11] This is what Samuel P. Huntington calls 'subjective control', as opposed to objective or institutional control.

5. *Consequences*

The appointment of General Chiabra did not have the desired effect within the army. As might have been expected, Chiabra — who had been commander-in-chief of the army until the day of his appointment as defence minister — continued to act as if he still was commander-in-chief. He encountered, at times publicly, resistance from the new commander-in-chief, General José Graham, a well respected conservative within the military establishment and someone who maintained a distance from the spheres of political power. In addition, Chiabra was unable to manage the army as Toledo wanted. This led to conflict and Graham's resignation in December 2004 only days before he was due to retire. Graham alleged that Toledo and Chiabra had manipulated the annual promotions, bringing in officers who did not deserve the positions they were given and taking out others who had been nominated by the military command.[12] The government ended by backing down, increasing the number of jobs available and then promoting both those the army had proposed as well as those hand-picked by the president and his minister.

What was clear here was the military's determination to recover the independence it had previously enjoyed in the key area of promotions. This clashed with political manoeuvrings to promote people for political and clientelistic reasons, not on the basis of professional merit. This conflict was a throwback to the perverse sort of relationship that had always existed between civilian and military authorities. Neither the military command nor the civilian authorities acted in accordance with the need for reform by re-establishing institutional hierarchies, encouraging professionalism and appointing senior officers strictly on the basis of merit.

The officer chosen to replace Graham was General Luis Muñoz, who appeared more malleable to the government's desires than his predecessor. However, he had the disadvantage of having appeared in one of the 'Vladivideos' thanking Montesinos for an earlier promotion and swearing eternal loyalty to him. Situations such as these encouraged rebellious actions, like that of Antauro Humala on New Year's Day 2005.[13]

6. The Andahuaylas Revolt

On 1 January 2005 Humala and some 150 of his 'reservists' assaulted the police compound in Andahuaylas, an impoverished town in the Peruvian *sierra*. Armed with roughly a hundred pistols and rifles, they took 15 policemen hostage. Humala demanded Toledo's resignation. In response, Toledo declared a state of emergency, but gave control of the situation to the interior ministry after the military had made it clear it did not wish to be involved. Several hundred police and troops were sent to Andahuaylas. The followers of Humala ambushed a police patrol and killed four policemen, while two of the Humalistas were shot by troops in circumstances that remain confused. Fearful after the killing of the policemen, Antauro Humala surrendered and convinced his followers to do likewise.

What was noteworthy about this episode was that hundreds of the inhabitants of Andahuaylas came out on to the streets spontaneously to support Humala, while no one emerged in support of the government. Subsequent opinion surveys suggested that up to a third of the people in the town supported the rising, although it was a move that had no possible chance of success, was led by someone who was mentally unhinged and had led to the senseless killing of six people.

The Humalista movement at the time enjoyed the support of a few hundred people nationwide, lacked any solid organisation and subsequently split. Rather surprisingly, a number of retired military figures who had identified themselves publicly with the movement became advisors to General Graham in 2004. This led some analysts and politicians to question the relationship between Humala and officers on active service. At the time of writing at least, this was still unclear.

The Humala movement was extremely nationalistic, militaristic and even fascist in orientation. Among its more far-fetched suggestions were the shooting of politicians and senior military officers, increasing the population of Peru fourfold, getting rid of money and producing more coca. It had an anti-Semitic trait and among its main platforms was a virulent hatred towards Chile. Still, in spite of these ideas, the advent of elections in 2006 would show it received a surprising level of support in the turbulent state of contemporary Peruvian politics.

7. Further Concessions

During 2004 the military won some important concessions. The first was the purchase of two frigates demanded by the navy, alongside the planned purchase of two more in 2005. The second was the approval of a Defence Fund, involving money to be given annually to the armed forces on an indefinite basis for the purchase of arms. In the first year, the Defence Fund was to be financed from budget resources, but subsequently from a percentage of the earnings from the Camisea gas project, which began operations in August 2004. Such an arrangement was similar to the way in which the Chilean armed forces received a portion of that country's copper earnings. It is worth noting that this sort of method to fund military expenditure has been on the decline in Latin America in recent times. The last country to eliminate it was Ecuador.

The Fund would transfer a quarter of the money thus raised to each of the three armed services, plus the police.[14] This sort of arrangement is yet another symptom of the process of military reform coming to an end. The establishment of a proper defence ministry would presuppose that it would decide upon budgetary matters. Under the Defence Fund, they would each receive a slice of the cake and then decide how to spend it. The Fund therefore simply reinforced their autonomy, leaving the ministry out of the picture. By early 2005 there had thus been a return to the status quo, in spite of advances in the legislative sphere.

Police Reform

1. Antecedents

The Ministry of the Interior and the National Police (Policía Nacional del Perú, PNP) were also institutions manipulated and utilised by Fujimori and Montesinos. From day one of the Fujimori government, the interior minister was an army general, and this remained the case almost to the end when, following Montesinos's flight from the country, Fujimori appointed the head of police, General Fernando Dianderas, as minister.[15] Montesinos used the Interior Ministry not just as one of his main sources of illegal money, but also to conduct operations on behalf of his mafia. When Peru returned to democracy at the end of 2000, the PNP was widely regarded as one of the most corrupt institutions in the country.

2. Police Reform

Although the team that took over the Ministry of the Interior in July 2001 lacked experience in public administration, it was fully aware of the deficiencies of the police and the need for reform. In October 2001 the Special Commission for the Restructuring of the National Police of Peru (Comisión Especial de Reestructuración de la Policía Nacional del Perú, CERPNP) was established, which produced a report on 22 February 2002.

The CERPNP worked in the most open way possible, seeking to take on board the views of individuals and institutions. It divided its work between eight sub-commissions, each of which met at least once a week. Public participation was encouraged by establishing mail boxes in the various law colleges around the country, as well as e-mail facilities and free phone lines for public consultation. Public opinion surveys were conducted to gauge people's views about the police. A weekly programme went out on state television to promote discussion of reform. Within the police, meetings were held at different levels, both in Lima and other parts of the country. Members of the Commission travelled widely to discuss issues with both policemen and civilians, and an opinion poll was also conducted among serving policemen.

In its diagnosis, the CERPNP laid things bare, highlighting the following key issues:

- Militarisation of the police and its distance from the community.

- Politicisation and subordination to an authoritarian regime.

- Poor living and working conditions for policemen.

- Poor management of scarce resources.

- High levels of corruption.

- Lack of openness to the community and poor relations with local government.

- Lack of public trust in the PNP.

From this analysis, the following priority objectives were set:

- To contribute to democratic consolidation.

- To improve relations between the police and the community.

- To improve living standards within the police.

- To confront corruption.

- To develop a modern educational system for the police.

- To bring in modern methods of administration.

- To apply state-of-the-art technology at every level.

- To combat sophisticated forms of criminality more effectively.

The report, which was over 200 pages long, provided detailed analysis. To avoid it simply gathering dust — as so many reports by special commissions tend to do in Peru — it provided a timetable for application, distinguishing between immediate, short-term and medium-term objectives.

3. Progress on Reform

Even before the Commission presented its report, a number of essential initiatives had been taken:

- De-politicisation of the promotions system and the adoption of objective criteria in this sphere. In particular, measures were introduced to reduce favouritism, clientelism and corruption among the committees responsible for recommending appointments.[16]

- Re-establishment of an institutional pyramid within the PNP. Under Fujimori and Montesinos, promotion to senior ranks had been conducted indiscriminately, packing them with people loyal to the regime. In 2001 there were 48 police generals, 751 colonels, 1,222 commanders, but only 597 sub-lieutenants and 1,495 lieutenants.[17] In December 2001, 600 police officers passed into retirement,[18] including a large number of generals and colonels, reducing at the same time the number of vacancies to be filled, a process that continued through till 2003.[19]

- The Catholic University was put in charge of running examinations for the officer school, thereby raising quality control and reducing the scope for corruption. Control over examinations for lower-level entry was given to the Ricardo Palma University.

- An ombudsman's office (*defensoría*) was established for the police under the control of a civilian.[20] This was to protect policemen and their families, especially in the lower ranks, from abusive behaviour on the part of their superiors. The ombudsman requires the support of the minister since he does not have enforcement powers.

- Steps were taken to improve the welfare of personnel. Extra-budgetary resources were used to establish a system of life insurance for policemen killed in the course of duty, to buy new uniforms,[21] and to pay off debts left outstanding since 1995 (holidays, removals costs, etc.). The police housing fund, a fruitful source of corruption under Fujimori, was reorganised. Salaries were improved in line with other public sector workers.

- In the attempt to deal with corruption, an Office of Internal Affairs (Oficina de Asuntos Internos, OAI) was set up, run by a civilian directly answerable to the minister. In 2003, during Rospigliosi's second period as minister, the OAI broke up a corruption ring involving a general and senior officers. They were dismissed.[22] A programme was organised called 'Respect for the Policeman' (A la Policía se la Respeta) to capture on film and prosecute those who tried to bribe policemen.[23]

- The National Citizen Security System Law was passed (a ministry initiative) to try to improve coordination between the police, local authorities and civil society.

- Laws were passed (also at the suggestion of the ministry) to raise the penalties for specific types of common crime and violations of public order. The judiciary was encouraged to ensure the presence of justices of the peace (*jueces de paz*) in police stations and for them to punish minor crime with community service orders.

- A new law modified the antiquated system of police discipline.

- The system for entry into officer and junior officer schools was changed, allowing university graduates and those finishing other types of higher education to qualify for careers in the police force more speedily than in the past.

- A new system of promotions was introduced in 2004 to be applied progressively over the following five years. Rather than rewarding years of service, this sought to promote younger and brighter people.[24]

In these and other areas, the police reform advanced in important ways, constituting probably one of the most successful reform programmes of the Toledo presidency. However, at the time of writing, many of the reforms had been abandoned and reversed.

4. The End of the Reform

The basic drive behind the reform programme came from the ideas and pressure of a team of civilians and policemen from within the Ministry of the Interior from July 2001 to August 2003, and from July 2003 to May 2004.[25] The government, and Toledo specifically, took little interest in these reforms, though it is true that they never sought to block them. When the team was replaced by others who had no interest in the issue, the more conservative sectors in the police took advantage of the situation to regroup, stop and then reverse the reforms.

Although Toledo took little interest in the reforms, he was concerned to maintain control over the ministry when he and members of his government were accused of involvement in shady dealing. It was for this reason that the president sought to sow discord between the director of the PNP and Gino Costa when he was minister.[26] This led to Costa being forced to resign and then replaced by Alberto Sanabria,[27] a member of the ruling party and personal friend of the president. Subsequently, a change in prime minister (Beatríz Merino, an independent) brought the return of Rospigliosi and his former team, albeit without the backing of the president. Following Merino's fall,[28] Rospigliosi was censured by Congress in May 2004 with crucial support from the ruling party benches.[29] Javier Reátegui, another member of the ruling party and friend of Toledo, became minister. The advantages of having direct control over the ministry became evident when it came to, for example, facilitating the illegal removal from the country of witnesses who had accused the president of criminal activities.

As a result of the Andahuaylas crisis in January 2005, Reátegui was replaced by a police general, Félix Murazzo, under whom the process of return to the status quo was complete. Under Reátegui and then under Murazzo, the reform programme was abandoned, and with it those institutions dependent on the minister such as the police ombudsman's office and the OAI. The campaign against corruption dissipated,[30] and with it there was a return to practices of populism and clientelism. In the 2004 round of promotions, 16 generals were promoted (and only two retired), raising the number of police generals to 44, a 50 per cent increase.[31] The number of appointments to the rank of colonel increased 100 per cent, with only very few retirements. The problem of an inflated number of senior officers thus returned. During 2004 some

US$1.2 million were spent on cars for the personal use of generals and colonels,[32] a figure which compares with a total ministry investment budget for 2005 of US$2.1m.[33]

5. Concluding Remarks

The experience of these years showed that reform was possible. A small team of civilians and policemen within the Ministry of the Interior had been able to do a great deal in a short time with few resources. However, experience shows that reform can be fragile and reversed almost over night. Generally speaking, such reforms do not generate excitement, either among the public or in the media. Even politicians, whether in the ruling party or the opposition, showed a lack of interest. Though they were not against reform, they are not in favour of it either. When the Toledo government committed the grave mistake of appointing a policeman as interior minister, no one criticised the move, just as no one raised their voice against nominating a member of the military as defence minister or as head of the National Intelligence Council (Consejo Nacional de Inteligencia, CNI). It became evident, though, that a policeman or member of the military — moulded by three decades of working in an institution with all the commitments, friendships and reciprocities that this implies — would be unlikely to spearhead far-reaching reforms. Probably the best that could be hoped for (and this has not been the case here) was that they would pursue policies of modernisation.

The Intelligence System

Reform of the intelligence service was another of the pressing tasks that faced the new democratic government. During the 1990s the SIN became an elephantine apparatus used unscrupulously to control other institutions: the armed forces, the judiciary, the police, Congress, the media. It became the main instrument by which the Fujimori administration maintained control.

From the intelligence point of view, the SIN had been a disaster. This was made clear by the 1995 conflict with Ecuador, when the country found itself in armed conflict with its neighbour without having any idea about the capacities of its adversary or its prime areas of weakness. In the war against Sendero Luminoso, the SIN showed its lack of intelligence capacity. Indeed, it was responsible for the worst single tragedy experienced when, in 1995, a helicopter was brought down (and various military personnel, including four officers, lost their lives) on a SIN operation to convince a terrorist group to surrender.

Nevertheless, Montesinos managed to make it seem that the SIN was an effective intelligence service by taking advantage of the successes of third parties and by using its control over the media and institutions to dazzle both government and opposition politicians alike. Partly for this reason, Montesinos had his imitators during the Toledo government.

In September 2000, when Fujimori first announced his intention to cut short his mandate and convene fresh elections, he announced that the SIN would be dissolved and restructured. In the months that followed, Montesinos and his minions removed everything from the SIN; files, equipment, vehicles, office supplies, the lot. At the end of the transition government a new law was hastily approved creating the CNI to replace the SIN. Valentín Paniagua appointed a retired admiral, Alfonso Panizo, to head it. In the period that followed there was such a swift succession of leaders that it was impossible to create a new intelligence service.

At the beginning of 2002, the Toledo government appointed Juan Velit to the post.[34] It had become by that time a highly bureaucratised entity with some 300 officials, mostly retired members of the armed forces or police. Velit lasted a few months and was replaced by Rospigliosi, who left in early 2003 when Gino Costa resigned as interior minister. He was replaced by César Almeyda, a lawyer, personal friend of Toledo and a member of the president's immediate entourage. Almeyda resigned shortly afterwards, the object of a major scandal,[35] and was replaced by Panizo who took charge once again. Months later Panizo resigned, himself involved in a scandal over infiltration within the CNI. He was in turn replaced by Daniel Mora, a retired general and leading member of the ruling party.[36] At the beginning of 2004, Mora was asked to resign in the midst of yet another scandal.

All this was too much, and the government found itself forced to declare the CNI to be in 'reorganisation'. Its dissolution was also announced, although this did not happen. Julio Raygada, a retired admiral, was put 'in charge', rather than being formally designated CNI head. Raygada had worked with Mora as an advisor. All in all, the CNI had had six heads (three of them civilians) between June 2001 and March

2004. This was an absurdity, particularly in a situation where a new intelligence service needed to be built almost from scratch. But more important than this was the idea — firmly held by both government and opposition — that an institution should exist to protect those in government from their various political adversaries, even by illegal means. There was also the prevalent belief that the service existed to conduct what the military call 'psycho-social operations'.

Following Mora's exit, the government named a commission, of three civilian intellectuals, to produce proposals for a new service. The commission came up with a conceptual plan and a draft bill. However, at the time of writing, neither the government nor the Congress had made any decision on this. According to some sources, the government had meanwhile resorted to using other institutions to undertake the espionage work it believed necessary to protect itself politically. In this setting, the intelligence services of the armed forces regained much of the ground they had lost since Fujimori's and Montesinos' fall. Although from the time of Paniagua they had been barred from domestic intelligence activities (except in areas such as terrorism), it is possible that they continued to undertake such activities. Indeed, the Toledo administration requested information from them, thereby encouraging them. The failings of the CNI have acted as a stimulus for this to happen.

To rebuild a real and effective intelligence service would have required a fairly lengthy period of time to develop the necessary structures and recruit and train staff. It should be part of a strategy to construct a professional and de-politicised civil service more generally like those of most developed countries and some Latin American countries. Given the sinister precedents of Montesinos's SIN and the history of exclusively military involvement in intelligence, it would have required a strong political will on the part of government to pursue such an aim, as well as support from the opposition. Such conditions did not exist. Both the government and the opposition shared the notion that intelligence should be in the hands of the military and that its purpose was to protect governments from their adversaries by whatever means possible.

Conclusions

As the Toledo government neared its end, it had become clear that institutional reforms in the area of security had failed and that the initiative would not be rekindled. One of the main reasons for this was the government's (especially the president's) lack of concern about the need for a thorough transformation. In more institutionalised countries, the importance of leadership for reform is perhaps less marked, but in countries like Peru it is vital. In general, the political class was indifferent towards, or even hostile to, change. Whether by conviction or fear, most shared this view that the military should control military matters and intelligence, while the police should do police work. With some exceptions, members of the military and police are conservative, resistant to change and unwilling to accept civilian authority. But as we have seen, change is possible, although it can easily be reversed.

With respect to civilian-military relations, there was a return to the situation prior to the Fujimori government, with a climate of mutual suspicion. The military seeks to gain the maximum budgetary independence possible. Civilian politicians try to control the military, often through manipulative means: keeping them happy without giving away too much, and letting them do what they like institutionally and in the use of their budgets. With regard to the police, the dismantling of the reforms and the lack of leadership has contributed to problems of citizen insecurity; the police are increasingly overwhelmed by the rise in ever more violent crime.

The agendas for reform, set out clearly at the outset of the Toledo government, therefore remained pending, awaiting the formation of a new government in 2006.

Notes

1   Specially appointed judges and prosecutors, carefully vetted and appointed solely to judge corruption cases from the Fujimori-Montesinos period, were appointed, along with an ad hoc Procuraduría to administer these cases and the passage of a number of special laws to this end.

2   To head the CNI, which replaced the SIN, the new government named first an army general and then an admiral, both retired.

3   Up until 1987 there had been three military ministries: those of war (army), the navy and airforce. In that year, these were replaced by a single Ministry of Defence. Nevertheless, the Ministry of Defence remained effectively an extension of the armed forces. The minister

was always an army general (and regarded himself as such) and was seen as the military's representative in government.

4   Toledo gave the impression of wanting to manage relations with the military himself. He accordingly appointed Waisman, who at this time did what he was told. In addition, Waisman was in poor health and lacked the physical vigour to assume the enormous burden that the job entailed. When Waisman withdrew, the ministry ended up in the hands of retired military officers and their advisors.

5   Officially, it was called the Working Group for Studying and Making Recommendations for the Integral Restructuring of the Armed Forces. Presided over by Dañino, its members included Francisco Morales Bermúdez (retired general and former president), Waisman, Fernando Rospigliosi (minister of the interior), Martín Belaúnde Moreyra (dean of the College of Lawyers), Aurelio Loret de Mola, Enrique Obando Arbulú, Luis Vargas Caballero (retired vice-admiral), Julián Juliá Freyre (retired general) and César Gonzalo Luzza (retired airforce general)

6   The attempt to sell a group of old Tucano airforce planes to an African country, initiated when Waisman was minister, ended in a congressional investigation and another by the public prosecutor's office. This involved Loret de Mola in considerable loss of time and energy and helped weaken him politically. Other cases had the same effect, although he finally managed to pass the law.

7   After the 1995 war with Ecuador, Peru bought 36 second-hand fighter aircraft (MiG29s and Sukhoi 25s) from Belarus, as well as three MiG 29s from Russia. In the process of these purchases, Montesinos received huge payments. Soon after purchase, two of the MiG 29s crashed. Most of these aircraft are currently unable to fly for lack of maintenance. Other arms were also bought, providing a source of illicit enrichment for military commanders.

8   These consisted of four decommissioned Lupo class frigates from Italy. They were on offer at US$15 million apiece, without arms. To equip them would have cost a further US$25 million each. Peru already possessed four such boats.

9   Chiabra, an officer with a prestigious track record, had been forced into retirement by Montesinos in 1998, following Hermoza's fall from power. In retirement, he quietly became a close collaborator with Toledo, at that time a presidential candidate. He was reincorporated into the army on active service under Paniagua. In 2002 he became head of

the second military region (the most important in the country), and thereafter promoted to commander-in-chief.

10   When Fujimori and Montesinos staged their coup against Congress in April 1992, they were obliged to replace the dissolved parliament with a new one, to maintain democratic forms and to uphold the freedom of the press. The *autogolpe* enjoyed widespread public support, as did the 1995 re-election of Fujimori as president. Both Hugo Chávez in Venezuela and Lucio Gutiérrez in Ecuador failed in their attempts at coups, but became rulers of their countries by virtue of clean elections. This shows how the international veto has failed to change the authoritarian urges in many Latin American countries.

11   For example (at the time of writing) the key central military region (Lima) which would be vital in the case of an attempted coup, was in the hands of General Hoyos Rubio, formerly head of Toledo's military household. Prior to him, the post was occupied by General Chiabra, and before that General Woll (an associate of Chiabra's).

12   The commander-in-chief of the airforce resigned for the same reason, although he still had a year of active service before him. He alleged that Toledo had promoted the pilot of the presidential jet, although he was not someone who had been in line for promotion.

13   Commander Ollanta Humala had rebelled against the Fujimori government in October 2000. He was detained along with his brother, Antauro, and dismissed. Ollanta was reappointed to the army shortly after Fujimori's fall, and was subsequently appointed military attaché in Paris and then in Seoul. He was dismissed from the army again in December 2004. At that point, Antauro established a political movement supposedly composed of retired members of the military, mainly unemployed young men who disguised themselves with military uniforms and took part in a variety of social protests.

14   The police were included to make the creation of the Fund more politically acceptable; increased citizen security is a demand that is enthusiastically supported by public opinion.

15   At the time of writing, Dianderas was still in jail, along with all those who were ministers of the interior during the 1990s — though some were still on the run — with only one exception. Also jailed was Agustín Mantilla, the vice-minister and then minister of the interior under the government of Alan García.

16   This got rid of the system whereby the committee could award points in favour or against specific candidates, which effectively gave them enormous discretion over promotions, thus enabling them to change the system of classifying merit. The president of the republic, the interior minister, the director of the PNP or anyone else with influence had been able to promote their friends or block the promotion of perceived adversaries. The system had also given rise to the sale of promotions. Elimination of such practices ushered in a veritable revolution in the PNP. The system of discretional committees continues within the armed forces.

17   With a similar number of policemen as Peru, the Colombian police had some 10 generals and 80 colonels.

18   This constituted the biggest purge ever in the history of the police force. Some of these were people who had worked closely with Montesinos and his mafia, but most were supernumerary officials without career prospects.

19   In 2001 promotions and retirements were handled by Rospigliosi and his team; in 2002 by Gino Costa; and in 2003 by Rospigliosi once again. This meant that the process of reform was sustained.

20   The first was the former women's minister, Susana Villarán

21   Policemen had not received new uniforms since 1997, in spite of a law that specifies that they should receive these free of charge.

22   This was the first time this had ever happened in the PNP.

23   Because of lack of budget, the US government helped finance the OAI, and the UK government the police ombudsman's office.

24   This was repealed in 2004 when Javier Reátegui and Félix Murazzo were ministers.

25   The ministers were successively Fernando Rospigliosi (July 2001 to June 2002), Gino Costa (June 2002 to January 2003), Alberto Sanabria (January 2003 to June 2003), Fernando Rospigliosi (July 2003 to May 2004), Javier Reátegui (May 2004 to January 2005) and Félix Murazzo (as of January 2005).

26   Costa was one of Toledo's ministers who generated most public confidence.

27   Sanabria was the Interior Government Director during Rospigliosi's first period as minister. He was the only person in the ministry appointed by Toledo personally. He left this job because of a scandal over the use of funds.

28   This happened in December 2003, following a campaign against her by
      members of the government.

29   Rospigliosi was the only minister to be censured by Congress. The pur-
      ported reason for this was the assassination of the mayor of Ilave by a
      group of opponents.

30   Opinion polls show that corruption heads the list of criticisms of the
      police. It is a major source of distrust. For this reason it is so important
      to deal with it.

31   In 2004, before the promotions, there had been 30 generals, and the
      reform programme projected lowering this to 28.

32   These are cars that officers are offered virtually free of charge when
      they retire.

33   For a more detailed analysis of the reversal of the police reform, see
      Basombrío et al. (2004).

34   From its original foundation in 1960, the SIN had been run by generals
      or admirals, in retirement or otherwise. Until the arrival of Montesinos
      in 1990, it had been a small organisation. In practice it was a subsection
      of the armed forces.

35   At the time of writing, Almeyda was in jail, accused of having sought
      to use extortion against Oscar Villanueva, a retired general, known as
      Montesinos's 'cashier', who was arrested and subsequently committed
      suicide. This supposed crime had been committed before Almeyda had
      become head of the CNI. The case became public knowledge after
      Almeyda had left the CNI. Almeyda was accused of having received a
      US$2 million bribe from the Colombian brewery Bavaria for helping in a
      trade dispute. According to the accusation, part of the bribe was for
      Toledo. Almeyda, Bavaria and Toledo have all denied any involvement.

36   Mora held important positions in the army during the period when
      General Nicolás Hermoza was commander-in-chief (1991–98). On
      Hermoza's fall from power, Montesinos took direct control of the
      army. Amongst those forced into retirement was Mora. He was an
      unsuccessful candidate in the 2000 elections for the Somos Perú party.
      Later, he joined Perú Posible.

5

Institutional Change and Social Programmes

Pedro Francke

There have been a number of books and studies in recent years that have highlighted the deficiencies of social programmes in Peru (for instance Vásquez and Mendizábal, 2004; Dubois, 2005). This chapter seeks to explore and explain why this has persisted over decades. It is argued that the explanation lies in the way the actors involved in the state's response to social problems interact. The key question to which this chapter seeks to provide an answer is why social programmes or the struggle against poverty have evolved the way they have institutionally. What is it that makes them so ineffective and so negative in supporting democracy? And how have recent changes, like decentralisation, changed the picture? The analysis focuses on the interaction of interests, incentives and relationships between the social and political actors involved in these anti-poverty programmes. We will show how the present institutionality is not something that has developed by chance, but rather is a product of the way in which democratic politics have evolved in Peru. For this reason, then, reforming the ways these programmes work involves changing not just the programmes and those who run them but changing the socio-economic and political underpinnings of democracy.

More than half (54 per cent) of Peru's population lives in poverty, and 20 per cent in conditions of extreme poverty. In rural areas, more than three-quarters live in poverty and around half in extreme poverty. The following table breaks this down by region and the rural/urban mix:

Table 1: Peru: Incidence of Poverty and Extreme Poverty (2003)

Geographic areas	Poverty			Extreme Poverty		
	Poverty rate (%)	Margin of error	95%	Poverty rate (%)	Margin of error	95%
National Areas	54.7	51.9	57.5	21.6	19.3	24.0
Rural	76.0	72.0	80.0	45.7	40.6	50.8
Urban	43.2	39.5	46.9	8.6	6.5	10.7
Natural regions						
Coast	40.6	36.0	45.2	5.8	3.4	8.2
Sierra	71.6	68.0	75.2	42.1	37.6	46.6
Jungle	63.8	57.9	69.6	27.8	21.4	34.1
Coast *	45.9	39.7	52.1	10.9	6.1	15.7
Sierra (urban)	51.4	44.7	58.1	12.7	8.9	16.5
Sierra (rural)	82.9	78.7	87.0	58.6	53.0	64.1
Jungle urban	63.8	56.8	70.8	30.6	20.3	40.8
Jungle (rural)	63.7	54.8	72.7	25.4	17.8	33.0
Greater Lima .	36.5	30.1	42.9	1.8	0.3	3.4
Capital and provincias						
Capital	36.5	30.1	42.9	1.8	0.3	3.4
Provincias	62.0	59.2	64.8	29.6	26.5	32.7
Rural	76.0	72.0	80.0	45.7	40.6	50.8
Urban	48.5	44.3	52.6	14.0	10.5	17.4

* excludes Metropolitan Lima
Source: Herrera (2004).
On the basis of the National Household Survey, 2003, IV Quarter.

State-Society Relations and the Efficacy of Social Programmes

A key point for analysis is the efficacy of social programmes. A large proportion of these are geared to providing food aid. There are currently a dozen or so such programmes under the aegis of Pronaa (Programa Nacional de Asistencia Alimentaria), a dependency of the Ministry of Women's Affairs and Social Development (Memdes). These programmes have overlapping functions and duplication of target populations, as well as low levels of coverage — with the exception of the Glass of Milk (Vaso de Leche) programme and School Breakfasts (Desayuno Escolar). Too many people are involved in the implementation of these programmes and there is not enough coordination between them. This leads to wastage of resources and a reduction in the efficacy of social spending overall (Cortez, 2001).

Furthermore, food aid tends to treat the poor as if they were homogenous. A distinction needs to be drawn between:

- The structural poor, who require policies to develop productive assets and resources over the long term in order to overcome want; and

- The occasionally poor, who require protection against shocks that affect their productive assets.

Another key issue relates to the way in which these programmes contribute (or not) to democratic governance. State-society relations are a critical problem area in Peruvian national development. Structurally and over the long term, these have been authoritarian and hierarchical, a product of the colonial inheritance (Portocarrero, 2005). However, state-society relations have recently undergone a process of democratisation (López, 1997). The failure of democracy in the 1980s and the subsequent authoritarianism of the Fujimori period in the 1990s have led to what Tanaka (2005) has called the 'destructuring without restructuring' of state-society relations.

Social policy is a key way through which the state responds to the people, providing them with basic services and assistance at critical junctures. It therefore impacts strongly on state-society relations. Students of social policy have adopted polarised positions in recent years, but many have been highly critical. Tanaka (2005) points out that 'women's movements organised around survival strategies have revealed a high degree of dependency on external agents and a reduction of their interests to ones of subsistence'. He goes on to show that 'grassroots leaders (…) are not so much *representatives* of communities or groups, but rather *intermediaries* (…). One of the consequences of this is that participative schemes that depend a great deal on a close relationship with such people do not really reach the average citizen who tends to regard such social leaders with mistrust.'

The approach adopted by the state is often characterised as one of clientelism, a practice whereby the delivery of social benefits is made conditional on support for the government in return. With respect to clientelism, some clarification is in order. If one of the basic principles of democratic politics is the quest for public support for government, why is it not possible for those who seek to improve the lot of the poor to seek to translate this legitimately into support for themselves? It is clear that if Peru suffers from chronic governance problems, part of the problem lies in the fact that the state does very little for the majority of people. To tackle this problem, it would seem reasonable and helpful for government to build up support for itself by accomplishing tangible and practical benefits for voters, especially the majority who are poor.

The critique of clientelism lies not with the search for public support, since this is one of the few (if not the only) reasons why the political system concerns itself at all with poverty and it is ultimately why the state does something about it. In contrast to its relationship with business, the government will never do anything for the poor on account of the monetary contribution they make to political campaigning. It only does so because it is looking for votes. The problem of clientelism lies not so much in the quest for public support and votes as such, rather how this quest is accomplished. The 'how' is all-important. The key issue here is that in democracy, the tie-up between social programmes and the search for votes should not be achieved via the partisan use of the state apparatus. It is quite legitimate that governments do things for people to win over support; what is not legitimate is that party militants make delivery of social assistance conditional on certain types of political behaviour or use state resources for party campaigning. The relationship between government and citizens cannot do away with such distinctions: a democratic government runs the state, but the party and the state must not be confused. Delivery of social programmes is a function of the state, not a party.

Clientelism has a number of negative consequences (Caballero, 2004):

1   It undermines democracy by encouraging a vertical relationship between parties and the mass electorate and confuses the distinction between parties and the state. In order to construct citizenship it is necessary to adopt the opposite formulation and to create rights which allow people to relate to the state on a horizontal basis.

2   It corrodes self-respect and self-confidence among the poor. This is because it teaches people that to improve their living standards they should abandon their political rights and not seek to widen and make use of their social and economic capabilities.

3   It reduces the effectiveness and efficiency of social programmes.
      This is because leadership roles are assigned to people who pro-
      fess partisan leanings and are prepared to be manipulated rather
      than to those with technical or managerial competence.

A Brief History of Social Programmes

Beginnings

From the time of Independence up until the 1960s the main means by
which assistance was given to the poor was through public charities
(Beneficiencias Públicas). These were organisations with their roots in
colonial times and were based on the charity of wealthy families. They
provided aid and medical attention to the elderly poor, the assumption
being that charity should go only to those without the physical capacity
to look after themselves through their own efforts. As the role of the
state grew during the twentieth century, the Beneficiencias became less
important. A system of social security took over as the main vehicle for
providing healthcare. A strengthened Health Ministry took care of
those unable to insure themselves.

The development of social programmes based on food distribution
began with the economic crisis of 1976–79. Without help from the
state, hundreds of soup kitchens (*comedores populares*) came into being in
Lima and other cities. They emerged as a response to public need
among large sectors of the population confronted with the difficult
economic situation of rising food prices, falling incomes and growing
unemployment. They also arose as a consequence of the search by
grass-roots movements in many areas of Lima to create a nexus
between trade union and neighbourhood organisation. The common
cooking facilities (*ollas comunes*) that the unions employed to provide sus-
tenance for striking workers and their families naturally transformed
into the *comedores* in nearby neighbourhoods.

Democracy Restored: Partisan Clientelism in the 1980s

The restoration of democracy in 1980 did not bring with it sustained
economic growth. On the contrary, in 1983 GDP underwent a 9.3 per
cent contraction and inflation raced ahead from 73 per cent to 125 per

cent. In such circumstances, survival mechanisms like the *comedores* became even more important for ordinary people. However, the dynamics of party competition were such that parties came to take great interest in such initiatives. While Violeta Correa, the first lady, promoted what she called 'popular kitchens' (*cocinas populares*), Alfonso Barrantes, the mayor of Lima, organised an extensive network of Glass of Milk Committees (Comités del vaso de leche) in the poorest districts of the capital. Both initiatives drew on the experience of the *comedores populares* but gave them a new twist by linking popular organisation to state-provided food assistance. For the most part, these programmes were not linked to public policy or development strategies.

The *comedores* themselves were moving in this direction. What had begun as a self-managing movement depending little on outside help became increasingly dependent on external assistance. Initially, help for the *comedores* had come from international donations, often through NGOs linked to the churches. For such donors, this sort of assistance had its advantages. It linked up the need to reduce excess food stocks from subsidised agriculture in their own countries with their promises for overseas development aid and also met a much-needed social demand in Peru.

The government of Alan García brought few major changes in this respect, and full use was made of the state apparatus for clearly partisan ends. At this time they called the new social organisations 'mothers' clubs' (*clubes de madres*), even though they amounted to much the same thing as the *comedores populares* and the *cocinas populares*. As under the Belaunde government before it, this sort of assistance fulfilled two objectives. It gave the impression of a government concerned about the poor and sensitive to welfare problems, thereby helping to prop up the popularity of the president. At the same time, it helped sustain a party structure, channelling assistance to places where party sympathisers or militants were taking the lead in social organisation.

Thus, during the 1980s there was a shift in the relationship between the political system and grass-roots social organisation, whether in the shape of *comedores populares, cocinas populares* or comités de vaso de leche. Political parties made use of state resources to build low-cost ties with an extensive social network. This was not so much a relationship in which the state developed policies for universal rights, rather one in which the political party in office, through the state, distributed benefits to those groups which they thought they could provide a political clientele. There is plenty of evidence to support this: the fact that control of the state agencies in charge of social programmes were always given to political leaders closely associated with the ruling party; that there was considerable scope for discretion in whether to include a community or not in programmes of state assistance; that different treatment was meted out between one set of *comedores* or organisations and others; that *comedor* organisations ended developing close ties to a specific party, etc.

For their part, the women involved in the *comedores* related to the 'party/state' perfectly aware of the need for political connections (through Tanaka's brokers) if they wished to obtain outside assistance. The mothers from the *clubes* who looked for state assistance spent a good part of their time seeking to establish links with people from the ruling party. Even so, there were some *comedores* that sought to maintain an effective autonomy and to portray themselves as a movement for the empowerment of women.

Under Fujimori: Authoritarian Clientelism

Fujimori's rise to power in 1990 took place in a context of acute crisis. However, the extreme impecunious nature of the public finances, added to the problems in organising a new government, made it difficult to launch an immediate programme of massive social assistance. Moreover, the government was primarily preoccupied with economic and security issues. This meant that in the first two years of the Fujimori government there was no clear response in this area; already existing mechanisms were used when evident that some urgent response was required.

Foncodes. The first major change in social policy occurred in 1992 with the establishment of Foncodes (the Fondo Nacional de Comensación y Desarrollo Social). This arose out of the confluence of two political necessities. On the one hand, *fujimorismo* required a new scheme for providing social assistance since it was essential to respond to the major social problems caused by both the economic and the internal security crises (the latter caused by Sendero Luminoso). The line ministries — education and health — were beset by the crisis, since hyperinflation had left them bereft of resources and their partisan operations under APRA had undermined institutional structures. In any case, the ministries did not extend into most rural parts of the country. On the other hand, international financial institutions, like the International Monetary Fund (IMF) and the World Bank, had re-established cordial relations with Peru. Consequently, they began to apply their recommendations with considerable acumen, and effectively refinanced the debts to themselves which had gone unserviced since the García government. Both the IMF and the World Bank saw the need for a mechanism that would attend to those worst affected by the adjustment — it is for this reason that Foncodes' name includes the word 'compensation' — and build political support for the regime. The World Bank thus brought in the experience it had developed elsewhere in Latin America with 'social investment funds'.

Foncodes brought two major innovations in institutional design. First, it was an institution that was not bound by the rules of the public sector for hiring and firing or buying in goods and services. It came under the direct authority of the office of the presidency. This gave it greater operational agility, both in improving efficacy and responding to the political demands on the regime. Second, it established as its main operational mechanism a system for carrying out small-scale projects and public works, through which it distributed money to communities so that they undertook projects subject to Foncodes' oversight and evaluation. This sort of modus operandi proved highly efficient for building small-scale infrastructure. Foncodes could reach remote rural communities traditionally ignored by the state and where transport and transaction costs were typically very high. Foncodes worked in a highly targeted way, especially because international funds were directed exclusively at rural areas. At the same time, Foncodes was able to verify whether communities had carried out projects efficiently and whether these were well adapted to local conditions.

At the same time, however, Foncodes had problems in the efficacy of its programmes, basically because of its weak relationship with the community, municipalities, NGOs and the ministries. Since Foncodes' links with communities were limited to carrying out public works and because it spurned contacts with NGOs, it found it difficult to include training and organisational strengthening in projects, aspects essential in providing sustainability and improving project impact. Foncodes was poorly linked with sectoral policy and the construction of schools or health centres did not form part of any organisational plan to optimise their impact. Moreover, because of its weak ties with municipalities and other local organisations, its small-scale community-based projects did not necessarily adhere to local development plans; so small-scale irrigation schemes were carried out without any attempt to provide training to peasants in productive techniques or marketing.

Foncodes also worked in providing clientelistic support for a dictatorial regime. Schady (1999) and León (2003) have shown how Foncodes spending rose significantly in the build-up to general elections in 2000, and how that spending was targeted at provinces where Fujimori stood to perform best. Within Foncodes, this worked in the following way. On the one hand, there was a great deal of discretion allowed over which communities and projects it was prepared to fund, allowing it to focus on places where there was a close rapport between community leaders and the government. Moreover, Foncodes did not work with leaders as such (which traditionally were key in peasant and jungle communities) but with what were called 'executive nuclei' (*núcleos ejecutores*) chosen for the purpose. It could choose to work with those leaders (among community leaders, *regidores*, mayors, local governors, etc.) whom it considered best disposed towards the government. However, the main clientelistic mechanism was the identification of all public works with the *persona* of Fujimori. Every project had a billboard with the words 'Presidency of the Republic' in large letters; each usually finished with a plaque that made clear it had been carried out when Fujimori was president; and each was usually painted orange, the colour of Fujimori's party.

This political logic to Foncodes' operations helps explain why its relations with other actors, like the municipalities and NGOs, were so limited. Had these been involved in the projects, they might have revealed the degree of political manipulation by the government. This lack of any relationship with other actors involved in rural communities was the most obvious and significant contradiction between its vertical political project (which required it to work in isolation) and the sustainability and impact of its programmes (which on the contrary demanded development of relations with all relevant actors: the community itself, the local municipality and the line ministries.

Comedores populares. The *comedores populares* underwent important changes over this period. First, Pronaa entered as a new organisation with responsibility for centralising food assistance programmes. Previously, Pronaa's responsibilities had been carried out by two entities: the Direct Assistance Programme (Programa de Asistencia Directa, PAD) and the National Office for Food Aid (Oficinia Nacional de Ayuda Alimentaria, ONAA). Like Foncodes, Pronaa stood out for the direct relationship it had (subsequently through the Ministry of the Presidency) with Fujimori. Second, international donors slowly changed the way in which they channelled aid. They stopped supporting the *comedores* and began to finance other programmes that did not work through community organisations. This meant that the government replaced funding for the *comedores* with Treasury funds. The reasons for this were primarily political: on the one hand, the women's organisations resisted any cuts to their funding; on the other, the Fujimori regime found these to be a fruitful area for clientelism.

Indeed, the authoritarian nature of the government and the crisis afflicting the political parties of the time enabled the regime to develop a network of clientelistic relationships through the *comedores populares*. Indications of this are included in Portocarrero *et al.* (1998), based on surveys conducted among officials who for a brief period tried to tech-nify Pronaa's work: 'those in charge of the main offices (*sedes*) acted as heads of the political campaign' (p. 197); 'the (...) *comedores populares* were perceived not so much as beneficiaries, rather as a political clien-tele whose demands had to be satisfied. In return, they had to collabo-rate and be present at presidential (campaign) meetings, for which free transport was laid on by the institution, laden with banners and placards as signs of their support for the president' (pp. 191–2).

At this time, reflecting a shift in the structure of power, a change took place in the pattern of incentives. In the 1980s each party had sought to build its own political clientele. Although the party in govern-ment had the means to push ahead with building up grass-roots sup-port, the parties in opposition could count on the loyalty that they had built up previously by having 'inaugurated' the *comedores* and using their presence in parliament and influence over the press to defend them against their detractors. The *comedores* also might expect that such and such a party would win the next elections and therefore they would be well-placed to receive special favours when it did. Clientelism was there-fore built up by inaugurating new *comedores* and widening the scope of the programme. In the 1990s, the political hegemony of Fujimori, the risk of disaccreditation on the part of anti-government leaders and the virtual disappearance of political parties enabled the regime to substitute the loyalty previously placed in other parties with loyalty to Fujimori himself. The majority of *comedores* that were resistant to this would have their arms twisted by a combination of 'carrot' and 'stick'. Under Fujimori, clientelism developed to such an extent that it turned into overt political manipulation. During the 2000 presidential elections, the Ombudsman's Office (Defensoría del Pueblo) registered a number of complaints of *comedores* being threatened with a cut-off in food supplies if they failed to put up posters of Fujimori and the head of Pronaa (who ran for Congress) in conspicuous places. All *comedores* moreover had to display orange-coloured billboards.

Other programmes. At the same time as Foncodes and Pronaa expanded their activities, a host of other programmes and organisations did likewise. The National Health Institute (Instituto Nacional de Salud) also had nutritional programmes for children. As well, there were organisations involved in infrastructural works, like the National Programme for Watershed Management and Soil Conservation (Programa Nacional de Manejo de Cuencas Hidrográficos y Conservación de Suelos, Pronamachs), the Institute for Educational and Health Infrastructure (Instituto de Infraestructura Educativa y de Salud, Infes), Caminos Rurales amongst others. These institutions were notoriously inefficient, duplicating programmes and expanding the size of the bureaucracy. Portocarrero et al. (1998, p. 141) note that in 90 per cent of schools in Ayacucho, both Foncodes and Pronaa were involved in distributing school breakfasts. How was it that a government organised so vertically and which had made so much of the virtues of efficiency could have programmes with such obvious shortcomings? Three reasons suggest themselves:

1   International donors and financial institutions, such as the Inter-American Development Bank (IDB) and the World Bank, each preferred to have their own independent programmes. Even different divisions within the same institution were interested in having their own projects. Faced with the need for resources, officials ended up accepting the proliferation of new organisations on the ground.

2   There was resistance from the bureaucracy which made it very difficult to close programmes down.

3   The methods for monitoring programmes were inadequate. This is explicable by the results being couched in overly technical terms or, alternatively in terms of the need to mobilise political support in favour of the regime. This lack of information made it difficult for those in charge to identify which were the least efficient. At the same time, in a context of clientelism and political manipulation, parallel networks became a way of stimulating competition between political operators.

The development of clientelism. Since popularity was a key point in sustaining the regime politically, it is important to analyse how it was generated. In the government's first few years, between 1990 and 1994, *fujimorismo* created political support by means of its anti-terrorist polices and by overcoming hyperinflation. Public order was a key political consideration at the time, and Fujimori derived support from people's perceptions about the need to take a hard line and from the positive results achieved. Though living standards did not improve, these were seen as being secondary to the need to reimpose 'order'. From 1994 onwards, by contrast, issues related to economic and social welfare became more important. Here, the Fujimori government had less to offer: although there had been economic growth, any improvements in incomes, employment and wages were modest at best. However, the return to growth plus the resources built up through the privatisation programme made it possible to increase public spending.

Social programmes thus became the most important element in sustaining the regime politically. The construction of schools by Infes, the public works of Foncodes, the distribution of food to poor families were all actions that followed a clear political logic: how to make sure that social programmes brought the maximum political dividends. The resultant system of clientelism had two aims. First was to propagate the idea that the benefits people received were not the result of state policies but of the personal intervention of the president. The second was the building of a political apparatus, based on public officialdom, to develop ties between beneficiary community leaders and organisations on the one hand and the party structure of *fujimorismo* on the other.

A structure therefore existed to build support for the regime, and work in this direction grew as time went by. It rested on the following conditions being met:

1   The possibility of fiscal easing, based on expanded growth and the receipts from privatisation.

2   The existence of institutions that could run programmes efficiently.

3   The organisation of a political apparatus that could infiltrate the state with the help of top government leaders, thereby enabling social programmes to be used for clientelistic purposes.

The experience of clientelism under Fujimori suggests that:

• The organisation of the state to this end (points 2 and 3) takes time;

• Condition 2 is a requirement for Condition 3; and

• In the medium term, the development of condition 3 (the political use of social programmes) affects condition 2 (efficacy of social programmes) in such a way that there is a trade-off between social and political efficacy.

Reforms to Social Programmes under Conditions of Democracy

Following Fujimori's fall, the democratic transition threw up important challenges for social policy. First and foremost, it was necessary to eliminate clientelistic practices, steering programmes towards the development of citizen rights. A second challenge was to restructure social policy and to improve both its efficiency and efficacy. Cutting across those objectives and affecting both were the twin issues of decentralisation and citizen participation. These had the potential to redistribute political power and enhance social oversight, contributing to greater democracy and efficiency.

The transition government of Valentín Paniagua managed to bring about some fundamental changes on the first of these objectives. In particular, it managed to 'cleanse' the organisations responsible for social policy of the political infiltration they had been subjected to under Fujimori. It passed a supreme decree that established the 'neutrality' that social programmes should observe during elections, with punishments for those that violated this norm. This was part of the transition government's prime aims of holding clean elections and ridding the state of the authoritarian remnants of the previous regime.

The Toledo Government: Clientelism Revisited

In July 2001 Toledo became president. He confronted a number of major challenges. The first was to continue with the transition to democracy, or rather to strengthen democracy. The second was to tackle poverty. Social programmes were key to both. At the outset, the new government's main idea was to bring in changes to enhance both efficacy and democracy, giving priority to citizen participation and building meritocratic institutions.[1] Social programmes were therefore put in the hands of a group of independent professionals with strong links to civil society.[2] Most of these had previously come from the left. At the same time, there was an increase in budget allocations for these programmes, although not that much since the government thought that it could raise money from the international aid community.

Before the end of its first year in office, between April and June 2002, the government ran into its first major policy dilemma, a dilemma that would affect social programmes in critical ways. The government called for municipal elections in November 2002, elections considered key in defining the future balance of political power in the country. At the same time, the government's popularity had nose-dived, whilst members of the ruling party, encouraged by Toledo's own declarations, had begun to agitate for quotas of power in the government. The government's 'To Work' employment scheme (A Trabajar), one of its first initiatives in the field of social policy, was under way in rural areas and was beginning to take shape in urban ones. Although poverty is more acute in rural areas, these had less political influence than urban ones, given their dispersion and their lack of impact on the media and public opinion. The A Trabajar programme was construed in such a way as to minimise its use for clientelistic purposes, involving communities, grass-roots organisations and civil society at various different levels.

It was in this context that Toledo decided to shift the policy orientation and to encourage militants of the ruling party to 'capture' the various programmes. Changes at the top within the ministries of women and education, as well as Foncodes, were proof of this changed attitude.

The objective was to galvanise support for Toledo and his party in advance of the elections. This meant mobilising party supporters within these programmes and in the social sectors more generally. Part and parcel of this was the aim to instil loyalty among congressmen and within the middle-ranking levels of the ruling party by accommodating their demands for jobs and influence.

The results of these manoeuvres were none too successful. In the political sphere, Perú Posible, the ruling party, won only one regional government (Callao), as did its ally the Frente Independiente Moralizador (Cuzco). After a brief upturn, the popularity of the president continued downwards. This raises the question then whether the system of clientelism was unable to work as previously because of social and cultural changes in Peruvian society, or whether Perú Posible simply lacked the level of party organisation required to make clientelism effective. It is worth remembering that it took the Fujimori government several years to organise efficient social programmes with a partisan organisation embedded within them. Perú Posible was a newly-constructed political formation with strong internal rivalries between groups with little loyalty to one another and whose leaders had their own personal agendas. Party militants appointed to social programmes thus belonged to different currents (with a view to keeping their various faction leaders happy) and worked in a poorly coordinated way. Moreover, ten years of *fujimorismo* had resulted in a paucity of practical policy experience.

This shift involved major costs for the efficiency and efficacy of the various social programmes. Most of the party people given jobs lacked suitable qualifications. Moreover, having been appointed for the political influence they possessed, they felt little identification with the institutions they were asked to run. Not only did this reduce efficiency and efficacy (i.e. the impact that programmes had on social indicators) but also reduced their usefulness for political ends. All this would suggest that the Toledo government's inability to use social programmes for clientelistic ends owed much to problems within the ruling party.

However, was it also the case that implanting clientelism was made more difficult due to the greater level of awareness of citizenship, changes in state-society relations or a greater independence on the part of the media? This remains an open question. Part of the answer lies in another question: if not through clientelistic social programmes, what other ways

are there of the Peruvian state achieving the popular backing and legitimacy it needs to govern? Here, some specific analysis is called for on the relationship between social and economic policy.

It is clearly the case that governability (or political sustainability) is
closely related to social policy and programmes. These establish a mechanism for constructing a rapport between government and people. It is
also clear that for the last 15 years or so, since neoliberal economic policies were first implemented in Latin America, these have not been conspicuously successful in reducing poverty in most countries. This is certainly true of Peru, and for this reason demand for social programmes
has increased. However, the problem resides in the fact that neoliberal
policies involve 'state shrinking'. States see their sources of income
reduced with the reduction of trade tariffs, the elimination of taxes on
capital gains and the reduction of taxes on the extraction of natural
resources to provide export incentives. This limits the possibilities for
strong social programmes. There is evidently a problem of 'squaring the
circle' with respect to governability. This has been made plain by social
rebellions in countries like Bolivia and Argentina, and by left-wing election victories in various countries of the Southern Cone.

Under Fujimori support for the government was maintained because
of the increase in the resources made available for social programmes and
because of the construction of an enormous apparatus of clientelism.
The 'political cost-effectiveness' for every sol invested was quite high. It
also helped to have under government control (through the use of threats
and other strong-arm tactics) organisations such as the teachers' and
health workers' unions. Under more democratic conditions, unions such
as these press for higher incomes; this has a high fiscal cost but is not of
much political benefit to the government. Control over the media also
meant that this sort of clientelism took place without producing major
shocks to public opinion. In short, Fujimori was able to maintain the governability of the country by means of public support (also aided by bringing terrorism and hyperinflation under control), alongside strong
alliances with the armed forces, the international financial institutions,
the United States and major private-sector conglomerates.

With the democratic transition it became essential to discover how to
square the circle of governability. Doing so implied changes of direction
in both social and economic policy. Regarding social policy, the alternative

to clientelism was to come up with other ways of making social programmes politically effective, namely by providing universal rights or entitlements to citizens. This is a democratically legitimate way of ensuring governability because people receive benefits guaranteed by the state. If a government can make the effort to increase or improve the quality of the services or programmes that respond to such rights, then it will generate the support it needs to govern. But this is not possible given the inadequacy of current social sector budgets. More resources need to be provided. How could this be achieved? Reduce military spending? Reduce the cost of servicing the foreign debt? Increase the tax yield through higher taxes, whether indirect or direct, or through better tax administration? In other words, the changes required to base social policies on rights involve increasing budgets; this in turn means modifying economic policy.[3]

Toledo's initial gamble was that he could overcome the budget problem by seeking foreign assistance. This was one of his first major errors. Even though there was considerable goodwill in many countries towards the recovery of democracy and a degree of regret for having supported Fujimori in the past, Peru would never become a priority given its status as a 'middle-income' country. With the problem of ungovernability at the end of the Fujimori period to some extent resolved by the Paniagua transition, there was little feeling of urgency among developed countries to provide an infusion of money to help resolve these problems. The chances of gaining additional funds from international donors were further reduced when Toledo decided to sack his original social team and to replace it with party loyalists, a move that generated strong misgivings within the donor community. The government's reluctance to push ahead with tax reform, raising direct taxation, then combined with union pressures in the education and health sectors to prevent spending on social programmes increasing.

In 2002 two factors therefore prevented the government from proceeding. Firstly, the government failed to take the tax measures required for a more redistributive fiscal policy. This reduced the chances of social policy eliminating clientelism and helping the government generate the political support it required. The initial approach — social reform without the necessary local funding but premised on support from the international community — did not last long enough to be put to the test. Secondly, the government decided to resort to the use of partisan and clientelistic social programmes within a limited budget. This decision undermined the efficacy of the programmes, reduced the chances of raising money from the international community, and (in the end) failed to generate the social support that the government wanted. Was the limited political effect of this return to clientelism a product of the lack of managerial competence of those brought in, or was it the case that changes in the domestic and international contexts made it difficult for such approaches to be successful? This remains an open question.

Decentralisation of Social Programmes: An End to Central Government Clientelism?

With the regional elections of November 2002 over, the government faced a new dilemma. It had given a great deal of importance to the need for decentralisation and had made a big issue about the formation of regional governments as a step in that direction. However, it lost the elections across the country, mainly to APRA, its principal political opponent. Decentralisation implies a substantial change in the way government works. Amongst the most important changes is that the transfer of responsibility for social programmes to the regional or local levels means that central government must cede the mechanisms of clientelism to these authorities.

In this predicament the government opted for an approach that seemed rational enough from the political point of view: to continue with decentralisation but at a much slower pace. This would enable it to maintain control over the budget and different areas of government, particularly over the social programmes, and avoid handing power to its opponents. However, it also meant side-stepping other possible approaches, such as pushing ahead with decentralisation to the municipal level. Municipalities had been working for over two decades as autonomous entities and they lacked the levels of cohesion that might enable them to become a strong source of opposition. Moreover, at the municipal level the government had fared far better in the elections than at the regional one, especially taking into account the performance of non-opposition groups like Somos Perú. Another possibility, in no way contradictory, was to use the budget for clientelistic purposes with the regional and local governments, acting as political intermediaries, or with popular organisations serving the same function.

The way in which decentralisation evolved, with all its significance for social sectors and programmes, obeyed dynamics that were both general and specific. The transfer of social programmes to local government, both provinces and districts, responded in large measure to central government initiatives. The pace was set mainly by the National Decentralisation Commission (Comisión Nacional de Descentralización, CND) and the MEF, but with some resistance on the part of Mimdes. This was because the dispersed nature of local governments means they exercise little effective pressure on their own. Also since the opposition won the regions, this was the terrain chosen by the government to make some timid advances with decentralisation.

In the case of the social programmes, decentralisation began with one of the food programmes (the *comedores populares*) and one of the Foncodes programmes (infrastructure). In each case, the transfer of responsibilities to the provincial and district governments respectively had to undergo a process of accreditation and the signing of management agreements. Accreditation aimed to provide some guarantees with respect to the quality of management, whilst management agreements were geared towards retaining a degree of control and policy input by central government. This was justified by the need for a national policy to guarantee basic rights and public goods.

So why, of the various food assistance programmes, did the government begin by decentralising the *comedores populares*? The answer lies in the fact that under conditions of democracy, such programmes are quite difficult to use for clientelistic ends. The delivery of benefits is seen by the women involved not as a gift but as an acquired right. Only spending at the margins can be used for clientelistic purposes, and in conditions of fiscal austerity this became more difficult. Decentralisation therefore involved the transfer to municipalities of the most complex programme and the one with the fewest political spin-offs.

In 2004 programmes had been transferred to only 63 provinces in the case of the *comedores populares* (around a third of the total), with a similar number of further transfers scheduled for 2006. In the case of Foncodes, only 241 districts were affected (around one-seventh of the total number of districts served). The process of accreditation was largely a formality, and the conditions attached fell considerably short of what would really be considered requirements for proper management. Nor was there any real oversight on whether the conditions were being met. Such shortcomings arose for a number of reasons: it was necessary to show that the whole scheme was going ahead; the requirements were only set after considerable delay and limited themselves to bureaucratic demands; and the weakness of the municipalities themselves. It is also worth mentioning that some provincial municipalities resisted the process. Some, like Metropolitan Lima and Piura, avoided accreditation. Others were accredited and then were reluctant to take on the programmes because of the conditions attached. Others only accepted the programmes because they believed it was a legal obligation. Beyond legal formalities, then, accreditation for the *comedores populares* lost any sense in practice of verifying whether standards were being met in the management of programmes. The management agreements, meanwhile, related basically to fulfilment of bureaucratic norms that had little to do with measuring results or critical outcomes. Furthermore, these agreements, made in the first year of transfer, no longer operated in subsequent years in enabling central government to influence the ways programmes were carried out. Once the municipalities had received the budget allocation and taken charge of the programme in 2004, there was no need to sign further agreements.

The way in which the decentralisation of social programmes developed can be summed up as follows:

1   It moved ahead in a partial way, affecting only a minority of programmes and a minority of municipalities. This was because the government decided to move ahead only very gradually, partly to ensure that promises were kept, partly to maintain political control.

2   The choice of the municipalities involved was arbitrary. This was the result of an accreditation scheme that did not work in practice. It was not run in a clientelistic way — whether by government decision or by its own organisational shortcomings is not clear — but could easily be used this way in future.

3   The management agreements have not been used as tools of political control or for influencing technical decisions. The idea prevailed that transfer involved complete autonomy for municipalities in the ways they manage the programmes.

The very limited progress made on decentralisation and the lack of effective oversight make it difficult to say with any degree of certainty whether or not it acts as a bulwark against clientelism in social programmes, or — to be more precise — how such practices may change.

Other than what I have discussed, the government did not develop any other new social programmes or schemes to turn these to clientelistic use. The Techo Propio ('Own Roof') programme is perhaps the most important initiative, but its coverage was very limited. There was no other explanation for this than the government's own problems in acting effectively in the field of government and politics.

Pro-Perú or Juntos

At the beginning of the Toledo government's last full year in office, a new social programme was under preparation, called Pro Perú or Juntos. This involved conditional cash transfers based on the model pioneered by Mexico (Progresa/Oportunidades). It gave rise to a good deal of debate. This is not the place to discuss its usefulness as a method for human capital formation or social protection, but rather focus on its significance in helping construct democracy. With elections not far away at the time of writing, the risks of clientelism seemed clear enough. Also the 'novelty' of the programme would allow the government to extract political benefits, since it stood to enhance its image not only by delivering specific benefits to certain localities and families but also from the idea and the name of the programme itself.

The signs were that the programme would begin without its *modus operandi* being properly discussed, and without debate about types of activity, budget allocations, the number of beneficiaries or how these would benefit. The decree that set up the programme placed it under the prime minister's office, which itself suggested that there was a political motive. There was no multi-party involvement on its board, nor the establishment of mechanisms for participation or oversight by civil society. Municipalities and regional governments had no established role to play, in clear contradiction to the whole idea of decentralising social programmes.

This all pointed towards a new clientelistic structure being erected. Who would benefit between one community and another, one urban district and another, would be entirely at the discretion of who ran the programme, at least at the outset. Assuming that responsibility would be placed in the hands of people from Perú Posible, the ruling party would be able to select localities to maximise the connections between the state/social benefit/political party/local leadership in such a way to ensure that it could be used by ruling party candidates and militants to electoral ends.

At the same time, and from what it was possible to discern, the system of targeting was to be based on what is known in the literature as the 'proxy means test'. This carried with it the risk of clientelism not only between communities but among them, undermining collective social bonds. A community in which people support one another is weakened when there are differential benefits between one persona and another, generating envy and misunderstanding. This was particularly likely where the differences between people classified as 'poor' and 'non-poor' were slight. Such categories can be very similar, and we know full well that the situation of families is constantly changing: employment opportunities are won or lost, children are born, young people leave home and the like.

Would such a clientelistic experiment be successful? Had conditions changed since the attempt to do something similar in 2002? On the face of it, it seemed fairly unlikely. Firstly, it would take time actually to implement a programme. Offices would have to be opened, people hired and budgets and procedures established. The government's previous administrative record did not commend it, whilst Peru Posible remained an inchoate political organisation.

Measures to reduce clientelism would involve the introduction of strict rules on political neutrality and strong punishments to deter the use of the programme for partisan ends. They would also involve the adoption of norms of transparency that would enable citizens to oversee procedures, with the programme placed in the hands of a pluralist and independent board capable of withstanding pressures on it from the ruling parties.

Conclusions

Looking back over 25 years, we have seen how the clientelistic management of social programmes has prevailed in Peru. It reached a peak under the Fujimori regime. Clientelism goes hand-in-hand with the weak development of democracy and citizenship; it has done little to promote them. Indeed, it represents a barrier to social programmes meeting their ostensible objectives, since it privileges political over social objectives, partisan designs over managerial and technical ones.

The return to democracy in 2001 raised great hopes that the situation would change. However, the policies of the Toledo administration in this respect differed little. Decentralisation was not forceful enough to provide a structural change, and the launching of Pro-Perú/Juntos in the build-up to the 2006 presidential elections seemed like an attempt to restore clientelist practices. Five years on from 2001, we could not be sure that such problems had been overcome.

However, even though the return to democracy may not have signified a break with the past in this respect, the Toledo government proved unable to erect its own clientelistic structure. The main factors here were the lack of coherence within the ruling party and growing resistance among citizens to this sort of practice. At the same time, the weakening of the democratic regime over these years was another basic reality. Just as the destiny of the democratic transition was unclear, so too was that of the social programmes. It would appear that these two situations — the snagging of social programmes which are neither fully clientelistic nor free from clientelism and the half-hearted nature of democracy — were linked.

The hypothesis therefore emerges that to put an end to the system of clientelism and affirm democratic governance, a new development path is called for — one that effectively reduces poverty and establishes genuine social rights for all. This would require changes in both social and economic policy. Put another way, clientelism will not be buried nor democracy deepened under the present exclusive patterns of social and economic policy. The next few years will show whether this hypothesis is borne out.

Notes

1   This was not the only orientation within the new government, however. For its first five months, with Doris Sánchez as minister for women's affairs and social development (the minister in charge of Pronaa), such institutions were filled with members of the ruling party.

2   For instance, Nicolás Lynch, the education minister, Fernando Villarán, the labour minister, and myself at the head of Foncodes. Shortly after-

wards, we were joined by Cecilia Blondet who replaced Sánchez as minister at Mimdes.

3   Other important changes in economic policy would be required, especially in spheres such as job creation, higher wages and support for small-scale enterprise or self-employment.

6

Agrarian Policy, Institutional Change and New Actors in Peruvian Agriculture

Fernando Eguren

More than four decades ago, in 1962, the Organization of American States recommended, at its conference in Punta del Este, the preparation of a comparative study on agricultural reform and agricultural development. The Inter-American Committee on Agricultural Development (ICDA) undertook this, guided by the following hypothesis:

> The main hypothesis of this study is that existing landholding systems in Latin America, dominated by *latifundios* and *minifundios,* can be changed to achieve more rapid social and economic development. The corollary here is these systems of landholding and land use are often an obstacle to development (Barraclough and Collarte, 1972, p. 10).

Peru over the years has not borne out this optimistic hypothesis.

In the section of the study devoted to Peru, it mentions that '0.4% of farms (…) account for 75.9% of the area included in the (1961) census, while 83.2% (…) have only 5.5% of that area' (Barraclough and Collarte, 1972, p. 395). In the period that followed, there were radical changes, and over the following 15 years there were three agrarian reforms. The last of these (1969–75) was by far the most important and most radical.[1] The Agricultural Census of 1994, the most recent available, bore witness to the changes that took place. At the time of the census, around 75 per cent of irrigated land and 62 per cent of non-irrigated land was in the hands of peasants and small-scale producers with plots of less than 20 hectares. In spite of the scale of the redistribution of land and its social consequences — among them the ending of servile labour and the gradual gaining by peasants of citizen rights — rural poverty persisted.[2] In 2003, 76 per cent of the rural population was considered to be 'poor', and 46 per cent 'extremely poor'.

From today's standpoint, the ICDA's prognosis seems somewhat naïve. This chapter seeks to contribute to an interpretation of why Peruvian agriculture remains, for the most part, poor and backward, in spite of this widespread redistribution of land. To this end, it offers a summary of sectoral policies over recent governments, arguing that these have not been politically neutral. They represent the fruit of often complex negotiations between different interests in the agricultural sector, and between these and the state. The course taken depends therefore on the relative power of different actors and the political and socio-economic contexts in which these find themselves. Once adopted, policies tend to be formalised in laws and other norms, with technicians then charged with implementing them. Policies can be seen as part of a continuum, the more extreme being those aimed at benefiting large numbers of social sectors (the 'win-win' choice), and those that benefit the few at the expense of the many (the 'zero-sum' choice). As we shall see, the policies of recent years are closer to the second of these.

The first part of the chapter deals with changes of orientation in agricultural policy, and it includes a hypothesis that seeks to explain the significance and logical coherence of this. This section finishes with a brief reference to the modernisation of Peruvian agriculture prior to the agrarian reform. The second part looks back at the key agricultural policies that help bear out the hypothesis adopted.

Changes in Policy Orientation and a Hypothesis for Explaining These

Under the Fujimori governments (1990–2000) sectoral policies in agriculture were subsumed by overall macroeconomic objectives. The so-called 'Fuji-shock', geared to re-establishing fiscal and monetary balance, led to a number of structural changes, including changes in the role of the state, the privatisation of state companies and market liberalisation. The radical nature of this structural adjustment was a response to the depth of the economic crisis, the roots of which go back to the late 1970s. The willingness of people to accept these

changes reflected their hopes that they would lead Peru out of the
nightmare of the late 1980s, in which the effects of economic crisis
were compounded by the political threat from Sendero Luminoso.

The neoliberal orientation of Fujimori's economic policies sought —
and achieved — to overcome inflation and establish fiscal balance. There
was consensus that the measures were necessary, although there were differences of opinion over the speed at which they should be applied. The
policies of structural adjustment that followed, however, revealed the links
binding the government's policy choices to those of private interest
groups. Market liberalisation, privatisation and the redefinition of public
policy (which remain in place today) had the effect of deepening social and
economic differences, not least in the agrarian sector. To offset these
effects, compensatory policies were introduced (such as the Fondo
Nacional de Compensación y Desarrollo Social, Foncodes) with the sup-
position that the benefits of liberal reform would follow afterwards.
However, such programmes as Foncodes have continued to exist, not just
because the expected benefits of reform failed to materialise, but because
it became clear that they were not going to happen.[3]

A Hypothesis

The macroeconomic policies and structural reforms pursued by
Fujimori with greater commitment and intensity than under his predecessors brought about important changes in the organisation of economic power in Peru (Vásquez Huamán, 2000; Durand, 2003). My central hypothesis is that agrarian policies over the last two decades have
been geared to the rebuilding of a business class, geared to the modernisation of Peruvian agriculture. This is particularly the case with coastal
agriculture. This process of modernisation excluded the huge majority
of peasants and small-scale agricultural enterprises. The new business
class is composed of businesses involved in large-scale commercial
farming, the marketing of agricultural produce and/or agroindustrial
goods. I am primarily concerned here with the former.

The strategic aim of rebuilding business agriculture — an objective
shared to varying degrees by all the governments since the military
regime — is based on an outlook that draws a sharp distinction between
production (mainly *costeño*) with the potential to be internationally competitive and an agriculture that is traditional, backward and peasant-

based (mainly in the *sierra*). A third area is the Amazon basin. This shares many of the characteristics of the latter but also includes the extraction of natural resources.

This breakdown is reflected at the level of state organisation: the Agriculture Ministry is principally concerned with modern agriculture on the coast (Ministerio de Agricultura, 2002); the social programmes with a highly distributive content — the National Programme for Watershed Management and Soil Conservation (Programa Nacional de Manejo de Cuencas Hidrográficas y Conservación de Suelos, Pronamachcs) and the National Food Assistance Programme (Programa Nacional de Asistencia Alimentaria, Pronaa) amongst others — deal with the *sierra*, and the National Institute for Natural Resources (Instituto Nacional de Recursos Naturales, Inrena) and the National Commission for Development and Life without Drugs (Comisión Nacional para el Desarrollo y Vida sin Drogas, Devida) focus their attention on the tropical Amazon basin.[4]

My hypothesis needs to be given an historical grounding which picks up on the different directions — or development paths — followed by the modernisation of rural Peru before and after the agrarian reform and the social sectors that led this modernisation. Classically, two development paths have been identified which reflect the experiences of Europe and North America: the *junker* path and that of the *farmer* (and its variant, the *campesino* path).[5] Schematically, the first of these, the Prussian model, involves the transformation of the large feudal or semi-feudal landholders into capitalist entrepreneurs and peasants into a salaried workforce. The second involves the transformation of peasants into agrarian capitalists, while those left over become part of the proletariat.[6]

The hypothesis supposes that both of these were taking place in Peru in the period before the first phase of the agrarian reform began in 1962. The *junker* path was being followed on the coast, and much less in the *sierra*. The same can be said about the *campesino* path mainly in the *sierra*, though this has been studied less and merits further research. The 1969 reform blocked both of these paths. The large landowners (and many medium-sized ones) were expropriated, while the peasant elites that led the mobilisations to increase their assets were in large measure co-opted by the government,[7] by political organisations (especially on the left), or were put in charge of the new associative units of landholding that came into being under the reform. The rural sphere was thus deprived of its modernising elites, and the state (unsuccessfully) sought to take the lead in spearheading modernisation and agricultural development. The agrarian reform failed in its attempt to develop agriculture. However, it did achieve a modernisation of social relations: it ended the semi-servile relations that had characterised *hacienda* agriculture.

Agricultural policy over the last two decades has striven to construct a new business elite. It has been this that has given a degree of coherence to what otherwise might be considered a lack of orientation in policy. Nevertheless, the possibility of achieving this objective depended on a number of conditions being fulfilled.[8]

The first is that the agrarian reform left a vacuum that needed to be filled. The reform did not eliminate all rural businesses, but certainly the most important and influential ones, depriving the rural sphere of a business class. In addition, in 1972 the military government abolished the National Agrarian Society (Sociedad Nacional Agraria) (Decree Law 19400) which had represented the interests of landowners and rural businesses. The most powerful rural organisations during and immediately after the agrarian reform were of peasants or small producers. These defended peasant interests, but were not able or oriented towards economic or technological modernisation (Monge, 1989). For their part, the associations of producers of specific crops lacked strength, in part because their demands were fragmented. The state ended up fulfilling a diversity of roles, thereby replacing the private sector — usually very inefficiently.

The second was the need for institutional changes, particularly with respect to property ownership. The agrarian legislation of 1969 imposed many limitations on property rights, discouraging investment and limiting the chances of the emergence of a rural business class. On top of this was the problem of rural violence, especially in the late 1980s and early 1990s.[9] Generally speaking, the economic, social and political contexts in the 1980s were unfavourable to business initiative. As we will see, a number of legal steps were taken that attempted to modify the rules of the game, especially with respect to property ownership. These began at the outset of the second Belaunde administration (1980–85). Such institutional changes provided a common denominator, giving a certain coherence and direction to agricultural policy.[10]

The third had more to do with the ideologies that became hegemonic after the collapse of socialist alternatives, concretely neoliberal policies. Although Fujimori has been identified with neoliberalism, in practice neoliberal proposals were circulating from the early 1980s, albeit not without difficulty and susceptible to reversal (e.g. under the government of Alan García). The neoliberal agenda helped frame a conception of agrarian development and modernisation that could only be achieved with free markets, free enterprise and minimal state intervention,[11] and subject to an international order in which competitiveness was the key criterion for judging the efficiency of producers and countries. Only internationally competitive private businesses matched the requirements. However, all peasants, the majority of small-scale producers and a significant number of medium-sized producers found themselves marginalised in this scheme of agrarian modernisation.

That this was the choice made is clear from the policies that were not adopted. In particular, the state backed away from trying to create conditions that would give viability to small-scale agriculture, other than those provided by private initiative. Such activities included the provision of informational or financial support or technical assistance. By contrast, the state sought to improve the conditions for export agriculture through the upgrading of transport infrastructure and port services, the simplification of export procedures, the provision of market information, the introduction of phyto-sanitary services to facilitate exports, etc. It was assumed that this sort of agriculture would have its own access to financial resources, information and technical assistance. The policy choice was therefore highly exclusive: to have a business class, whose members were small in number and linked to the export market, and not to have a policy to help debilitated small-scale commercial agriculture. As for peasant producers, they found themselves wholly marginalised from the development mainstream, dependent largely on substantial hand-outs from the public purse or donor contributions.

This policy choice provoked a reaction from medium and small-scale producers, who see themselves as excluded and are prepared to fight for agricultural development to become more inclusive. These sectors were hard hit by the withdrawal of the state in the early 1990s. It was they who had been among the main users of Agrarian Bank (Banco Agrario) lending, who had bought subsidised inputs from the state or who in the case of some crops had sold their production to state companies. Mostly, they consisted of coastal producers, but also included producers in the more fertile valleys of the *sierra* and from certain regions in the *selva alta*. Generally speaking, their production was geared to supplying the domestic market, and they included producers of rice, maize, cotton, potatoes, sugar cane, fruit and vegetables.[12] Although only some had their own producer organisations, these were among the strongest in the sector. Many of them came together in the National Agricultural Convention (Convención Nacional del Agro, Conveagro), an entity that gained importance in helping to formulate policy proposals, channel interests and provide an effective lobby towards the Ministry of Agriculture and other public offices.[13] Conveagro's relative success can be appreciated with the establishment of a Consejo Nacional de Concertación Agraria (Conaca) in 2002[14] and the so-called Carta Verde, a set of proposals made by President Alejandro Toledo to the agricultural sector in 2004. Conveagro also gave rise to local initiatives, with local Conveagros being set up at the regional level. These made use of the spaces opened up by decentralisation in seeking to influence and negotiate with regional governments.

However, in spite of these organisational advances on the part of small and medium-sized producers, the overall orientation of state policy under Toledo did not change in essence. The Agriculture Ministry sought in a fairly limited way to link up smaller-scale producers with larger agro-exporters or agribusinesses in productive 'chains'. In order to take advantage of available loans from Agrobanco, small-scale producers had to make themselves part of such chains. There were a number of reasons why these sorts of linkages failed to establish themselves, including the lack of sufficient finance for the purpose, a lack of respect for contractual agreements, judicial shortcomings in enforcing agreements and huge asymmetries between the links in the chain (such as access to information, educational levels, disparate negotiating power, etc.)

Key Measures in Agrarian Policy

The main characteristic of the measures taken as part of agrarian policy in the 1990s — and they have not changed much since — was the reduction in the role of the state and the liberalisation of markets, both for land as well as products. In the Table that follows, I include a summary of the main measures taken, before, during and after the 1990s. I then develop further those of specific importance for the purposes of this chapter.

Table 6.1: Changes in Sectoral Policies in Agriculture

Sectors	Before the adjustment measures and structural reforms (1980s)	Adjustment measures and structural reforms (1990s)	From 2000 onwards
Finance	Banco Agrario. State-owned development bank, with low rates of interest. It was the main formal source of finance for small-scale agricultural producers. Also the main channel for subsidies.	Liquidation of the Banco Agrario. Much more selective in loan policies, as commercial banks marginalise small-scale agriculture. Appearance of small, rural financial institutions, set up by NGOs and others (*cajas rurales*). Informalisation of finance becomes the norm. Increase in lending rates.	Creation at the end of 2001 of Agrobanco, a two-storey financial entity. Lack of resources prevent it from playing any significant role.
Agricultural research and technological dissemination	Carried out on a very small scale, either public or private sector, through the Instituto Nacional de Investigación Agraria (INIA).	Virtually eliminated. The supposition (unmet) is that private sector will take this over. NGOs and some special programmes undertake small-scale programmes. Universities and specialist faculties maintain low profile.	Establishment of Innovación y Competitividad para el Agro Peruano (Incagro). INIA restructured with a view to it giving leadership in research. Subsequently given role in technical extension.
Access to land and property rights	Land market restricted by legal norms and socio-economic context. Limits on legal extent of landholding. Community and peasant land protected under the constitution. Promotion of sub-division of associative agrarian holdings.	Liberalisation of land markets through legislation. Elimination of limits on landholding. Enabling of transfer of communal land to third parties. Programmes to regulate title deeds. (Proyecto Especial de Titulación de Tierras y Catastro, PETT). In contrast with past practice, initiation of auctions of land created by irrigation projects to medium and large-scale producers.	Continuation of PETT. No major changes in policy.

Table 6.1 continued

Administration of access to and rights regarding water	Regulated by the state, but with a tendency to transfer these to irrigation committees.	More assiduous policy of transfer to the irrigation committees. Aim (never carried out) to enact law creating a market in water. Carrying out of Subsectoral Irrigation Project (PSI) in the coastal valleys to improve irrigation systems.	New draft law for water, for the first time multi-sectoral. No change in overall policy. Continuation of the PSI.
Pricing	State intervention in fixing prices of certain agricultural products (staples)	Liberalisation of prices. Occasional (and erratic) intervention through the Programa Nacional de Apoyo Alimentario (Pronaa) for Andean crops, rice and fibres (alpaca)	Previous policy generally maintained.
Marketing	State intervention through public companies involved in marketing of specific products (staples). Regulation of food imports through annual quotas. Subsidies on food imports, favourable to consumers but not domestic producers.	Liberalisation of domestic and external marketing. Scrapping of subsidies. Liberalisation of imports. Imposition of surcharges on the importing of some products subsidised by country of origin. Overvaluation of dollar neutralises effects of this. Sporadic intervention by Pronaa for Andean crops.	Establishment of price bands that provide a degree of protection for specific national products in response to foreign subsidies. Pronaa takes on more active role in sourcing its food aid programmes from local producers.
Special programmes	Temporary employment schemes.	Compensatory schemes like Fondo Nacional de Compensación y Desarrollo Social (Foncodes); for food distribution (Pronaa); for expanding educational infrastructure (Instituto Nacional de Infraestructura Educativa y de Salud (INFES). Maintenance of important programme for natural resource management in the *sierra* (Pronamachcs). These programmes become politicised.	Programmes maintained and depoliticised (with difficulty).

Table 6.1 continued

Investments	Investment in special irrigation schemes. In general limited public investment for lack of fiscal resources. Very limited private investment.	Important investment in road infrastructure. Extension of the energy network and telephone system (private). Increase in private investment for agroexports and agribusiness.	Limited public investment. A moderate amount of private investment.
Relations with producers			Establishment of the Consejo Nacional de Concertación Agraria. Brings together produc er *gremios* and relevant ministries. Pact between executive and *gremios* (Carta Verde)

Note: Updated version of scheme included in Eguren (2002).

The most important of these policies for export-oriented businesses were those gradually modifying agricultural property rights, as we see below. These were also connected with water rights and management, the fate of the associative entities created by the Agrarian Reform, and the liberalisation of domestic trade.

Property rights

Land

Reconstituting a group of actors to drive agricultural development involved institutional changes. Prime among these was a redistribution of assets, particularly land, the main factor of agricultural production. In the wake of the agrarian reform and the subsequent subdivision of associative units of landholding into small parcels, land was mainly in the hands of small and medium-sized producers. More than 97 per cent of units of irrigated land — those of most interest to investors — were less than 20 hectares in size in 1994, and these accounted for three-quarters of the total. The agrarian reform legislation not only placed limits on land property rights — maximum limits on landholding, restrictions on sale and renting, the personal nature of property holding, obligations about its exploitation and restrictions about its use — but also included requirements which if unfulfilled led to the loss of property rights. Such norms were a far cry from those likely to attract investment. However, in addition, the unfinished legal and administrative red-tape surrounding the transfer of expropriated properties to tens of thousands of family lots arising from the subsequent subdivision of the land, created a panorama that was at once confusing and uncertain. Still, 15 years were to pass between the first changes to the reform legislation in December 1980 and the promulgation in 1995 of the extremely liberal Law 26505 (known as the Ley de Tierras).

There were various reasons why this process was so slow. For a large number of people, both urban and rural, the agrarian reform had been a necessity. Though legally questionable, it was seen as wholly legitimate. This legitimacy, based on the notion that land had a 'social function' and that 'the land belonged to those who work it', made it difficult for the governments that came after the military regime to adapt the agrarian reform law in any far-reaching sense. Changes only became possible in as much as new options opened themselves up, giving a degree of legitimacy to rather different principles. Concepts such as 'efficiency' and 'competitiveness' eventually became alternative sources of legitimacy for property rights as time passed; those best placed to achieve these were investors and businesspeople.

This 'legal odyssey' began only four months after Belaunde became president in 1980, twelve years after he himself had been deposed as president by General Juan Velasco. The new Belaunde government announced Legislative Decree 02, whose Article 82 put an end to the agrarian reform, a process initiated by Belaunde himself in 1964 during his first administration. It validated the restructuring of the reform's associative units, a process that had in fact begun back in the mid-1970s. This decree also changed part of the legislation about the Amazon jungle (Law 22175 of 1978) which prohibited commercial companies (*sociedades mercantiles*) from owning land unless they entered into a sort of joint venture with the state.

A second step consisted of a number of legal norms, announced during both the Belaunde and García governments, about the use of uncultivated land in the irrigated valleys of the coast. The Private Projects for Integral Development (Proyectos Privados de Desarrollo Integral, PRIDI) of 1982 created a special regime for concessions of uncultivated land, initially for studies and public works and then for distribution. This was a way around the legal and practical restrictions that had prevented land concentration, since it allowed areas to be granted of between 100 and 50,000 hectares, even though the private individual concerned could hold between three and 150 hectares. The PRIDI did not have the results hoped for, bringing into cultivation a mere 512 hectares. Its objective had been to produce vegetables for export.

In 1988, during the García government, Supreme Decree 029-88-AG tripled the limits of landholding on the coast — which had stood at 150 hectares — to 450 hectares. From that point on, any type of firm legally constituted under the Ley General de Sociedades, could register a claim to uncultivated land on the coast, in the *sierra* or in the jungle fringe (*ceja de selva*).

Under Fujimori, some of these norms were confirmed, even though several of them bordered on unconstitutionality.[15] In 1991, a decree was issued that allowed commercial firms to own and manage agricultural land. It also allowed land to be rented, sold or mortgaged. The upper limits on landholding were retained, but properties of up to 1,000 hectares were allowed where these were brought into cultivation through irrigation by private enterprise.[16]

Further norms complemented the legal framework that finally culminated in the 1993 Constitution. In August 1991 Legislative Decree 653, the Ley de Promoción de Inversiones en el Sector Agrario, called by Fujimori himself 'the reform of the agrarian reform', dealt mainly with aspects related to property and the market for land, principally in the *costa* and *selva*. It openly allowed commercial firms to be owners of agricultural land; it abolished obstacles to the renting of land; it paved the way for the abolition of specialised land tribunals; it laid down the principle of equal treatment for Peruvians and non-Peruvians; it brought rights to rural land under the Civil Code; it raised the limits on landholding on the coast to 250 hectares, as well as raising those in the *sierra* and *selva*. It declared that uncultivated land was state property, implicitly including that of peasant communities. Finally, it allowed for community land to be rented for periods of up to 30 years (renewable), a first step towards the elimination of the special protection afforded to communities under the 1920 Constitution, reaffirmed by those of 1933 and 1979.

It will not have passed the reader by that in spite of their crucial importance, hardly any of these norms passed by three successive governments — which effectively repealed the 1969 agrarian reform — were approved by Congress. They were not presented to, debated or justified in parliament. Those working in agriculture knew nothing about them, and had no opportunity to register any opinion before they became a *fait accompli*. Furthermore, in spite of the different styles and outlook of the three governments concerned, there was a logical consistency between these norms; all pointed towards the liberalisation of the land market.

By this time, it had become clear that a decade or more of legislation — some of it on the borders of unconstitutionality, some clearly unconstitutional — needed to be made constitutional if it was to provide any real guarantees to investors. The 1993 Constitution, approval of which was marred by a referendum seemingly rigged by the government, provided such guarantees. It validated the institutional norms passed over previous years and banished the concept of agrarian reform. Furthermore, it allowed for communal property rights to be transferred to third parties.

On the basis of the new constitution, the government moved in 1995 to pass the Ley de Tierras (Law 26505). This removed any limit on land ownership and all restrictions on land use (including the previous restriction on cultivated land being used for construction). It enabled land held communally by peasant communities or tribes in the Amazon jungle to be owned by private individuals or sold to third parties. Further new norms were announced for peasant communities. Although much of the land held by communities in the *sierra* was not very fertile, much of that belonging to communities in the *costa* had a potentially high commercial value, and if irrigated was attractive to investors. In 1997, the Fujimori government approved the Ley de Titulación de las Comunidades Campesinas de la Costa. This introduced the idea that land left uncultivated by communities on the coast would be taken over by the state. As well as violating the constitutional principle of equality before the law, this also violated the autonomy of communities to chose freely and democratically how to organise themselves and dispose of their land.[17]

Effects on the Market for Land

What effects did these changes in legislation and property rights have on the market for land? There are few studies on this. It is known that there were transactions in land even during the period when the agrarian reform was at its height. But, as would be expected, it was only after the military government, under Belaunde, that the rhythm of land transactions increased. The agricultural census of 1994 showed that of the total number of land units with private owners, 62 per cent had been acquired by inheritance, 27 per cent by purchase and 6.5 per cent by adjudication (mainly under the agrarian reform). However, a study based on surveys in Chancay-Huaral, one of the most 'modern' valleys on the Peruvian coast, showed an increase in 'market transactions' but indicated that it was not 'possible to register the majority of land contracts as market transactions' rather as 'bilateral transactions agreed between economic agents who know one another well' given the high transaction costs involved (Alvarado, 1996, p. 14; Trivelli and Abler, 1997). If the market in land was incipient in this valley — the study concluded — it must be even more so in other places where the conditions were less propitious. An extension of this research to include the northern valley of Piura concluded that the market for land was segmented by demand, due to the different ways in which those on the demand side were inserted in the markets for credit and products, there being two circuits in the market, one a business circuit and the other a more informal one (Ugaz, 1997).

These studies were conducted prior to the Ley de Tierras. However, even after this law, research showed that institutional problems continued to be major obstacles in developing a market for land. Informality in property rights, the lack of legal security, the absence of information, the atomisation of property all prevented the emergence of such a market (Zegarra, 1999).

One of the main limitations of these studies is that they focused on transactions for small properties and failed to analyse properly the 'business circuit' within the land market and the formation of larger units of landholding. Any significant concentration of property would have to involve contacts between both circuits, since most of the irrigated properties on the coast were still in the hands of small-scale agricultural owners.[18]

Some of the new agricultural businesses, geared towards export markets, were formed out of pre-existing properties, either through purchase or rental agreements. Some others established themselves on uncultivated land brought into cultivation by publicly-financed irrigation projects. Towards the end of the 1980s, many of the most important of these belonged to national economic conglomerates of non-agricultural origin, such as the Romero, Brescia and Nicolini groups (Eguren, 1989). In the years since 1989, a number of others have arisen. A study undertaken in 2001 estimated that, on the basis of the 1994 Census figures and more recent information, there were some 400 agricultural businesses with 80 hectares or more, mostly geared to the export market, out of a total 200,000 agricultural units in this region (CEPES 2002).[19] A census on asparagus production at the end of the 1990s showed there were some 200 firms in the *costa*, at an average of 140 hectares each. Most were engaged in producing asparagus for export.[20] A smaller group geared to export crops have land extensions of more than 500 hectares; they have become Peru's new, modern *latifundios*.

Research still needs to be carried out in analysing the land market within the 'business circuit'.

On Water Rights and Management

The defeat of legislative reforms over water for agricultural use is a different story. Attempts to develop a market in water rights repeatedly failed. The water legislation, the Ley de Aguas, passed by the military government in 1969, just after the enactment of the agrarian reform, is still extant, albeit subject to important modifications. The main modification came about in 1987, introduced by the APRA government, which transferred water management from the hands of the state to those of Committees of Water Users (Juntas de Usuarios) and their Irrigators' Committees (Comisiones de Regantes) made up of agricultural producers themselves (Apaclla et al., 1993). During the Fujimori government, this transfer was consolidated and further changes to the law were brought in. They included giving guarantees of water to those who had drilled their own wells and creating autonomous authorities within hydrographic watersheds.

A second important reform was introduced in January 1994, by which the government offered the private sector concessions to operate and maintain large-scale hydraulic projects. Those who acquired these concessions were allowed to finance services in future by charging water users through a canon system, and to sever supply to those who failed to make regular payment.

Possibly the most important feature of the 1990s was the fact that there was no new Ley de Aguas. A succession of draft laws produced heated discussion, and one of the few clear things to emerge from this was most agricultural producers' objections to any attempt to create a market in water. Their fears were twofold: that a market would increase the cost of water and that it would create a separation between the own-ership of land and the right to use water, the concern being that this would lead to monopolisation and hoarding.

There are several studies of water management in different parts of Peru, but so far as I can detect, none on the impact of water policy. Nor are there studies on the socio-economic impact of other aspects of water policy, such as irrigation. Still, it is worthwhile noting that tradi-tionally the new land brought under cultivation thanks to publicly-fund-ed irrigation projects has been distributed among small and medium-sized agricultural producers. Since the 1980s, however, the method used for handing over larger areas has been through auction, with small-scale producers effectively excluded. Nor has there been any proper research into competition for access and use of water by different types of user: agricultural producers, mining or other extractive industries, and urban populations. These are a permanent source of conflict.

The Dissolution of Associative Enterprises

One of the main obstacles to the development of a market in land was the existence of associative peasant forms of enterprise created under the agrarian reform: the so-called Agrarian Production Cooperatives (Cooperativas Agrarias de Producción, CAPs) and the Agrarian Societies of Social Interest (Sociedades Agrarias de Interés Social, SAIS). At their height, these included the country's most productive land, both arable and pasture. It was the members themselves who began the process of dismantling these associative enterprises as a way of dealing with their economic difficulties and the accumulation of management problems that had built up. The CAPs were divided up into small family units, and most of the SAIS were forced to disgorge a significant proportion of their lands to peasant communities. Whilst these associative enterprises lasted, the transfer of these lands to third parties was restricted by a series of norms established by the Velasco government.

I will mention just a few of the norms that sought to put an end to this experiment in associative enterprise. Decree Law 02 has already been mentioned. Promulgated in 1980 by the Belaunde government, it gave legal recognition to the restructuring of these enterprises, permitting the adoption of the model 'that was most convenient to the associates'. The APRA government, under pressure from peasant communities, issued a Supreme Decree (DS 006-86-AG) that required the 43 associative enterprises in Puno department to be restructured. In September of the following year, through DS 049-87-AG, the Ministry of Agriculture declared that the associative enterprises of Cuzco department were also to be restructured. Political violence was widespread in these areas of the country at the time, and this was probably the main reason for these moves since they would remove points of tension that Sendero Luminoso would otherwise use to consolidate its presence.

Years later, during Fujimori's second term in office, the government decided to privatise the shares it held in the huge coastal sugar plantations in order to capitalise their tax debts. This began in October 1996, and was the first of a series of measures, proposals and counter-proposals to transfer the ownership and management of the country's largest agricultural businesses from the workers to private investors, an objective that was met at least in part. At the time of writing, private capital accounted for the majority shareholding of these agroindustrial complexes.

Trade Liberalisation

Just as the changes in the legislation on property ownership favoured the development of the export-oriented agricultural business, other institutional changes sought not to stimulate small-scale production but rather to enhance its exclusion. Changes in the rules of the game contributed to this. The liberalisation of trade in certain agricultural products had begun at the time of the APRA government. The liberalisation of trade in rice was decreed in mid-1989.

However, it was during Fujimori's first year in office that state intervention in domestic production and imports was brought to an end. The ending of commercial intervention did not necessarily lead to 'the right prices', owing to the continued existence of 'non-competitive market structures and (…) externalities, both positive and negative, (that) affected the operation of markets for agricultural products' to the special detriment of small-scale producers and peasants (Escobal and Agreda, 1994). A study on the marketing of rice carried out in an important production area on the northern coast concluded that once the Food Trading Company (Empresa Comercializadora de Alimentos SA, ECASA) had been closed down and the Banco Agrario liquidated, new agents began to appear — local intermediaries, wholesalers and importers — who used their control over credit and information and their superior organisational powers, to appropriate most of the profits from production and marketing rice (Escobal and Agreda, 1994, p. 125). In certain valleys where hard yellow maize was produced, a product previously marketed by state companies for the poultry industry, there were clear examples of the abuse of market power by oligopolistic commercial interests to the detriment of mainly small-scale producers (Aparicio, 2004). The same sort of effects were seen with fruit production for the domestic market, where marketing and wholesale was in the hands of oligopolistic transport providers (Valdivia and Agreda, 1994).

As regards foreign trade, this was almost completely liberalised in March 1991. A single tariff of 15 per cent was established on food imports, and ECASA and the National Company for Trading Inputs (Empresa Nacional de Comercialización de Insumos, ENCI) were shorn of their exclusive right to import specific products. They were abolished shortly afterwards. Owing to the opposition of producer associations and due to the 'dumping' prices at which many products were imported, the government adopted a compensatory surcharge (later eliminated). For the rest of the 1990s and up to the time of writing, a variety of compensatory instruments had been adopted, but there were no restrictions placed on imports. The maintenance of such compensatory mechanisms to offset the effects of US subsidies to agricultural producers was one of the points of greatest contention in Peru's negotiations with Washington over a Free Trade Agreement (FTA).

Concluding Observations

Modernisation of agriculture and rural society, prior to the agrarian reform, involved a wide range of actors: large and medium-sized *hacendados* — mainly producing crops but also livestock; peasants living in communities; small-scale producers on the coast who had ceased to be *yanaconas* (a type of tenant farmer working on the haciendas). The intervention of the state in providing a variety of services was much greater than it is today. This sort of intervention was underpinned by a way of thinking about the future of the country and how to achieve future objectives; it implied a much more decisive role for the state than neoliberal ideology is prepared to contemplate.

Besides this process of modernisation in advance of the agrarian reform, there were forms of economic exploitation (exacerbated by the concentration of landed property) and socio-political oppression that by mid-century had become quite unacceptable. They included the most modern agricultural businesses. The political class and the wider public believed that this situation could not continue. Mobilisations by peasants and the huge migration to the cities was indicative of a crisis in the agricultural sector. The support provided by the state at the time to tens of thousands of agricultural producers was riddled by inefficiency and favouritism. By the end of the 1950s, agrarian reform was no longer a demand just on the left; there were no politicians with ambition who did not include agrarian reform on their platform. It was not just seen as a necessity, but something that the US government, scared by the prospect of a repetition of the Cuban revolution elsewhere in the hemisphere, was pushing. Agrarian reform was thus not a contentious matter.

However, this does not obviate the need to analyse it in its many different dimensions, not simply to understand better a key development in the history of Peru, but because it continues to exercise a huge importance for the present day. Nevertheless, for researchers into agricultural matters, the main issue is not just to review a process that was radical, extensive and which had such important implications over time (and still does); the important thing is to analyse current developments from the point of view of long-standing and complex transformations, thus adding to the significance of specific studies that are delimited in space and time.

For most of the Peruvian political class today the 'actors of development' are not the social sectors as a whole but those who profit from the market, in other words those who are 'efficient' or 'competitive'. In a country that is so heterogenous and polarised and has such a tradition of social exclusion, this is a project that further deepens exclusion. The efficient are relatively few, especially if the state fails to invest in improving the efficiency of the many small-scale producers. The overall verdict of agricultural policy over the last few decades has been negative if one defines as positive those policies that generate welfare, lead to sustainable development, that generate positive externalities, that are at once inclusive and equitable.

Agricultural policies today are more exclusive than those of 30 years ago. Replacing policies geared towards equitable and sustainable development with those geared to the workings of the market exclude large numbers of people who are in no condition to compete successfully. They are out of the game. Neither market mechanisms on their own, nor the restricted private interests of the 'efficient' can incorporate them without state intervention. It is quite clear that making market mechanisms the key objective is not a decision that is disinterested, rather the justification of a specific power structure for those mechanisms that help uphold and prolong it.

Research carried out over the last ten years confirms a number of things: that policy has not benefited peasants and small-scale producers; that trade liberalisation has tended primarily to benefit intermediaries; that the organisation of small producers can offset the range of disadvantages arising from the lack of individual bargaining power; that on rare occasions business initiatives can act to the benefit of small-scale producers if these manage to become properly organised.

Apart from a very few modest but promising instances, research over the last decade has yet to uncover any notable successes on the part of small-scale producers and peasants, even though their resilience and ability to resist is well documented. In no part of Peru have the majorities of rural people managed to improve their living conditions. Those success stories that might be worthy of mention are so few that they simply dissolve in a sea of poverty and backwardness.

What I have proposed here is the need for an overarching hypothesis, albeit limited in terms of its design, that makes some sense of norms and processes which otherwise seem to lack coherence or logic. This hypothesis suggests that the winners from the last decade have been the agricultural investors and businesses that export. But these have not tended to attract the interest of researchers. Nor have the policies that benefit them, both within the agricultural sector and more generally, been properly examined. Such actors seem to exercise no interest for researchers. This is a serious deficiency. One can argue, at least hypothetically, that they are ever more important among the *poderes fácticos,* those who wield power not because they are elected by ordinary people but because of what they own and the political relations this creates.

Notes

1   The last agrarian reform gave peasants and rural *hacienda* labourers 595,000 hectares of irrigated land, more than one million hectares of non-irrigated land, more than 5.5 million hectares of natural pasture, 222,000 hectares of forest land and more than 1 million hectares of non-agricultural land. The total distributed was more than 8.7 million hectares (Matos Mar and Mejía, 1980, p. 184).

2   That these changes were insufficient has been clearly demonstrated by the Comisión de Verdad y Reconciliación, which researched the results of the internal war during the 1980s and early 1990s. The report estimates that 70,000 persons perished, three quarters of them Quechua-speaking peasants (Comisión de la Verdad y Reconciliación 2003).

3   According to INEI, the percentage of poor people in Peru went from 42 per cent in 1985, to 43 per cent in 1991 and 54.7 per cent in 2003. This last figure is not directly comparable to the others because of changes in the methodology used.

4   Devida is the state entity in charge of designing and implementing the National Anti-Drug Strategy. It operates in areas of coca production (estimated at 40,000 hectares). Although the substitution of coca is central to its strategy (at least formally speaking), in practice its role is more repressive and geared to coca eradication. It offers few real alternatives to the many thousands of peasants involved in growing coca.

5   See, for example, De Janvry (1981, p. 208 and *passim*). From the beginning of the twentieth century, Lenin used the idea of the two paths as options for transforming the Russian countryside. Carmen Diana

Deere uses the two concepts to describe agrarian modernisation in Cajamarca (Deere, 1992).

6   Clearly there have been other ways throughout history, as Barrington Moore shows in his analysis of the English, French, US, Indian, Chinese and Japanese experiences (Moore, 1973).

7   In particular under the Sistema Nacional de Movilización Social (Sinamos).

8   The overall context was conducive. Neoliberal policies brought important changes in the structure of economic power. The privatisation of state companies was of great importance, as was the privatisation of pensions and the removal of limits to foreign participation. Francisco Durand summarises these changes in the 1990s as follows: 'What changed was that both the market and the state changed the structure of property and the weight of different economic groups [...]. In the 1990s, it [the process] revolved increasingly around the multinationals, and Peruvian or Latin American power groups which practically took over [all] economic sectors [...]. The structure of economic power ended up primarily as primary-exporting, with private hegemony and the overwhelming presence of private capital' (Durand, 2003, pp. 125–6).

9   See note 2.

10   On the liberalisation of the market in land and its effects on property concentration, see Zegarra Méndez (1999).

11   On public sector institutions and the agrarian sector, see Santa Cruz (1999).

12   The exception here is the Junta Nacional de Café, which brings together coffee cooperatives, producing mainly for export. By virtue of their origins, lifestyle and production methods, coffee producers are more *campesinos* than businessmen.

13   As well as 18 national agricultural *gremios*, Conveagro also consists of 16 entities that are associated with rural livelihoods, such as NGOs and professional bodies (Conveagro, 2004).

14   Conaca was set up in July 2002. Those that took part included *gremios* and ministries covering five sectors. The ministries include the Prime Minister's Office, the Ministry of Economy and Finance and the Agriculture Ministry.

15   The 1979 Constitution confirmed some of the principles established by the 1969 agrarian reform.

16 Alerta Agraria 49, April 1991.

17 Alerta Agrario 120, July 1997.

18 According to the 1994 Census, three-quarters of all irrigated land involved properties of under 20 hectares. Of this total, 39 per cent were under five hectares.

19 The complete study can be accessed at www.cepes.org.pe. A summary of the conclusions is to be found in Gorriti (2003).

20 Peru is one of the world's foremost exporters of asparagus, and it has become the flag carrier for modern agricultural businesses.

7

Judicial Reform in Peru (1990–2005)

Eduardo Dargent Bocanegra

Introduction

In Peru, as elsewhere in Latin America, the judiciary and the public prosecution service (Public Ministry or Ministerio Público) are institutions that are a long way from fulfilling their constitutional mandate either efficiently or effectively. Latin American judicial institutions suffer from a number of problems, among them lack of finance, lack of access to the justice system for people living on low incomes, corruption, obsolete procedures, poor levels of professional competence and management difficulties. Low levels of public confidence have been compounded in recent times by a widespread perception that the justice system is incapable of confronting criminality.[1]

This lack of public trust in the justice system is but an aspect of distrust in democratic institutions more generally. Mainwaring believes that this lack of faith in democracy resides in what he calls 'state failure'. The Latin American state has failed effectively to confront the many serious problems that affect ordinary people, among them poverty, political violence, corruption and the violation of human rights (Mainwaring 2005). This is also the case regarding the gap between the legal system and the informal means by which the great majority of people resolve their conflicts. As a consequence, the formal channels for conflict resolution do not work for those who, theoretically, should see these as a guarantee of social peace.

This lack of confidence in the justice system forms part of a broader mistrust on the part of citizens towards democratic institutions in Peru. This breach between institutions and citizens is both a result of ineffectiveness as well as the discriminatory way they operate. As else-

where in Latin America, in Peru there is first class citizenship and second class (López, 1997). Access to justice in many parts of Peru is
unavailable, and where this is not the case the cost of justice is such that it
is effectively unavailable to those on low incomes. The service provided is
in any case low-quality, lengthy and riddled with bureaucratic red tape. As
Drinot points out at the beginning of this volume, norms in Peru are
applied partially and inequitably. Such criteria as wealth, social status, political contacts and race are determinant in the way in which institutions
relate to citizens. This sort of discrimination is particularly harmful in an
institution like the judiciary whose constitutional purpose is to resolve conflicts between citizens with independence and impartiality.

   Starting with this notion of institutional failure as a key issue for
democratic legitimacy, this chapter revises the ways in which judicial
problems have been confronted in Peru over the last two decades. After
a brief critical assessment of the previous period, I analyse the changes
that came about in the wake of the 1992 *autogolpe*. I thus seek to discuss
and evaluate the judicial reforms introduced under the Fujimori administration and how these developed over time. Finally, I will look at the
justice system during the interim presidency of Valentín Paniagua and
under the government of Alejandro Toledo. This will help us identify
the key problems that currently afflict judicial reform in the country.
Although there have been some instances of progress, the main structural defects of the justice system remain the same as they were in previous decades. Though plans for reform may exist to tackle these, the
chances of these being adopted are slight, given both the lack of concern on the part of political authorities and resistance to changes within the judiciary that might upset vested interests.

Antecedents: The Military Government, the Return to Democracy and Political Violence (1968–90)

Although Peru's judicial system has long been an object of criticism, in
the past it managed to meet the needs of a small society, where judicial
disputes were mainly concentrated in provincial capitals (Hammergren,
2004, pp. 293–4). This situation changed during the 1960s when deep
social changes revealed the limitations of the courts in dealing with larger issues. During the Velasco government (1968–75), the judicial system

tended to be considered as an ally of the dominant classes and opposed to the popular revolution initiated by the government. This led to far-reaching reforms in the justice system, including purges of judges, changes in the way the court system was organised and overt intervention in judicial decisions. Consequently, those who became magistrates distinguished themselves more by their support for the regime than by their professional capacities.[2] Furthermore, whilst supposedly anti-elitist, the reforms did nothing to prepare the judiciary to confront the social demands that were bound to arise

With the return to civilian government in 1980, it was hoped that governments would give priority to a judiciary that had been overwhelmed by the social changes of previous decades and which had suffered greatly from a lack of autonomy. The expectation was that there would be a real overhaul of the workings of the justice system, and that based on the 1979 Constitution the judiciary would act as guarantor of the political liberties existent under a democracy. However, apart from further purges of magistrates and a few isolated changes, the democratic governments of the 1980s and the political parties of the time gave little priority either to the judiciary or to the newly-created Ministerio Publico. Apart from reincorporating judges dismissed under the military regime, little else of substance was done.

The proof of the weakness of judicial institutions was the way they behaved during the internal war against Shining Path (Sendero Luminoso, SL) and the Revolutionary Túpac Amaru Movement (Movimiento Revolucionario Túpac Amaru, MRTA). Partly because of its own institutional weaknesses and partly the pressures on it from outside, the judiciary failed to fulfil two of its prime objectives. Firstly, it was unable to respond to the terrorist phenomenon, punishing within the law those who had committed criminal acts. Secondly, it failed to provide guarantees for citizens whose human rights were violated by the military authorities or to organise trials that would guarantee due process (Comisión de la Verdad y Reconciliación, 2003, vol. 3, chapter 2; De la Jara 2001; Dargent, 2000).

As well as the problems made manifest by the internal war, also important was the way in which political parties increasingly sought to influence judicial decisions. Though the Peruvian justice system was not exactly autonomous in the period prior to the military government, it enjoyed a degree of independence (Hammergen, 2004). Traditionally, judges were nominated by the president, except in the case of members of the Supreme Court whose nominations by the president needed to be ratified by the Senate. Generally speaking, judicial decisions were respected. Under the 1979 constitution, the National Justice Council (Consejo Nacional de Justicia), an organ created under the military government, was made responsible for the nomination of judges, whilst the executive branch continued to nominate and propose to the Senate members of the Supreme Court. Especially under the APRA government (1985–90), this faculty was used to politicise the workings of the judiciary.

The hyperinflationary crisis through which Peru lived in the late 1980s also had a profound impact on the judiciary. One of the articles of the 1979 Constitution stipulated that the judiciary should receive no less that two per cent of central government current spending, but this was never adhered to. During the late 1980s, the value of a judge's monthly salary fell as low as US$50 (Hammergren, 2004). Lawyers, litigants and judges all agree that the economic crisis of these years raised the threshold of corruption enormously, both in the judiciary and in other institutions (e.g. the penal system) linked to it.

During this period, the drive to reform and strengthen the justice system gained momentum, inspired mainly by the donor community, the academic world and civil society organisations. In the view of multilateral banks, some academics and the business community, any genuine economic liberalisation to make the country more competitive presupposed the existence of an efficient judiciary with the ability to establish clear and predictable rules for investors.[3] At the same time, those institutions involved in the defence of human rights believed that the institutional weakness of the judiciary was one of the main causes of human rights violations in Peru. As already mentioned, the justice system came in for searching criticism for its failure to guarantee basic citizen rights against abuses from the state. Judicial review with respect to the constitutionality of laws, as well as the idea that the constitution was a norm to guide judicial decisions, were concepts that became increasingly common in law schools and among judges (Eguiguren, 1990). Also, from the end of the 1970s US foreign policy — notably through USAID — came to focus on conflict resolution over and above more traditional support for the military and police. The need to build an effective and independent judiciary was therefore strongly argued from both of these different perspectives, the economic and the democratic. It was to receive even more attention in the 1990s (Pásara, 2004a).

Autogolpe, Autocracy and Judicial Reform (1990–2000)

From the outset of his presidency in 1990, Alberto Fujimori was highly critical of the justice system. Indeed, he was scathing about judges in his very first speech as president in July 1990, lambasting them for their responsibility for the crisis which the country was suffering (De Belaunde, 1998). From such remarks, it might be thought that judicial reform would therefore have been among his priorities. However, beyond such criticisms, his government did little or nothing to spearhead reforms during its first few years in office. In 1991, a new Framework Law for the Judiciary did little more than tackle some overlapping judicial and administrative functions and improve some aspects of management. The law had a very limited impact, not least because of the intervention of the judicial branch with the *autogolpe* of the following year.

One of the main justifications for the *autogolpe* was indeed the scale of inefficiency and corruption within the judiciary. In his message to the nation on 5 April 1992, Fujimori stressed that his objective was to reorganise not just the legislative function but the judicial branch as well. The opinion polls conducted at the time showed huge public support for this. The need for judicial reform was supported by 95 per cent of those interviewed in Lima, with a mere two per cent expressing opposition (Hammergren, 1998, p. 3). However, the reorganisation that took place consisted merely of a purge of 134 magistrates in both the judiciary and in the Ministerio Público accused of corruption or for being political placemen. As lawyers, litigants and magistrates privately admit, many were indeed linked to political parties and had come under suspicion of corrupt activity. Yet, the purge also got rid of judges who were independent and who had attracted criticism from the armed forces on account of decisions they had made in upholding human rights (Planas, 1999).

The purge left many positions vacant in the judiciary, and many junior judges found themselves in senior posts on a provisional basis. In order to resolve the difficulties caused by the purge and to counteract some of the criticisms to which it gave rise, the government created the Honorary Magistrates Jury (Jurado de Honor de la Magistratura), composed of five jurists who were well-known for their autonomy. The purpose of the Jurado was to revise requests for reincorporation from Supreme Court judges and prosecutors who had been dismissed; to arrange an open competition for nominations to these posts; and (once these tasks had been completed) to initiate nominations for other appointments lower down the judicial hierarchy. In all cases, the decisions of the Jurado had to be ratified by the Democratic Constituent Congress (CCD) elected in 1992 to re-write the 1979 Constitution and to act as a legislature until the 1995 elections. At least initially, the CCD respected the decisions made by the Jurado (De Belaunde, 1998),[4] whose functions were then widened, managing to make several appointments to the Supreme Court as well as judges for the Lima judicial district. Still, despite the Jurado's labours, the number of provisional judges remained very high.

The 1993 Constitution brought a number of changes in terms of institutional design, and on paper at least these appeared to be positive. To resolve the problem of political nominations for judges, the National Magistrates' Council (Consejo Nacional de la Magistratura, CNM) was set up, its allotted task being to nominate judges directly. It is made up of seven representatives, none of them from the executive or Congress. Also, in the case of Supreme Court judges, the CNM was given a disciplinary role. At other levels, the CNM acted only at the second tier, vetting dismissals imposed by the disciplinary boards of the judiciary and the public prosecutor's office. However, apart from these constitutional innovations and the appointment of government confidants in the judiciary and Ministerio Público, Fujimori did little about judicial reform during the rest of his first term in office.

Fujimori's judicial reform began in earnest on 21 November 1995 with the promulgation of Law 26546. This established an Executive Commission to manage the judiciary for a period of 360 days with the express purpose of developing judicial reforms. The law got rid of the judiciary's Executive Council and its general management office. The government argued that the judicial reform constituted one of the 'second generation' reforms that followed on from the 'structural reforms' of its first term of office. The Executive Commission was made up of three Supreme Court magistrates who, in theory at least, would spearhead the reforms. These were appointed on an individual basis, not because of the posts they occupied in the judiciary. The same law also set up an executive secretary, who would be in charge of budgetary allocations.

In view of what we know now about the levels of corruption in the Fujimori administration and the corrupt activities of many judges, it is difficult to view objectively the beginnings of the process of reform and the government's reasons for supporting it. Although most now share the view that the government had no interest in having an independent judiciary, it is still debatable whether the reforms were vitiated from the very beginning by the desire to guarantee impunity for corrupt government officials and to hold on to political power indefinitely, or whether the reform progressively degenerated.

My impression is that there was a plan from the start, at least in the National Intelligence Service (Servicio de Inteligencia Nacional, SIN), to have a judiciary and public prosecution service that was subordinate in order to avert certain eventualities and to guarantee regime continuity. As we shall see, the road to eventual re-election would necessitate control over these institutions. Such a plan, however, does not necessarily imply that there was no interest in other areas of government in reforming the justice system and making it more efficient, or that the degree of control grew progressively as the need for having a subordinate justice system became clearer. In other words, it is quite possible that some in government thought that the judiciary could be run more efficiently without becoming a risk for the regime. However, by 1997, it had become quite clear that the changes were not forthcoming and that the regime had little real interest in having an independent judicial system.

It is difficult to follow all the various laws passed by Congress to guarantee the continuity of the Executive Commission. Many of these norms came about as a consequence of what became known as 'dawn laws'.[5] The initial law was followed up in June 1996 by Law 26623, which ostensibly aimed to create a Council for Judicial Coordination (Consejo de Coordinación Judicial). In the small print, this included interim provisions (*disposiciones transitorias*) to increase outside control over the Consejo and to give further new functions to the Executive Commission and the executive secretary. These included the right to regulate aspects of judicial administration and appointments, as well as the status of judges. Also included in the judicial reform was the Magistrates' Academy (Academia de la Magistratura), whose governing body found itself suspended (Comisión Andina de Juristas, 2003; De Belaunde, 1998).

Law 26695 of 2 December 1996 then further widened the powers of the Executive Commission, allowing it to regulate other aspects related to judicial administration and appointments amongst other things (Comisión Andina de Juristas, 2003, p. 106). This further increased the government's power over judges since, under the pretext of taking steps to reorganise the institution, it enabled decisions to be made that increased control in sensitive areas. On 10 December 1997, Law 26898 gave equal rights to full and provisional judges. This gave the latter the right to occupy elected internal positions as well as to vote for these appointments or for judicial representatives on other constitutional bodies like the National Elections Jury (Jurado Nacional de Elecciones) or the CNM. As we shall see, this not only increased the degree of control over the judiciary but helped pave the way for Fujimori's second re-election in 2000. During these years, the time limit on the Executive Commission was repeatedly extended. The last extension took it to 31 December 2000; but before then the regime collapsed.

Law 26623 also brought other surprises in its interim provisions. They declared that the Ministerio Público was 'under reorganisation'. The creation of an Executive Commission was announced for the Ministerio Público, with Nélida Colán Maguiño, hitherto the attorney general, in charge. The Commission was given similar duties as its counterpart in the judiciary, and these were subsequently extended. In 1997, a new attorney general was chosen in spite of manoeuvres by Colán to keep the post. However, as head of the Executive Commission, Colán in effect enjoyed most of the functions formally reserved for the attorney general (De Belaunde, 1998, pp. 326–7).

It is important to recognise that some aspects of the reforms of this period were positive and could prove useful if applied free of political manipulation. It is also important to see the judicial reform as a complex issue requiring action across a number of different spheres. The spheres in which there were more or less positive results included: the training of judges, improvements in administrative and management methods, improvements in court infrastructure, reductions in the backlog of cases for trial, improvements in information systems and better controls over the incidence of corruption at lower levels in the judiciary. Although some of these advances were turned on their heads and the only evaluations we have were conducted by those in charge of the reforms, a few of these measures did seek to address institutional problems in quite novel ways.[6]

Such positive innovations apart, the effect of the reforms was on balance negative. At the outset, the reform process had been trumpeted as being a genuine attempt to grapple with the structural deficiencies of the judiciary. The government invested some US$50 million. However, not only did the main problems persist, but even in the areas in which the reform was focused the results proved unsustainable over time. The problems of the reforms were twofold: problems of design and those relating to political control over the justice system.

First, the reforms sought to introduce changes as if the judiciary was an office or a factory, irrespective of the sorts of functions that judges should fulfil (Hammergren, 2004). No-one doubts that efficiency is important and that delays in providing justice are a central problem. However, this sort of approach ignored many other factors that need to be borne in mind, such as the quality of sentencing. Linked to this problem of design was the lack of participation of judges in the reform process. In other words, the reform sought to improve the product, but paid little attention to (indeed confronted) those who should produce it.

The key problem of the reform was that it did not seek to strengthen the institution or to make it more independent and professional. On the contrary, it sought to subordinate it to political power. It is worth concentrating for a moment on analysing how this control was achieved. The existence of provisional judges dated from the 1992 *autogolpe*, and helps explain how the judiciary came to be controlled. The problem was made worse by the creation of some 400 temporary tribunals and courts under the reform to reduce the backlog of cases. Provisional judges were those nominated at lower levels by more senior judges on a 'provisional' basis. At the same time, lawyers from outside the judiciary were contracted to act as 'deputies' (*suplentes*). During the Fujimori period, these provisional judges and *suplentes* accounted for up to 80 per cent of total appointments (Comisión Andina de Juristas, 2003). The significance of such nominations was that they meant higher salaries for those involved and that they were directly dependent on the Executive Commission.

The wide powers of the Executive Commission enabled the regime to appoint magistrates that would do its bidding in important positions.

The Commission, as we have seen, could get rid of nominations for provisional judges or *suplentes* at will. It could also shift full magistrates to new posts that came into being so as (at least in theory) to reduce the backlog. In this way, judges with a reputation for independence could be put in charge of unimportant jobs in the bureaucracy, far removed from any politically sensitive matters. In the same way, magistrates with no professional experience could be put in charge of tribunals in which cases of political interest to the government were heard.

To maintain this level of 'provisionality', bodies like the CNM and the Academia de la Magistratura saw their functions eclipsed. The CNM began once again to select and nominate judges in 1995, seeking to deal with the high number of provisional judges working in the judiciary. It came forward with new nominations until 1996, but thereafter these were interrupted by an ambitious programme to train candidates in the Academia de la Magistratura. The rules at the time made it compulsory for those who sought to become judges to pass the Academia's training course. However, the programme which had originally been for six months was extended to two years. In the end, the class of students who passed the course was never nominated. The CNM was therefore prevented from carrying out is constitutional role to make nominations for the lack of any suitably qualified students.

The final blow came for the CNM when it initiated proceedings to remove a number of Supreme Court judges for having issued a highly questionable sentence and thereafter making it known that they had done so without reading the details of case. As this trial got going, the pro-Fujimori majority in Congress responded by approving Law 26933, reducing the punitive powers of the CNM in such a way that it could no longer initiate proceedings directly against senior judges, but only act at a secondary level in revising disciplinary proceedings initiated by the judiciary itself and then only in cases where the judiciary sought to remove them. This decision was justified by yet another pretext on the part of pro-Fujimori congressmen: the need to respect the right of appeal in judicial disciplinary proceedings.[7] The real reason was the concern that the CNM might open proceedings against those judges most loyal to the government. At the same time, the CNM also had its power to nominate judges suspended until 2002. In this predicament, the members of the CNM resigned, and were replaced by their *suplentes*, many of whom were government loyalists (Comisión Andina de Juristas, 2003).

We have already seen how giving provisional judges the same rights as full judges made it easier to achieve the election of people close to the government to bodies where the judiciary had powers of appointment. Chief among these was the JNE, the body which would have the last word in pronouncing the legality of whether Fujimori could stand for re-election in 2000. The way in which the Executive Commission augmented the number of chambers in the Supreme Court and the Ministerio Público (ostensibly to improve efficiency in hearing cases) also enabled it to appoint provisional judges to these posts. Able to count on a large number of votes in both institutions, the government was able to ensure that those close to its interests were elected to the JNE. The paradox here was that the 1993 Constitution had been written ostensibly to guarantee the independence of the JNE by ensuring that it was composed of people removed from the direct influence of government. With its control over the Supreme Court, the Ministerio Público and the public universities (overseen by the government at the time), Fujimori could count on the support of at least three of the five members of the JNE.

The same sort of way in which an originally good idea for heightening institutional autonomy was stood on its head was revealed in another area. The creation of specialist courts in the judiciary responded to a need that had been evident since the 1980s to improve the quality and independence of judicial rulings. To avoid the corruption arising from drug trafficking, it was suggested that a specialist tribunal be created for judging crimes in this area. Similarly, to provide better protection for human rights, it was recommended that a specialist court be established to deal with demands for constitutional guarantees. Fujimori's reforms responded to these initiatives, and initially cases about drug trafficking and public rights were dealt with successfully. However, the system began to go awry when judges who were poorly qualified or known for their subordination to the government were nominated to these potentially sensitive areas. Furthermore, specific courts within the Supreme Court were given the task of organising and exercising discipline over these specialist courts to ensure that they were not controlled by the judiciary's usual procedures. In this way, the government was able to ensure that all potentially embarrassing cases were dealt with not by specialist judges of known autonomy but by judges faithful to the government.

Hence, by the end of the Fujimori period, the process of judicial reform had lost all semblance of political neutrality. Even the government no longer sought to justify it. Although some judges resisted this tide and raised their voices in protest, they had little impact. Once again, the weakness of the judiciary and the ease with which it could be manipulated was made manifest.

The End of *Fujimorismo* (2000–01)

Following Fujimori's re-election in 2000, a round-table for negotiation (Mesa de Diálogo) was established between the government and the opposition with a view to democratising the country. This was brokered by the Organization of American States (OAS).[8] The decision to negotiate represented a sort of compromise on the part of both parties, between whom the battle lines had been clearly defined following the scandalous way in which the 2000 elections had been conducted. Also present as observers were institutions from civil society and the Church.

One of the main issues discussed was the need to get rid of the Executive Commissions in the judiciary and the Ministerio Público. Progress was made in the first few meetings specifically in the area of the judiciary, and timetables were suggested for scrapping the commissions. This could be interpreted as being a ploy by the government to gain legitimacy without taking any concrete steps to relax its grip over the institutions concerned. At one point it seemed that there was deadlock and this heralded the collapse of the negotiations. However the screening of the Kouri-Montesinos video in September 2000 led to the speedy unravelling of the regime. In the weeks that followed the video, in September and October 2000, the Mesa de Diálogo played an important democratising role. Reforms to dismantle the system of control over the judiciary were agreed, and these were subsequently legislated on by Congress. They repealed the equal status that had been granted to full and provisional judges, and delimited the jurisdiction of provisional judges. At the same time, the Executive Commissions in the judiciary and the Ministerio Público were abolished, and were replaced by Transitional Councils (Consejos Transitorios) composed of Supreme Court judges (elected by full judges) and professional people from outside the judiciary who met with the requisites for appointments to the Supreme Court.[9] These councils were given competence to govern both

institutions. They were given 90 days in which to come up with measures to eliminate all remnants of the Executive Commissions and to
produce an evaluation of the main problems within both institutions.
The functions of the CNM were restored and norms introduced to
resolve the problem of provisional judges.[10]

Owing to their brief duration, the councils were not in a position to
undertake important structural reforms. However, they did manage to
complete a number of important tasks in abolishing outside controls
over the judiciary. They also carried out a certain amount of diagnostic
work that was to play a part later on in reforming the justice system. It
is worthwhile finally pointing out that the majority of those judges who
had taken part in both Executive Commissions, as well as judges at all
levels, were put on trial and in some cases convicted for corruption.

The Toledo Government (2001–06): A Transition?

At the outset of the government of Alejandro Toledo there was widespread expectation that judicial reform would be given priority. Because
of the way in which justice had been manipulated over the previous
decade and the awareness of the danger that this represented for the
future of democracy, the issue was among those at the top of the political agenda. The need for reform of the justice system, for instance, was
included in the National Accord (Acuerdo Nacional), a document
signed by political groupings and a variety of civil society organisations
containing recommendations for reform over the medium-to-longer
term. But in fact, four years later, at the time of writing, what had been
thought of as a 'transitional' government had achieved little with
respect to judicial reform. Little seemed likely to be achieved of any
substance in what remained of Toledo's term.

There is a source of tension, difficult to resolve, that repeatedly
blocks the way for comprehensive reform to tackle structural problems.
The new authorities in the judiciary and the Ministerio Público, as well
as the media and public opinion in general, remained rightly suspicious
of proposals for reform that come from outside the institutions themselves. From the beginning of the Toledo government, there were accusations that the government wanted to manipulate the justice system to
its own ends, and the government also accused APRA of the same. As
often as not, such accusations had little basis in fact[11] — even if it had

wanted to the government lacked the ability to manipulate the justice system — but it remained a highly sensitive topic.

This helps explain why, from the very beginning of the Toledo government, questions of judicial reform were left in the hands of the judiciary itself. Since the time of Fujimori's fall, the judicial authorities have repeatedly expressed their ability and desire to push ahead with reform. The process re-emerged whereby reform was to be kept in the sphere of the judges since they 'knew the judiciary best'. This meant that proposals from outside the institution were looked upon askance. However, such 'self-reform' did not prosper under Toledo; few advances were made and there was no movement from within the judiciary to push forward with the structural reforms required.[12]

Notwithstanding, some positive changes came about during these years. They need to be analysed with some care as they too reveal shades of black and white. The most significant include:

- **Wages and salaries.** In 2005 wages in the judiciary were raised substantially. The budget for the year rose to 645 million soles, up from 553 million the previous year. This compares with 288 million in 1996, 405 million in 1999 and 486 million in 2000 (Justicia Viva, 2004b). Because of the criticisms of the low pay received by judges, they were awarded a pay rise in 2002. Judges' salaries in 2003 varied between US$1,000 and US$7,600 a month (Hammergen, 2004). Although this hike responded to longstanding complaints among judges, the increase was not awarded to other sectors (such as administrative staff). This led to prolonged strikes in 2003 and 2004.

- **The Consejo Nacional de la Magistratura.** Following the resignation of the members of the CNM in 2000, these were replaced in line with constitutional mandates. The task of selection and nomination began swiftly, bearing in mind constitutional procedures and the need to grapple with the large number of provisional judges. Between 2001 and 2004 the proportion of provisional judges fell from 73 per cent to 35 per cent. Although this is generally regarded as a positive development, there was no shortage of criticisms about the way it was handled. The basic problem resided in the fact that the appointment of full judges to reduce the number of provisional ones tended to take precedence to heeding the academic and ethical qualifications of those appointed. Criticisms were directed in particular at the way in which examinations of candidates were designed to reward rote learning more than professional or academic experience. Some of these criticisms led to changes in methods of selection with consequent improvements in standards of transparency (Justicia Viva, 2004b, p. 18). There were also criticisms of the degree of discretion enjoyed by the CNM in ratifying appointments and in exercising its disciplinary functions.

- **Judicial independence.** After 2000, the institutions of the judiciary operated with more independence of the other powers of the state, especially compared to the 1990s. There was no overt instance of outside interference that compromised the autonomy of the courts. However, there was no guarantee that this would continue to be the case.

- **Justices of the peace.** From the 1990s onwards the system of justices of the peace gained legitimacy in providing alternative methods for conflict resolution at the local level. Although the system involved contacts with the judiciary, it was largely autonomous. Its relative success in dealing with minor legal issues gave rise to various attempts to study ways in which the judiciary could function in ways that brought it closer to the community. Although their spheres of competence were much more limited than those of regular judges, the justices of the peace fulfilled a very important function, and the system showed that it was possible to create institutions that were seen as legitimate in the eyes of the communities they served when these undertook a valuable service that responded to people's everyday requirements.

- **Civil society and oversight.** It is important to stress the ways in which non-governmental organisations have contributed to discussion about reform in the judicial system. Since the 1980s, and especially during the 1990s, the Andean Commission of Jurists (Comisión Andina de Juristas, CAJ) and the Institute for Legal Defence (Instituto de Defensa Legal, IDL), for example, became critical voices developing research into key aspects of how the justice system works. In more recent years, the Justicia Viva consortium also played an important part in monitoring and developing aspects of judicial reform.

- **Anti-corruption and anti-terrorist tribunals.** The development of specialised systems of justice in the fields of corruption and terrorism proved to be a positive move. Criticisms can be made in both spheres, however. In the case of anti-corruption, there was a problem of slowness. Rather than inefficiency, this showed the defects of the Peruvian justice system in dealing with the complexities and sophistications of high-level criminality. In that of anti-terrorism, it was regrettable that the court in which the leaders of Sendero Luminoso were tried in 2004 did not take more precautions in preventing the proceedings getting out of control. Even so, the trials provided scope for new types of judge, capable of dealing with difficult cases firmly but in a transparent way.

- **Reducing the profile of military courts.** Two cases in 2004, one in the Constitutional Tribunal and the other in the Supreme Court, laid the basis for what should constitute the role of military justice in a democratic society. The Constitutional Tribunal's ruling restricted the previously wide ambit of military justice in Peru. Amongst other things, the ruling established that military justice could only be applied to crimes committed on active service and only when related to military issues.[13] Subsequently, on 17 November 2004, the Supreme Court ratified this in ruling on a case of competing civilian and military jurisdictions in Coronel Portillo province in Ucayali involving the torture and killing of a civilian by a military patrol. These two rulings represented an important challenge to the previous superiority of military justice.

The most interesting and significant contribution to the debate over reform of the justice system has been the Special Commission for Reforming Judicial Administration (Comisión Especial para la Reforma de la Administración de Justica, better known by its acronym Ceriajus). As we have seen, there were a number of statements by members of the judiciary that the justice system could only be overhauled from within. In his inaugural speech as president of the judiciary in January 2003, Hugo Sivina Hurtado adopted an extremely self-critical tone, recognising the need for comprehensive reform. This led people to believe that at last a judge would take the lead. He announced what he called a National Accord for Justice (Acuerdo Nacional por la Justicia). His plan was for both judges and jurists from outside the judiciary to undertake a critical evaluation of the various problems confronting the justice system. Whilst this was under way, the executive launched the proposal to set up Ceriajus. This came into being under Law 28083 on 24 October 2003. Its objective was to come up with a comprehensive set of reform proposals for the justice system as a whole. The commission was given 180 days to report back on its conclusions.

Sivina reacted to this initiative by countering that it represented an excessive interference into the affairs of the judiciary. This was a somewhat exaggerated stance since the role of Ceriajus was simply to propose measures, and that it was to play no role in putting these into practice. Also, the judiciary would be well represented within Ceriajus. It was widely believed at the time that the Acuerdo Nacional por la Justicia would be used as a pretext not to take part in Ceriajus. In fact, events did not turn out quite like this and the work undertaken by the Acuerdo was finally incorporated in Ceriajus as a specific contribution from the judiciary.

The composition of Ceriajus helped provide it with a broad view of the problem of the justice system, involving a wide range of institutions with an interest in judicial reform. The commission was composed of the president of the judiciary (who presided over it), the chief public prosecutor (Fiscal de la Nación), the president of the CNM, a representative from the Constitutional Tribunal, the president of the Academia de la Magistratura, the minister of justice, two members of the congressional justice commission, the ombudsman (Defensor del Pueblo), a representative from the Peruvian bar association, a representative of the six oldest public and private university law faculties and five members appointed by the civil society institutions represented in the Acuerdo Nacional.

Although some of the conclusions are open to criticism, the work of Ceriajus was important in providing a pluralist basis for future change (Justicia Viva, 2004a, p. 8). There were two basic reasons for such a positive assessment. Firstly, the conclusions of Ceriajus mapped out a reasonably realistic plan for the various different spheres that have a bearing on the administration of justice. These acknowledged both the limitations and obstacles to change, recognising the failures of the Courts to match up to the expectations of a democratic society. Being realistic about the scale of the challenge, it recommended the adoption of a gradual approach that would take into account the operational capacities of the institutions involved. It set out a well-ordered and prioritised plan of action that was agreed upon by judges, political figures and representatives of civil society.

Secondly, it produced an estimated budget covering the costs of the reforms (1.34 billion soles or around US$385 million) over the medium term. Although only an approximate figure and one that excluded various programmes that would involve further spending, it was important that the effort was made to quantify how much the reforms would cost. Although this total would need to be revised, at least it enabled funding to be sought both from the executive and foreign donors.

All in all, Ceriajus contained 170 proposals for reform. In many cases, these were agreed upon unanimously. This meant that modifications were accepted by those working in the judiciary itself whereas previously they had been resisted. Among the main agreements reached were a number of proposals on key issues. Recognising the enormous gulf between institutions and ordinary people, these included measures to improve access to the justice system, to help root out corruption, to modernise the administration of justice, to improve judicial training, to raise levels of consistency in jurisprudence, to reform the penal system and to take on board the conclusions of the Truth and Reconciliation Commission.

Among the recommendations arrived at by consensus were:

- a bar on the executive interfering with the budget of the judiciary, except in so far as this exceeded four per cent of overall Treasury expenditure;

- the incorporation of the system of military justice within the judicial system;

- the granting of full autonomy to the Academia de la Magistratura; and

- allowing peasant and indigenous communities to judge issues arising within their communities, subject to certain provisos about observance of human rights.

Notwithstanding these agreements, Ceriajus met resistance from the judges to two basic aspects of the proposal: key aspects of constitutional reform, and reform of the framework laws for the judiciary and the Ministerio Público. These were precisely the areas in which the main obstacles lay in achieving an effective judicial reform and where the main institutional decision-makers involved had most to lose. The proposal for constitutional reform was approved against the opposition of the president of the judiciary, the chief public prosecutor, the president of the Academia de la Magistratura and one member of the Supreme Court. Given the opposition from the heads of the two institutions most involved, it was considered most expedient for the Congress — taking on board both the recommendations as well as the observations made by both institutions — to approve the framework laws.

Also, even though the judges involved approved many of the proposals, there were others who did not. As a consequence, the agreement to reinforce the CNM and to make it responsible for discipline in both institutions was made against the will of the judiciary, as were moves to reduce the size of the Supreme Court (to 11) and change its responsibilities and procedures. Similarly, the decisions to create Consejos de Gobierno in both institutions and to appoint members of civil society to these were also resisted.

Ceriajus wound up its proceedings in May 2004, but a year later its recommendations had been largely ignored by the judiciary and the Ministerio Público. In spite of movement on one or two specific points — such as widening the areas of competence of anti-corruption judges or waiving payment of judicial fees in areas of extreme poverty — the bulk of the plan remained on ice. Within the Toledo government, interest in judicial reform languished after the departure of Fausto Alvarado and Baldo Kressalja as ministers of justice. In Congress, the Ceriajus proposals did not receive much attention from either legislators or the political parties. In the case of the latter, they made no serious comments on any of the suggestions made, still less did they comment on what position they would adopt in the event of winning office. Nevertheless, in early 2005 the Congressional Justice Commission resumed its discussions on the proposals and created a sub-commission to study them further. This was at least a positive development, and contrasted with the lack of interest of most other actors.

With no enthusiastic support from the government, ignored by the political parties and facing strong resistance within the judicial establishment, progress on reform therefore looked implausible. The reformist tide had ebbed.

Conclusions

In spite of its shortcomings, the recommendations of Ceriajus provided a starting point and some sense of orientation for reform. It was the first time that a reform plan had been adopted that acknowledged the problems facing the judiciary in meeting its constitutional responsibilities and had involved senior judges. However, it seemed improbable that it would lead anywhere in the near future. This raised the question of how best to confront the lack of interest that is palpable within the judicial hierarchy without infringing the autonomy of the judicial institutions. The only way would seem to be to 'push' the judges in that direction. Hammergren puts it well:

> It is unlikely that this mindset will shift among judges or other sections of the judiciary, so it may be necessary for pressure to be placed by other branches of the state, civil society or even the foreign donor community. Such pressure does not necessarily imply restricting judicial autonomy, simply to insist that the financing of the reform agenda is worked out in a coordinated way and that externally assessed measures of improvement become the conditions for accessing available funds (Hammergren, 2004, p. 330).

The future therefore depended on making the judges understand that the reform meant much more than just an increase in funding and that the goal was to give people the means to resolve their social problems; it did not mean 'better wages or more imposing buildings' (Hammergren, 2004, p. 331). The changes would clearly have an effect on them, but they had to learn to distinguish their own interests from those of the institution. Finally, as with other reform processes, it was important not to think of reform as if it were some sort of bubble, disconnected from Peru's other problems. It remained difficult to think of a reform that sought an autonomous justice system, with professional, well-paid judges, well managed and free of corruption in a country in which these were problems that plague most institutions and society itself (Pásara, 2004b, 2004c). We face a 'chicken and egg' problem, in which the judiciary should be an engine of change but is caught up in a reality of power relations from which it cannot easily escape. In Pásara's words:

> In Latin America, conditions of life make it impossible for men and women to recognise themselves as being equal before the law. There is no equality before the policeman, the judge or the public prosecutor. This inequality is socially conditioned, and cannot be remedied either by a normative declaration or by an institutional body like a public defence lawyer that seeks to mitigate it (Pásara, 2004b, p. 541).

Yet, as the experience of SUNAT suggests, along with the attempted police reform at the beginning of Toledo's presidency, this does not mean that with the right policies and transparent procedures you cannot improve the workings of institutions that appear to be basket cases and to change some aspects of the social context in which they operate. Rather than make us pessimistic, the size of the task should make us aware of the urgency of reform.

Notes

1   According to Magaloni (2003, p 276) the Latin American region 'not only presents the highest international homicide rates, but together with Sub-Saharan Africa, has shown the highest increase in criminal behaviour during the last decade'. The number of homicides in the Andean region is 22.7 per 100,000 inhabitants, compared to a world average of 10.7 (Carrión, 2004, p. 217).

2   See, for instance, Hammergren (2004, pp. 296–9 and 1998, pp. 142–7).

3   As Pásara points out (2004b), these changes were often presented with excessive optimism based on their short-term impact.

4   There are those who are highly critical of the contribution of the Jurado de Honor de la Magistratura. See, for example, Pease (2003).

5   These were laws suddenly sprung on the Congress and approved by the pro-Fujimori majority in a matter of hours. Usually they did not appear on the congressional agenda and were designed to avert debate or scrutiny.

6   For a more detailed analysis of the positive impact of the Fujimori reforms, see Comisión Andina de Juristas (2000); also Hammergren (1998), De Belaunde (1998) and Rubio (1999).

7   As the CNM was the only institution that could take measures against
        members of the Supreme Court, it was claimed that another level
        should be involved. Rather than violate the constitution on this point,
        another level of oversight could have been created within the CNM.

8   The OAS intervened after an electoral observation mission, dispatched
        to oversee the 2000 elections, reported on the large number of irregu-
        larities which vitiated the outcome.

9   Law 27367, 4 November 2000.

10   Law 27368, 6 November 2000.

11   It is worth pointing out here the case of the Supreme Court judge Silva
        Vallejo who demonstrated the habitual subordination of the judiciary to
        executive power by going to the home of the president to press the
        demand that Toledo acknowledge the paternity of his illegitimate child.
        This was one of the first of a string of embarrassing scandals that sullied
        the reputation of the president.

12   The Ministerio Público alleges that it has evaluated and reformed its
        internal workings. Good intentions apart, this is not something that is
        generally recognised, and what is known does not lead us to think that the
        institution's critical weaknesses have been tackled.

13   This ruled out the possibility of military courts having jurisdiction over
        crimes such as torture or assassination.

8

Promoting Human Rights: NGOs and the State in Peru

Coletta A. Youngers

Since its foundation Peru's National Coordinator for Human Rights (Coordinadora Nacional de Derechos Humanos) — an umbrella organisation of the country's human rights organisations — has earned a reputation as one of the most effective country-based human rights movements in Latin America. Over the years, the Coordinadora has managed to function effectively as a coalition even as the situation in Peru dramatically changed.[1] It was consolidated during a period of extreme political violence, emerged at the vanguard of civil society groups advocating democratic change in the face of President Alberto Fujimori's decade of authoritarian rule and supported the reform efforts undertaken by Peru's transitional government following Fujimori's fall in November 2000. Of particular significance, the Truth and Reconciliation Commission (Comisión de la Verdad y Reconciliación) formed by the transition government was the result of a concerted advocacy campaign on the part of the Peruvian human rights movement. The Coordinadora and other civil society groups are now essential voices for implementation of the Commission's recommendations.

A key factor in explaining the Coordinadora's relative success over the years is the constructive approach it has taken to engagement with the state. This stands in stark contrast to the situation in other Latin American countries, where civil society groups often came to see the state solely as an adversary, primarily due to its repressive role. In Peru, however, the idea that the human rights community should seek to influence and collaborate, when possible, with state institutions became widely accepted within the Coordinadora. This was largely due to the nature of the Shining Path (Sendero Luminoso) insurgency, responsible for horrific atrocities against the civilian population.

Even when in a confrontational and antagonistic role, the Coordinadora sought out opportunities to collaborate with government initiatives. When conditions allowed, communication existed with a range of national and local authorities of state institutions. More often than not, such communication was ignored, but occasionally a local official could be found who would respond. Within the justice sector, the Coordinadora and its member organisations sought out officials within the Public Ministry (Ministerio Público) — from the attorney general, to the special prosecutor for human rights, to local prosecutors — sending denunciations and follow-up requests for information. Mid-level judicial and police personnel received training from Coordinadora member organisations. Human rights lawyers interacted with judges hearing cases of civilians charged with terrorism, while social workers worked with local prison officials to improve conditions.

From its inception until the fall of Fujimori, Coordinadora activists faced tremendous hostility from successive governments, as well as threats on their lives from state security forces. Over time, however, through public denunciations and repeated contact with government officials, the Coordinadora and its member organisations gained a reputation as political players, and they were increasingly able to influence certain state policies. Human rights groups successfully sought to have the office of the Human Rights Ombudsman (Defensoría del Pueblo) enshrined in the 1993 Constitution and then lobbied for its eventual creation in 1996. As the situation of political violence waned, Coordinadora member organisations began formulating and advocating legislation and other human rights-related reforms to promote human rights and democracy. For example, they sought and obtained legislation making both torture and disappearance a criminal offence in Peru. Finally, as noted above, the Coordinadora carried out a successful campaign to create a truth commission charged with investigating the past, seeking justice and reparations for victims, and proposing reforms. While many challenges remain, the human rights community has contributed significantly to incorporating human rights into law and government institutions.

Peru's Human Rights Movement

In May 1980 a vicious cycle of political violence began in the Peruvian countryside. Just as a civilian president was elected after 12 years of military rule, the Shining Path insurgency launched its bloody revolution. The Belaunde government largely abdicated its responsibility for maintaining internal public order, allowing the military to carry out a scorched earth campaign, which largely targeted poor rural peasants (Gorriti, 1999; Stern, 1998). According to the statistics compiled by the Truth and Reconciliation Commission, over the next two decades an estimated 69,000 Peruvians were killed or disappeared as a result of political violence (Comisión de la Verdad y Reconciliación, 2003).

In response to the violence, Peru's incipient human rights movement proliferated. Small human rights groups, often called Human Rights Committees (Comités de Derechos Humanos, Codehs) were formed in small towns and cities around the country. The Catholic Church played an important role in supporting local human rights efforts; pastoral offices called *vicarías* were formed in many dioceses. In the emergency zones, organisations of family members (*familiares*) of victims of violence were formed. Most had family members who had disappeared; they were overwhelmingly poor, Quechua-speaking peasants from isolated rural areas — the most marginalised sector of Peruvian society. The organisations of *familiares* offered both solidarity and possibilities for joining together with others to take actions.

Like much of Peru's peasant population, human rights activists increasingly found themselves caught in the crossfire between the military and the insurgents. Even as more information became available about egregious abuses committed by state forces, conservative political leaders continued to view human rights as an obstacle to waging a successful war against the subversives. Human rights defenders were branded as direct or indirect supporters of the insurgents — either as the legal arm of subversion or as unwitting accomplices. The Peruvian military and police routinely targeted human rights activists, mistakenly linking them to the Shining Path. In Peru as in other Latin American countries, state agents were responsible for most of the attacks on the human rights community. However, the terrorist tactics employed by the Shining Path and its unabashed targeting of grass-roots and left-wing activists and the human rights community set it apart from other revolutionary movements in Latin America. By the end of the 1980s, scores of popular leaders were killed each year by its 'liquidation squads' (Basombrío, 1998).

Being caught in the crossfire gave greater impetus to the need for unity among Peruvian human rights groups and was significant in determining both the nature and activities of Peru's human rights movement. In 1985 human rights groups across the country came together to form the Coordinadora Nacional de Derechos Humanos. At its founding, the Coordinadora and its member organisations adopted a firm and unwavering condemnation of acts of terrorism committed by the Shining Path. The role of the progressive church, Catholic and Protestant, was important in this discussion. Over half of those present were affiliated to the churches and they successfully advocated the condemnation of all political killings and the rejection, at least in the case of Peru, of the idea of taking up arms as a way of achieving societal change.[2]

However, one issue of debate was not resolved quite so rapidly: the approach to the 'state'. Was the state 'the enemy' or was it an ally? Debate ensued as to whether or not human rights groups should work with the state to address the human rights crisis. There was also the question of whether or not equal resources should be put into documenting and denouncing abuses by the state and by insurgent groups. Traditionally, human rights groups focus on state-sponsored abuses given the obligations of governments under international human rights law. This debate came to the fore as the decade drew to a close and the Shining Path surpassed the state security forces in responsibility for the number of killings committed annually.

Ultimately, each group within the Coordinadora adopted its own approach in dealing with the state. Some focused on denunciation and protest while others sought constructive engagement. But the overall philosophy of most was that one must confront, but also seek to influence, combining the two strategies.

The internal debate on relations with the state reflected, in part, the tremendous diversity of groups within the network. The initial Coordinadora membership was very broad, encompassing peasant, union and other grass-roots groups as well as more traditional human rights groups. The bulk of the members came from the provinces, particularly small church-based groups or Codehs. Over time, some of these groups that were based in provincial capitals became large institutions. However, in general, the Lima-based groups — such as the Episcopal Commission for Social Action (Comisión Episcopal de

Acción Social, CEAS), the Institute for Legal Defence (Instituto de Defensa Legal, IDL), the Asociación Pro-Derechos Humanos, Aprodeh) and Human Rights Commission (Comisíon de Derechos Humanos, Comisedh) — were the largest and best-connected politically. Other differences affected the movement as well: some were urban based and others rural and they were spread out between the coast, the highlands and the jungle regions. Given these vast cultural differences and the physical distance between Lima and many other parts of the country, it is a testament to the political will of those involved in the Coordinadora that a functioning coalition was maintained (Youngers and Peacock, 2002; Youngers, 2003). Yet it was this very diversity that gave the movement its strength: the Coordinadora spoke on behalf of members that represented the tremendous diversity in Peru. It connected human rights work at the local, regional and national and, ultimately, international level. Today, other social movements, facilitated by computer technology, also serve that function; however, the Coordinadora was the pioneer.

The García Years

One of the first acts undertaken by the newly formed Coordinadora Nacional de Derechos Humanos was an initiative to insert human rights issues into the 1985 presidential and congressional electoral debate. On 6 April 1985 the Coordinadora published an open letter to all of the presidential candidates, calling on each one to make a statement prior to the voting on proposed policies to deal with the complex problems of political violence and human rights.[3] While few of the candidates complied with the Coordinadora's request for specific policy proposals, upon taking office, Alan García of the APRA party promised to prosecute those responsible for human rights violations, called on the judiciary to review cases of those in jail on terrorism charges and reorganised the police force.

He also created a pluralistic Peace Commission to seek a democratic solution to the problem of political violence. Installed in September 1985, the first set of commissioners was viewed as plural and relatively independent.[4] What it lacked in terms of economic resources was offset by the political will of its members. Although the Coordinadora had been in existence less than a year, it was designated an official adviser to the Peace Commission. Within a few months, the Commission presented a series of legislative and other proposals that were widely endorsed by the human rights community.

Yet these proposals went unheeded. Frustrated with President García's lack of sustained attention and unwillingness to move forward on even part of its recommendations, four of the six Commission members had resigned by the beginning of 1986. In February, García reconstituted a second Peace Commission, this time with only three members, all perceived as loyal to the APRA party. By this point, the Commission was looked upon sceptically by most outside APRA and had little impact on public opinion. Following the June 1986 prison massacre —— in which nearly 300 prisoners and guards were killed after a bloody assault by security forces to put down a riot — its members again resigned and that marked its end (Ames, 1988). The Commission was never able to realise the lofty goals for which it was created. Nevertheless, the first Peace Commission provided the Peruvian human rights community with its first significant experience of a state-sponsored initiative, which in turn provided access to a range of government institutions.

Coordinadora member organisations worked with the few members of the Peruvian Congress willing and interested to work on behalf of human rights issues. The human rights commissions within the Congress continued to play a key role in documenting atrocities and forcing public debate on particular incidents and the problem of political violence more broadly. While final reports were often thwarted from being approved by APRA members of Congress, the minority reports still served an important purpose (Ames, 1988; Piqueras, 1989 and Bernales, no date). In addition, Congressman Javier Diez Canseco and others undertook investigations of numerous massacres and other individual atrocities. Human rights groups often assisted in gathering evidence and documentation in these investigations and in disseminating the final results.

In addition, human rights advocates continued to interact with state officials in order to seek redress in individual cases, communicating with national and local authorities and with judges hearing cases of civilians charged with terrorism. In emergency zones, a disappearance often necessitated a visit to the regional or local military commander — if nothing else to put them on warning that the case had reached the human rights community. Given the political situation, the impact of these initiatives was limited; however, they were important for at least two reasons. First, some cases were resolved. People who were disappeared did on occasions reappear; some detainees reported that they were tortured less after human rights groups began inquiring about them; and some of those who were unjustly charged were ultimately released from jail. Some violations were likely prevented due to the vigilance of human rights activists. Also of importance, family members of victims of violence received support from the human rights community that they were denied elsewhere. Finally, over time the Coordinadora and its member organisations gained a certain public profile through the public denunciations and repeated contact with government officials. While they faced a constant uphill battle in winning over public opinion, human rights activists were slowly becoming political players.

At the same time, space for human rights work continued to be very restricted and closed altogether in the areas afflicted with the highest levels of violence. By the end of the decade, there were only two significant victims' organisations, both of which encountered significant obstacles to their work. Provincial groups, particularly the organisations of *familiares*, often complained of being marginalised from activities in the capital, yet had to rely more and more on Lima-based organisations for assistance. Meanwhile, the national organisations continued to grow, become institutionalised and to become more sophisticated in developing effective advocacy strategies. These differences sometimes strained relations between Coordinadora members.

The Coordinadora was evolving institutionally as well. Initially, its diverse membership afforded it a broad base of grass-roots support; however, that same diversity made consensus-building more difficult. In addition, many grass-roots groups were not able to commit time or resources and ultimately dropped out. By the late 1980s the Coordinadora membership consisted almost exclusively of organisations with a straight-forward human rights mandate, although it maintained a combination of faith-based and secular NGOs, totalling around 50 members (Youngers, 2003; Youngers and Peacock, 2002). At the same time, many groups felt that the network needed a formal coordinating office in order to insure follow-through on agreed activities and strategies. In 1987 a Secretariat was established and an executive secretary chosen. Coordinadora activities increased substantially as a result, and over time the executive secretary became a visible and prominent spokesperson, greatly enhancing the human rights movement's visibility and impact. Of particular significance, because the Coordinadora represented groups across the country, this gave a voice to groups that otherwise would not have had access to Lima's highly centralised political structures and communications media.

The Early Fujimori Years

Both political violence and the economic situation continued to deteriorate over García's term in office. Peruvians appeared increasingly sceptical of the traditional political parties' ability to govern the country. In the 1990 presidential elections, independent candidate Alberto Fujimori exploited this sentiment and won handily in the second round of voting.

In his first inaugural speech to the nation, Fujimori emphatically stated: 'The unrestricted respect and promotion of human rights will be a firm line of action by my government.'[5] Yet that promise was quickly forgotten; no new initiatives were put into place and within months some of his cabinet members were showing themselves openly hostile to the human rights community. In a November 1990 statement, Peru's then minister of justice, Augusto Antonioli, talked of the need to 'avoid the obstruction of police and military actions by human rights organisations in zones affected by subversion'. In an October 1990 meeting with the minister of defence, General Jorge Torres Aciego, members of a World Council of Churches delegation were accused of being 'international missiles of Sendero Luminoso' (Washington Office on Latin America, 1991, p. 5).[6] During Fujimori's first year in office 224 Peruvians were disappeared at the hands of state agents, extrajudicial executions began to rise and the areas of the country declared to be in a state of emergency were expanded to include 56 per cent of the population (Washington Office on Latin America, 1991, p. 6.). The human rights crisis continued unabated (Amnesty International, 1992).

Tension between the human rights community and the government was steadily increasing and bubbled over in mid-1991. In a speech before the commanding officers of the armed forces, Fujimori referred to human rights groups as 'useful fools' of terrorist groups, 'that will be unmasked'. Such statements were extremely dangerous in the context of the military's counterinsurgency campaign, where anyone seen as aiding the subversives was considered a legitimate target. Simultaneously, the Shining Path stepped up its anti-human rights rhetoric.

In the Peruvian Congress, there was increasing dialogue across the political spectrum on how to develop a more comprehensive plan to end the internal conflict. By this time, the Coordinadora's proposal for ending the conflict was an integrated approach that encompassed three major elements. First, while accepting the state's role in combating armed groups operating outside the law, the Coordinadora emphasised that military action should be under the direct control of civilian authorities and carried out within the context of the constitutional order, the rule of law and respect for human rights. Second, the human rights community emphasised the need to alleviate the underlying conditions of poverty and discrimination which fed the conflict. Finally, the Coordinadora underscored the need for a strategy that was developed with and had the support of the population and that sought to work with popular organisations, treating them as allies and not as enemies.

This very approach, however, itself indicated that for all practical purposes the debate over the 'state' had been resolved. According to Carlos Iván Degregori, the Shining Path dramatically changed the perception of the 'bad state' that characterised previous progressive thinking.[7] The question as to whether or not the state was an enemy or ally clearly remained murky — in fact, the relationship between the state and the human rights community was increasingly adversarial as the Fujimori government's authoritarian tendencies became increasingly evident. However, the idea that state institutions should play a fundamental role in addressing the problem of political violence had become widely accepted within the human rights movement. This was true at the popular level as well. As more and more grass-roots leaders were killed, many activists saw the need to build bridges with the state in order to protect themselves and to prevent a Shining Path victory. Of particular significance in Lima was Sendero's brutal killing of María Elena Moyano, a very popular local leader in the Villa El Salvador neighbourhood, which provoked massive indignation against the insurgents (Burt, 1998).

The demise of the left as a political force also contributed to this tendency. In addition to ensuring that Peruvian human rights groups operated independently of any political party, this phenomenon also allowed the continued development of a human rights discourse neutral from left-wing political discourse. Moreover, this situation allowed many social sectors, including the human rights community, to move beyond the previous left-wing debates to embrace fully the concept of deliberative democracy. As one Peruvian analyst notes, 'The end of the left-wing project allowed for the entrance into the democratic game ... the Coordinadora bought directly into the idea of fighting for democratic values.'[8]

Finally, the authoritarianism found on both sides of the conflict underscored the need to promote democratic alternatives. The circumstances of extreme political violence in Peru and the very possibility of the rigidly centralised and dictatorial government that would be established after a Shining Path victory — at the time perceived as a real possibility — led to a growing acceptance of the democratic rules of the game. As a result, the Coordinadora's discourse was increasingly oriented towards defending democratic principles, as well as human rights.

The Official Dialogue

During his first 18 months in office, President Fujimori issued numerous decrees that strengthened the hand of the military and further restricted human rights guarantees (Amnesty International, 1992; Coordinadora Nacional de Derechos Humanos, January 1993). Then, in what became widely known as the *autogolpe*, or presidential coup, on 5 April 1992 President Fujimori dissolved Congress, suspended the constitution and temporarily closed the judiciary. Political avenues for compromise and consensus building were closed as a period of authoritarian rule began to take shape (Bowen, 2000).

While Fujimori's hard-line tactics remained popular at home, they were not well received by the international community. Action on the part of the Organization of American States (OAS) forced Fujimori to concede elections for a new congress and the drafting of a new constitution. Increasingly sceptical of the Fujimori administration, international actors looked towards the Peruvian human rights groups as a crucial source of information and analysis. The election of President Bill Clinton, who assumed office in January 1993, cemented the Coordinadora's position with US policymakers. Clinton brought individuals sympathetic to the Peruvian human rights community into key positions related to Latin America. The first high-level Clinton administration delegation to visit Peru in January 1994 met first with the Coordinadora and only afterwards went on to meet Peruvian government officials (Youngers, 1994, p. 45). While a purely symbolic gesture, it provided powerful media images to bolster the Coordinadora's prestige and sent a strong message to the Peruvian government that it could not so readily dismiss the concerns of the human rights community.

The Clinton administration was in a particularly good position to influence the Peruvian government directly, as Peru was at a crucial point in its 'reinsertion' into the international financial community. (Former president García had defaulted on the country's international debt payments and the new government was seeking to regain the support and confidence of international creditors.) Two steps needed to be taken to complete the reinsertion process: a Support Group meeting of Peru's major donors and the provision of a short-term, $2.1 billion bridge loan to be provided jointly by the United States and Japan.

The Clinton administration immediately linked these two steps to four concrete actions by the Fujimori government: guaranteeing the International Committee of the Red Cross access to detention centres, accepting advisory services from the UN Human Rights Commission and an on-site visit by the OAS's Inter-American Commission of Human Rights, initiating a formal dialogue with the Coordinadora and publicly recognising the importance of the work of national and international human rights groups. Having no other viable choice, the Fujimori government quickly indicated its willingness to comply with Washington's demands and both the Support Group meeting and the bridge loan went forward.

The official dialogue became the Coordinadora's only point of access to high-level Peruvian government officials. The executive branch's tight control over its ministries and its increasing control over the judiciary made it ever harder to maintain contact with and find allies in the government bureaucracy. Likewise, as the military was brought more directly under the control of de facto national security adviser, Vladimiro Montesinos, local commanders lost the freedom to operate more independently. According to one internal evaluation, the most difficult years for promoting human rights were right after the *autogolpe*, from 1992 to 1994 (Heinz and Pedraglio, 1997, p. 33).

Not surprisingly, the Peruvian government showed an unwillingness to enter into good-faith discussions. In fact, the minister of justice, the president's representative to the talks,[9] began the first meeting in April 1993 by reiterating that Peruvian officials were sitting at the table with Coordinadora representatives only at the insistence of Washington. The government did initially accept an agenda laid out by the Coordinadora, which included seven specific points, including anti-terrorist legislation, the situation of the displaced, assistance to victims of terrorism, prison conditions, and investigations and sanctions of those responsible for human rights violations. Meetings were initially to take place on a monthly basis, though that only happened the first two months. Then in June 1993, Minister Vega made statements to the press — possibly intending to provoke the Coordinadora into withdrawing from the dialogue — in which he said that human rights reports, including those of the Coordinadora, 'lack objectivity because their sources are not reliable'.[10] On 2 September, Coordinadora representatives sent a letter pointing out that in five months, they had had only two meetings, neither of which led to any action. They reiterated their desire to continue discussions, but only if they resulted in concrete improvements to the human rights situation; otherwise, they would be forced to withdraw publicly from the dialogue.

The minister convened another meeting at the end of September 1993 and then proposed that he be replaced by a personal representative of President Fujimori. Although this was widely interpreted as a way to downgrade the level of the dialogue, the Coordinadora member organisations decided to accept the proposal. After the government named the widely-respected priest, Hubert Lanssiers, as the president's representative to the talks, the Coordinadora representatives adeptly shifted their strategy. They ceased efforts to promote judicial and other reforms and instead focused on attempting to resolve concrete cases of unjust imprisonments on terrorism charges, leading to the release of six detainees. These cases had great symbolic importance, as being the first official recognition of the problem. The Coordinadora representatives continued to participate in the dialogue for several more months, but as authoritarian actions by the government and military increased, they felt that they could no longer endorse the dialogue and withdrew.[11]

Although the dialogue failed to achieve its intended objectives, the Coordinadora emerged from it as the key interlocutor on human rights issues, both at home and abroad. Though some on the political left criticised the human rights groups for sitting down at the same table with the representatives of an authoritarian regime, the very fact that they were at the table changed the opinion of some who had seen the Coordinadora as too radical, allowing member organisations to make inroads with more moderate political sectors. This strengthened their position vis-à-vis the human rights debate and enhanced their ability to utilise communications media to their advantage. Finally, the strong and visible backing of Washington also provided local activists with some protection, albeit limited, from intimidation and threats by the Peruvian government.

The Human Rights Ombudsman's Office

In October 1993 a referendum was held in which a new constitution was officially adopted by a narrow margin. The official vote was widely questioned, however, and well-founded allegations of fraud further weakened public support.[12] The new constitution allowed for presidential re-election to a second term in office and contained other measures that would later be used to consolidate Fujimori's power even further; however, some positive changes were incorporated. Of particular importance for the human rights community, the constitution mandated the creation of a Human Rights Ombudsman's Office (Defensoría del Pueblo), an autonomous state organ tasked with promoting protection of basic human rights and monitoring the government and its provision of basic services.[13] When finally created, the Office of the Human Rights Ombudsman became a powerful ally of Peru's human rights community and ultimately one of Peru's most respected and effective institutions (Youngers, 2000, pp. 26–7).

The inclusion of the Ombudsman's Office in the new constitution was the result of a concerted lobbying campaign by Peruvian human rights groups, with the support of grass-roots organisations and many local church groups. The international environment was conducive to their effort, as such offices were being created in other Latin American countries (Unger, 2004; Domingo and Sieder, 2001). However, implementing legislation languished for years. Peruvian human rights groups sought the support of international actors, including the World Bank and Inter-American Development Bank, both of which supported the initiative and pressured the Fujimori government to move forward.[14] In 1996, the Congress finally voted to name the Human Rights Ombudsman, Dr Jorge Santistevan de Noriega, a former high-ranking UN official, and the office was opened in September 1996.

The Fujimori bloc in Congress sought to limit the powers of the new office. The implementing legislation prohibits the staff from entering military installations, in effect curbing its control over the military. Empowered with the ability to present draft legislation to the Congress, in practice its proposals were routinely ignored by the Fujimori-controlled Congress. That combined with the gutting of the Constitutional Tribunal greatly limited the ability of the Human Rights Ombudman's Office to move beyond denouncing illegalities or human rights violations and to advocate either the derogation or adoption of human rights-related legislation.

Nonetheless, it has had significant impact in various realms. First, it was the only state institution over which the Fujimori government was unable to exert significant control. Santistevan proved extremely adept at moving initiatives forward, despite the difficult operating environment; his effective leadership and political savvy was key. He also benefited from foreign sources of funding for the office (including European governments and USAID), hence mitigating the impact of the government's failure to provide it with sufficient resources. As the office had no real authority over the executive branch — just a capacity to bully — Fujimori may not have been willing to risk the political fall-out (particularly internationally) that actions taken to rein in the office would have provoked. As a result, the Ombudsman's office quickly gained a reputation for being independent and reliable among much of the population, and the Ombudsman and his staff became an important and respected voice for democracy, human rights and justice.

Second, the main office in Lima along with the provincial offices have contributed greatly to generating public awareness of the importance of filing formal complaints and how to go about it. Since its creation, people have become more willing to come forward and make their demands heard. The publication of the Human Rights Ombudsman's major report on the disappeared in Peru contributed greatly to the cause of the *familiares* and in many ways prepared them for the work that lay ahead in presenting cases and testimony to the

Truth Commission (Defensoría del Pueblo, 2000). Third, its staff is often able to resolve complaints by working with various government agencies. This is particularly true in dealing with issues such as inaccurate water or electricity bills, but has also proven to be the case regarding complaints of human rights violations lodged against personnel in some military and police installations.

In other words, the Human Rights Ombudsman's office has significant moral stature in the country and has shown that human rights and other civil society complaints can be resolved. This combination of moral voice and efficacy greatly boosted the legitimacy of the human rights cause in Peru, thereby strengthening the work of the existing human rights community.

At times, human rights activists have said that the Ombudsman's office did not go far enough on certain issues and that it was too timid in confronting the Fujimori regime. In some areas of the provinces, relations with the local human rights community got off to a rocky start as roles and relationships were defined and the presence of the new office generated a series of unexpected demands on local human rights workers. Finally, the Ombudsman's office also brought into its ranks many key staff people from Coordinadora member organisations and may have siphoned off some funding as well. Overall, however, the benefits have far outweighed the costs, and the relations between the Ombudsman's office, its staff and the human rights community remain strong.

Jorge Santistevan, the Ombudsman until he launched a failed presidential bid in late 1999, saw his role as being a 'bridge between the human rights movement and the state'.[15] Santistevan is also quick to point out that human rights organisations proposed many of the themes that he focused on during his tenure. 'The best example,' he says, 'is the case of the innocent Peruvians in jail on terrorism charges,' as described in greater detail below. Another example is the issue of forced recruitment into military service. Church-based groups and other Coordinadora member organisations were of particular importance in raising the issue and stimulating action by the Human Rights Ombudsman's office, which led to a law to end mandatory military service and hence forced recruitment that went into effect in September 1999.[16] There are times when the Coordinadora successfully acts on its own — for example, in the case of the legislation making torture a crime. However, when the Human Rights

Ombudsman's office is also involved in a campaign or legislative initiative, it brings 'value added', says Santistevan.[17]

Following Santistevan's resignation, the Peruvian Congress failed to agree on his successor, a situation primarily resulting from the overall poor performance of the Congress rather than any political motivation. His former deputy, Walter Albán Peralta, continued as acting Human Rights Ombudsman until 2005. This has weakened the office politically, but has allowed for continuity in its functioning, and it continued to grow. There are now 28 offices around the country and five divisions: state administration, constitutional matters, human rights and persons with disabilities, women's rights and public services. There are also two additional programmes, one on prisons and one on native communities. In short, the Ombudsman's office has considerable reach and impact and as a result, public opinion polls consistently give it high marks for its performance (Unger, 2004, p. 179.). In addition to its impact on promoting human rights described above, these efforts have led many Peruvians to embrace the notion of citizens' rights, thereby furthering efforts to promote citizenship, and ultimately democratisation.

'In the Name of the Innocent'

Perhaps one of the best examples of effective collaboration between the human rights community and the Human Rights Ombudsman's office is the campaign to secure the release of innocent Peruvians in jail on terrorism charges. After the *autogolpe,* Fujimori decreed draconian anti-terrorist laws that violated fundamental due process guarantees. Military courts were established to try those accused of 'treason' and certain forms of terrorism, and 'faceless' civilian courts, where the identity of the judges was not known, were set up to try terrorism cases. Legal safeguards for defendants were essentially eliminated; one was presumed guilty until proved innocent. Sentences were notably harsh (Coordinadora, 1993; De la Jara, 2001; Youngers, 1994). The number of people detained on terrorism and treason cases skyrocketed. By the end of the decade, an estimated 22,000 Peruvians had been unjustly detained or imprisoned as a result of the anti-terrorist legislation.[18]

In response, the Coordinadora launched a campaign, 'In the Name of the Innocent' to secure the release of innocent Peruvians in jail on

terrorism charges. A multi-year effort, it began to take shape shortly
after the anti-terrorist legislation was adopted in mid-1992 (De la Jara,
2001; Youngers, 2003). The campaign focused on promoting sympathetic press coverage and gaining the support of prominent Peruvians
and key sectors of Peruvian society.[19] By the mid-1990s, public sympa-
thy was clearly on the side of the innocent, upon assuming office the
Human Rights Ombudsman had embraced the issue and even President
Fujimori himself began to recognise publicly that some mistakes were
made, hinting that he might be open to reviewing some cases. The question became what sort of review process was politically feasible.

With the Human Rights Ombudsman's Office working to craft an
acceptable approach, the government finally said that it would go forward
with an Ad Hoc Commission, composed of three members[20] charged
with reviewing individual cases and making recommendations to the president for granting a pardon in any case where a conviction was based on
fabricated, coerced or insufficient evidence. All three members of the
Commission had to agree to recommend a pardon and whether one was
granted was ultimately left to the discretion of the president.

This was far from the outcome that the Coordinadora had lobbied for.
The use of presidential pardons was ripe for Fujimori's manipulation and,
most importantly, the process continued to treat those involved as guilty.
Those who were pardoned would still have a criminal record and at the
time the government made it clear that it would not agree to reparations.
However, as this was the most that could be hoped for under the circum-
stances, the human rights community threw its weight behind the Ad Hoc
Commission, which was formally established in August 1996.

Once in operation, the lawyers working for the Ad Hoc Commission
appeared to err on the side of caution, reviewing in exhaustive detail cases
that had already been documented by human rights groups. They argued
that this was necessary if the cases were going to pass the litmus test of
unanimity, particularly given the hostile stance of the Justice Ministry. This
slowed down the process considerably, however, and by the time the
Commission's mandate expired permanently at the end of 1999, there
were still an estimated several hundred cases pending. Nonetheless,
Fujimori pardoned over 500 individuals, and hundreds more were declared
innocent via the courts, as the creation of the Ad Hoc Commission created a more propitious environment for judges to acquit individuals

accused of terrorism.[21] In 1998, the Congress finally passed a law eliminating the criminal records of those pardoned.

When the Commission's mandate expired, the Human Rights
Commission of the Ministry of Justice took over the task of reviewing
the remaining cases. For all practical purposes, the process was put on
hold until the transition government of Valentín Paniagua, when a new
Pardon Commission was created within the ministry to complete the
process of releasing the innocent who remained in jail. The Justice
Ministry also began developing a set of proposed reforms to the anti-
terrorist legislation in order to bring it in line with due process standards. The Coordinadora's campaign, 'In the Name of the Innocent',
had become one of its most successful endeavours.

Confronting Authoritarianism

The hybrid nature of the Fujimori regime created an unusual situation
whereby human rights and other groups could have absolutely no impact
in some areas, while for the first time achieving important gains in others.
The human rights community was increasingly sophisticated at effectively
putting forward concrete alternatives. Fujimori's desire for a popular mandate meant that at times his government bowed to popular opinion, as was
the case with the campaign just described. On the other hand, the government was not willing to bend with regards to efforts to alter the fundamental character of the regime, its actions to perpetuate itself in office, or its
primary sources of power, the military and intelligence services.

Slowly, the work of the Peruvian human rights community was
undergoing an important transformation. In some other Latin
American countries, human rights movements largely fell into crisis
with the end of violence and hence their original *raison d'être*. In the case
of Peru, however, there was no political transition marking the end of
the period of intense political violence, which had largely subsided by
the mid-1990s, and its legacies remained. In addition, a new crisis — the
crisis of democracy — quickly became the focus of attention and activity. In stark contrast to the situation faced by colleagues in other Latin
American countries, the authoritarian nature of the regime increased
proportionally to the decline in the levels of violence.

In 1997 the Coordinadora membership officially adopted a pro-
democracy platform. The increasingly authoritarian nature of the

Fujiimori regime, the steady dismantling of civilian institutions and its manipulation of the electoral process all made promoting human rights more difficult than ever. It was clear that in order to institutionalise human rights guarantees, the country had to return to a more democratic path. Nowhere was this clearer than in the judiciary, where Montesinos ensured impunity for his allies and manipulated cases to punish or co-opt those opposing the Fujimori administration, and in the growing power of the National Intelligence Service (SIN), which routinely threatened civil liberties. 'You had to be blind', noted Carlos Basombrío, 'not to see that the issue of democracy had become the fundamental barrier to any effort to advance human rights in the country.'[22]

Moving in this direction implied working with many other sectors of civil society, including other social movements, student organisations, influential groups such as the Lima bar association and the political opposition (and hence the more traditional right-wing political parties). In the 2000 elections, Coordinadora member organisations played a role in helping to document and denounce the electoral shenanigans taking place and, most importantly, in mobilising civil society and shaping public opinion. While Transparencia, an independent electoral watchdog, was the primary civil society organisation reporting on the electoral process and mobilising election observers, Coordinadora member organisations in the provinces became an important source of election monitors at the local level. After the elections, the Coordinadora was a key actor in denouncing the fraud and mobilising the OAS, helping to pave the way for the fall of the authoritarian Fujimori regime.

The Paniagua Government and the Commission for Truth and Reconciliation

The power structure so carefully assembled by Fujimori and Montesinos crumbled quickly. On 16 September 2000, Fujimori announced that new elections would be held, that he would not run, and that the SIN would be dismantled. In mid-November, Fujimori fled into exile, attempting to resign via fax. Congress refused to accept the resignation and on 21 November 2000 declared the presidency vacant due to Fujimori's 'moral incapacity' as allowed by the 1993 Constitution. Valentín Paniagua, the next in the line of succession, was sworn in as President of Peru.

His transitional government was charged with carrying out free and fair elections in order to pass the torch to a democratically elected president in July 2001. President Paniagua pulled together an impressive cabinet, which began laying the groundwork for an ambitious reform agenda affecting almost .all aspects of government and civil-military relations. For the first time, the Peruvian human rights community encountered a government that shared much of its agenda. Perhaps the most visible sign of the dramatic change in the political environment was the number of prominent human rights activists who became part of the new government. Two were included in the cabinet. Susana Villarán, former executive secretary of the Coordinadora and later on the staff of the Institute for Legal Defence, was named Minister for Women. Diego García-Sayán, who founded and directed the Andean Commission of Jurists, became minister of justice.

One of Paniagua's last acts before passing the presidential sash to Alejandro Toledo — who won the 2001 elections — was to create a truth commission. Its creation was largely the result of a concerted advocacy strategy designed and led by the Coordinadora.[23] By Fujimori's fall, the Coordinadora member organisation's systematic work over nearly two decades to promote justice and confront entrenched impunity had borne fruit and the idea of a truth commission was on the political agenda. In addition, the stature gained by the Coordinadora by the end of the decade meant that it had both access to and influence in the media. Likewise, its proven ability to convene significant sectors, representing diverse political viewpoints, allowed it to bring together an important group of civil society actors and leaders in support of a truth commission. Finally, the political mood was propitious: the extent of corruption within the Fujimori government that was revealed after its fall led to vocal demands for justice and accountability.

The truth commission's mandate was to investigate the period of political violence in Peru, as well as specific human rights violations committed by both state agents and insurgent forces, determining, when possible, responsibility for such acts. It was also tasked with making recommendations for reparations and institutional reforms.[24] The implementing decree creating it followed most of the guidelines recommended by human rights groups and the Human Right's Ombudsman's office. Upon taking office in July 2001, President Toledo pledged to abide by the Commission's recommendations. He renamed it the Commission for Truth and Reconciliation and added five new members, including Sofia Macher, who at the time was just finishing her term as executive secretary of the Coordinadora. The twelve commissioners were presided over by Solomón Lerner Febres, rector of the Catholic University.

The Truth and Reconciliation Commission brought together a large staff, opened offices around the country, began consolidating the information already available and initiating its own investigations. One advantage that Peru's commission enjoyed was the existence of a cadre of well-trained and experienced human rights lawyers and advocates, who provided much of the staff. It also benefited from the existence of sound political analysis of the period of political violence by Peruvian academics and intellectuals, significant and solid information on human rights abuses compiled by Peru's human rights community and advances already made by the Human Rights Ombudsman's office. Perhaps far more than was the case in other countries, Peru's truth commission already had a solid base of information and analysis on which to build.

Peruvian human rights groups opened up their files to the commission and collaborated regularly with its staff. Of particular importance was the role of human rights groups in supporting the commission's efforts in the countryside. Local groups helped Truth and Reconciliation Commission staff gain access to local communities, assisted in interviewing community members and victims of violence and played a very important role in disseminating the Commission's conclusions and recommendations. This in turn helped empower some local human rights groups. On the other hand, the human rights community as a whole was also affected negatively, as staff and international funds were redirected towards the Commission. Moreover, the Truth and Reconciliation Commission occupied much of the space in the public debate and media formerly enjoyed by the Coordinadora and its member organisations.

The process initiated by Peru's Truth and Reconciliation Commission differs from that in other Latin American countries in two important ways. First, the Peruvian commission adopted the South African model of carrying out public hearings around the country, where victims and particular groups victimised by the violence were provided a platform on which to testify. These proved to be both cathartic for some victims and also an important public education tool; media coverage of these hearings, particularly at the local level, proved to be significant in educating the public about Peru's violent past and the victims' plight. It was also the first step in opening a path towards reconciliation between victims and society at large.

Second, Peru's commission took a novel approach to the issue of justice. In previous cases, debate centred on balancing truth, justice and reconciliation — in other words, some sort of amnesty was viewed as necessary both to obtain the information necessary to carry out effective, but limited, prosecutions and in order to promote reconciliation more broadly. Although Argentina was the first country in Latin America to put military generals on trial, governments in countries like Chile and Guatemala argued that prosecutions would jeopardise fragile democratic transitions.[25] In contrast, the Peruvian commission was the only one in Latin America to date to have a department charged with preparing cases for presentation to the justice sector for prosecution. No amnesty law was passed, though Peruvian law allows for reduced sentences for accused who collaborate with investigations. Recognising its limitations, the Commission for Truth and Reconciliation adopted a strategy of focusing on 'emblematic' or representative cases where sufficient evidence existed to allow for trials to go forward. Over 40 cases, implicating more than 150 military and police officials, were presented to the Public Ministry.

The Peruvian Truth and Reconciliation Commission presented a nine-volume report that provides an official history of the period of political violence in Peru. It encompasses broad political analysis, detailed description of human rights abuses committed by both sides in the conflict and documentation of specific cases. The exhaustive list of recommendations — from individual reparations to justice sector and military reform — presents a blueprint for meaningful change in Peru. A lengthy book summarising the report was produced for broader distribution (Comisión de la Verdad y Reconciliación, 2004) and various popular education-style pamphlets were disseminated. A curriculum guide on the Commission's conclusions and recommendations is being implemented by the Ministry of Education. Finally, a photo exhibition (and a book of the photos) — another novel development now being looked at by newly-formed truth commissions in other parts of the world — was created for both national and international viewing.

The Legacy of the Truth Commission

While it is far too soon to evaluate fully the impact of the Commission's work, the track record to date has been mixed at best and disappointing at worst. Both the Commission and those trying to implement its recommendations face considerable political obstacles. Peru's democratic transition has moved at a snail's pace, with both poor governance and continued bickering between the leading political groups hampering reform efforts. Moreover, important political and economic elites opposed the Commission from the start. They have used their influence with the media to generate negative coverage of the Commission, particularly at the time of the release of its final report in August 2003. Key members of Congress opposed to the Commission's work blocked legislation needed to carry out the commission's recommendations.

Also of significance, the terms of the debate in Peru about the insurgents and terrorism have not changed significantly. In contrast to Central American countries, no peace accord was signed and no process of reconciliation was taking place between government and insurgent forces when the Commission was formed. While political violence has largely subsided, small pockets of insurgent activity continue and alleged members of the Shining Path continue to be arrested.[26] Various political forces, including the remnants of the Fujimori regime, keep the alleged threat of terrorism alive in the national debate. The Toledo administration has failed to change the terms of that debate and tries to present an image of being tough on terrorism. As a result, the fear of terrorism continues to be very real for much of the population, a situation exacerbated by the post-September 11 environment.[27] Opponents of the Truth and Reconciliation Commission criticise it as naïve or misguided in the face of this alleged terrorist threat.

Implementation of the Commission's recommendations depends largely on the three branches of government, all of which have shown serious deficiencies in carrying out their respective mandates. As noted, the opposition of key political sectors has stymied legislative action. The judiciary continues to operate with extreme inefficiency and often ineptitude. While the number of cases working their way through the courts is unprecedented, the court proceedings are advancing at a snail's pace. Finally, the Toledo government faced one political crisis after another — many of its own making — which left it extremely weak.

Whether or not it had the political will to promote the Commission's roadmap for change, it proved incapable of doing so. Indeed, all of the reform processes initiated after Fujimori's fall — including justice sector, police, military and intelligence reform — are stagnating. Of particular concern, the victims of violence — the most marginalised sectors of Peruvian society to begin with — have yet to see significant concrete results of the Commission's work.

Nonetheless, some progress is being made. The Toledo government finally created a 'multi-sectoral commission' to study and advance the implementation of its recommendations. While its progress is slow, according to one human rights activist, it provides 'a space for dialogue … a space where one can go and push for advances'.[28] The health ministry has developed programmes to provide health-related services to victims of violence and is the only ministry at the time of writing to have incorporated a line-item for the programmes into its budget. The regional government in Huancavelica — one of the poorest areas of the country and one of those most affected by violence — has adopted laws to implement the Commission's recommendations and has allotted resources within its budget for reparations to victims, showing that progress is possible even with scarce resources. Regional governments such as Apurímac, Huánuco and San Martín are also moving forward, albeit at a slower pace. Finally, within the justice sector, a sub-system for human rights cases is now in place and judicial reform plans include human rights training for judges.[29]

Of particular significance is the fact that the Commission's work has stimulated the role of civil society at various levels. As noted, historically in Peru, the organisations of victims and their family members have been small and largely unheard. Today, there are more than 150 organisations of *familiares* and they are increasingly demanding that their voices be heard. As the Coordinadora's executive secretary points out, 'We are beginning to hear the direct voice of those affected by violence in the process of implementing the Commission's recommendations.'[30] Likewise, a network of human rights and other NGOs, church and grass-roots groups from around the country have formed 'Para Que No Se Repita',[31] a loose coalition engaged in creative and persistent efforts to keep the Commission's conclusions in the public debate and to promote compliance with its recommendations.

A Truth and Reconciliation Commission is the initiation of a process that can take decades, as is evident in Chile and Argentina today. It is the beginning of a process to ensure 'that the future is not continually hampered by an unresolved past' (Hayner, 2001, 254) and ends with a far more democratic and just society. Many governments will come and go as the process unfolds. It falls to civil society to keep the struggle for truth, justice and reconciliation alive. In that sense, Peru's human rights community has a formidable task ahead. An immediate challenge was to make the Commission's findings an issue of debate in the 2006 elections and commit candidates to carrying out its recommendations. Its longer term challenge, and that of Para Que No Se Repita and other civil society movements, is to build popular support and bring political pressure to bear on processes of democratic reform that will further consolidate human rights guarantees in Peru.

Notes

1   The Coordinadora Nacional de Derechos Humanos is referred to in this chapter as the Coordinadora; it is not intended to identify it as the only *coordinadora* in Peru, as there are many '*coodinadoras*' of different sectors of Peruvian civil society that function as coalitions.

2   Interview by author with José Burneo, 26 October 2001.

3   Open letter of the Coordinadora Nacional de Derechos Humanos, *La República*, 6 April 1985.

4   The commission was headed by Mario Suárez, a former Supreme Court member, and its members included Fernando Cabieses, a doctor and member of the APRA party; Diego García-Sayán of the Andean Commission of Jurists; Alberto Giesecki, a respected geologist; César Rodríguez Rabanal, a psychologist; and Monsignor Augusto Beuzeville, auxiliary bishop of Lima.

5   President Alberto Fujimori, *Mensaje a la Nación*, 28 July 1990.

6   The author participated in the World Council of Churches delegation.

7   Interview by author with Carlos Iván Degregori, 28 May 2001.

8   Interview by author with Aldo Panfichi, 14 November 2000.

9	In addition to Justice Minister Vega, representatives of the Ministries of the Interior and Foreign Relations were present, as well as the Public Ministry.

10	Quoted in *Exigimos Aclaración del Gobierno*, Press Release by the Coordinadora Nacional de Derechos Humanos, 7 June 1993.

11	*La Cantuta: Indignante Impunidad*, Press Release by the Coordinadora Nacional de Derechos Humanos, 8 February 1994.

12	In fact, one member of the National Electoral Board publicly called the vote tally fraudulent (McClintock, 1998, p. 8).

13	For additional information, see www.ombudsman.gob.pe.

14	Both international institutions were able to use funding for justice sector projects as leverage.

15	Interview by author with Jorge Santistevan, 13 April 2000.

16	Interview by author with Jorge Santistevan, 25 February 2001.

17	*Ibid.*

18	'22 mil inocentes estuvieron detenidos,' *La República*, 5 July 2002.

19	The campaign began with an exhaustive survey of prisons in order to document the number of innocents in jail. Other stages included gaining public support for the release of the innocent from prominent Peruvians, generating positive media coverage, seeking international support and finally, obtaining official recognition of the problem.

20	These included the minister of justice, the human rights ombudsman and a personal delegate of the president, Father Hubert Lanssiers.

21	Written communication from Juan Rosas, Instituto de Defensa Legal, 8 July 2002.

22	Interview by Jo Marie Burt with Carlos Basombrío, 8 August 2000.

23	In the spring of 2001 the Coordinadora pulled together a coalition of civil society organisations to develop an advocacy campaign that combined popular education activities at the local level, media outreach and securing the support of prominent Peruvians. Their efforts were greatly facilitated by the presence of Susana Villarán in the cabinet, as she had easy access to, and the confidence of, President Paniagua and helped sway him in support of the truth commission.

24	The government created the Truth Commission via Supreme Decree 065–2001 PCM, published in *El Diario* on 4 June 2001.

25	For a review of truth commissions around the world, see Hayner (2001).

26 Almost all political analysts in Peru agree that at the present time, the Shining Path does not present a significant threat to the Peruvian state. Its main actions have been limited to certain jungle areas where drug trafficking is prevalent and many of these are attributed to collusion between the remnants of the Shining Path and illicit logging and drug trafficking interests.

27 Since September 11, the US government has viewed Latin America through a counter-terrorist lens. US policy toward Peru is focused on eliminating the production of coca, the raw material for cocaine, and dangerously distorts the distinctions between coca farmers, drug traffickers and terrorists. Lumping all into one basket has led to a dramatic deterioration in relations between the Peruvian government and coca farmers, as well as increased protests and confrontations. Peru has sought to comply with US demands for reduced coca production through forced eradication efforts, but as viable economic alternatives are not in place, farmers continue to replant. Peru's anti-drug tsar claims that coca production in the country increased significantly in 2004.

28 Interview by author with Erika Bocanegra, 18 April 2005.

29 *Ibid.*.

30 Interview by author with Francisco Soberón, 27 October 2005.

31 This translates roughly as 'So we do not repeat the past'.

9

The Problem of Strengthening Business Institutions

Francisco Durand

Concern about the institutional development of the state in Latin America has centred on its modernisation as a precondition for growth. This was a notion that first gained force in the years after 1945, during the 'populist' phase when the state became a tool for development. Its interventionist powers were enhanced and its size grew. In the 1980s, as the populist state entered into crisis, the influence of neoliberalism took root. From the neoliberal point of view, state intervention is a problem that needs to be resolved; the functions of the state need to be reduced. As the state 'shrinks' the institutional power of the private sector is strengthened (Moore, 1997).

However, when neoliberal policies failed to generate the welfare they had promised to deliver — a situation made clear by the emergence of a number of social, political and economic asymmetries — the question of state reform was 'rediscovered'. During the 1990s a variety of international organisations and specialists suggested reforms, but these proposals conflicted with the resurgent power of the business sector. Today such proposals have lost importance and have largely been abandoned.

What interest does business have in institutional development? It appears to be the case that large businesses have grown accustomed to working with a corrupt and inefficient state, but one that defends their interests. Still, over the longer term, a new state — one that is efficient and transparent — is crucial to the consolidation of the neoliberal institutional matrix, although in the short term its weakness may be functional to business interests.

This chapter focuses on this dilemma, reflecting on the problem of unequal institutional development and the existence of such asymmetries from the viewpoint of economic elites. To this end it analyses the impact of neoliberalism on the structure of property; changes in how economic interests are represented and defended; the shifting relations between business and civil society (and its effects of contemporary Peruvian politics) and the ways in which the economically powerful perceive social problems.

It is argued that the issue needs to be seen from all these various viewpoints, including the efforts by a strengthened private sector to build bridges with civil society through 'corporate social responsibility'. This angle is important since these sorts of initiatives are insufficient to provide long-term stability to the new matrix. The example of extractive export industries — which are the most important in the Peruvian economy today and which operate in poor, remote areas where 'there is no state' — is particularly illustrative. These industries show how limited programmes of 'social responsibility' are in their effects, and how they can, indeed, generate conflict (political 'noise') rather than being a source of social peace and business legitimacy. The alternative is to strengthen the technical capacity of the state to deal effectively with social problems.

The central problem lies in the fact that corporate power has achieved hegemony, but without legitimacy. Because its role is questioned and because it does not foster institutional change, business has grown accustomed to living 'divorced' from politics, The business class enjoys a privileged access to the state, with more influence over it than any other social group, but yet gives little importance to the idea of reforming it. In practice, it is fearful of change because it would lead to more technically solid state management with enhanced regulatory capacities. Strengthening the technocracy and democratising the state would mean a relative loss of influence on the part of the private sector.

Positive institutional change within the state would therefore act as a counter-weight to market forces and would be a source of support to a new, more proactive civil society. Today, a variety of social organisations are fighting to defend the rights of clients, pensioners, savers and consumers, a new situation that has arisen out of the growing strength of the private sector. Also, unions are trying to defend the interests of wage earners, whose rights have been cut back and whose union strength has been eroded. A stronger state and a more active civil society, increasingly conscious of the asymmetries caused by neoliberalism, are not likely to benefit the private sector in the short run. At the same time, a better state, more attentive to social problems, gives greater stability to the new matrix. It provides a counterweight to the private sector, but without depriving it of its place as the gravitational centre of the market economy.

Economic Interests and Institutional Development

In view of the meagre medium-term results of neoliberal policy since the mid-1990s in terms of growth and employment, its proponents 'discovered' the institutional weaknesses of the state and called for reform. This concern was at the heart of the World Bank's publication 'Institutions Matter' (World Bank, 1998). Typically, Peru's neoliberal economists linked to the private sector — led by Roberto Abusada — only followed this line in part. Rather they argued the need to 'deepen' policies of privatisation and trade liberalisation, positing that state reform had not and would not go far (Abusada et al., 2000).

One of the reasons for this apparent lack of interest in reform is that in the new institutional matrix, large businesses and their technicians and experts in public policy, work in a way that is contrary to reform. Strengthened by the change of policy, these have made full use of the institutional weakness of the state and the political dispersion of civil society to develop a pattern of relationships that greatly helps them defend their economic interests. However, they do so in a way that introduces instability into the matrix because it prevents other actors from developing themselves institutionally.

Economic power groups and their political allies at once reject change and turn a blind eye towards growing signs of social discontent, referring to this in a deprecating way as 'political noise' emerging from civil society which frightens off investment. They demand order and authority, complaining about attempts to control or regulate their activities. They are worried about the state spending too much and warn of excessive taxation. They neither suggest nor demand institutional reform, but rather insist on deepening the policies of trade liberalisation and privatisation.

The new economic power structure has thus accommodated itself to the status quo; indeed it *is* the status quo. It depicts the current political problems and the new correlation of forces within the matrix as being a 'divorce' between the economy and politics, in which the former (represented by the private sector) carries on regardless of the latter in view of the huge power it has acquired.

Illustrative of this approach is the view taken by José Antonio Colomer, the managing director of the Banco Bilbao Vizcaya Argentaria (BBVA). Confronted by the outburst of social conflict, he publicly declared that happily 'the Peruvian economy has disconnected itself from political noise' (*La República*, 7 January 2005). At the same time, leaders of the private sector openly admit that 'businessmen have a more important role than politicians in running Peru' (*La República*, 28 November 2004). Since the economy continues to be managed and dominated by large corporate interests, 'politics' and the irritating 'noise' it produces become less important. This is because the state and politicians can be co-opted or otherwise prevailed upon to 'guarantee investment'. This sort of attitude persists even though it is clearly the case that large private businesses are operating in a climate of increasing political instability and growing social malaise.

It is for this reason that they view state reform, and even strengthening civil society, as problematic and risky. The lack of any appetite for reform therefore poses a dilemma: so long as it is does not take place, it becomes impossible to consolidate the institutional matrix. However, the neoliberal status quo does not bring stability or legitimacy, since the rest (of the matrix) remains weak owing to asymmetries both within the business class and the matrix itself. Such asymmetries consist of:

- widespread poverty;

- significant differences between different social groups in terms of access to and influence over the state; and

- the progressive displacement of national capital.

These problems end up generating dissent among those excluded. Such dissent transfers itself to the political sphere and even builds up within the private sector. Peruvian businessmen, especially those in small or medium-sized firms, have their own complaints. It is here that the increase in the power and influence of large corporations and the displacement of Peruvian capital comes in. Trends towards concentration and the de-nationalisation of the economy are particularly strong in Peru, as is also the case in Bolivia and Argentina. There are a number of reasons for this: (a) the non-democratic and intense way in which neoliberalism was imposed from 1990 onwards; (b) the historical weakness of the Peruvian business sector; and (c) the economic decline brought about by successive bouts of high inflation and deep recession between 1978 and 1990.

The asymmetries within the private sector are especially important because they generate even greater problems of legitimacy, placed as they are within the gravitational centre of the matrix. Because the nationally-owned component of capital is marginal instead of being protagonistic, such marginalisation can become an issue that expresses itself as a nationalistic reaction, adding its own voice to that of the majority of people and the middle class in questioning the power of large corporations.

Changes within the Economic Power Structure

The dramatic way in which the structure of economic power has changed is exemplified by the displacement of the state as well as by the strengthening of the corporate world, particularly multinational companies and the power groups from neighbouring countries. This strengthening of the private sector took place principally in the 1990s, thanks to the authoritarian Fujimori government which privileged and protected large-scale capital. The process continued afterwards under Alejandro Toledo, but in conditions in which Congress and civil society began to question things; in the latter case on the street.

Excessive Privatisation

With the exception of a handful of large public companies that remain as such, the state has no direct role in the productive economy. Privatisation involved a massive transfer of public sector assets to the private sector. The main purchasers were multinationals and power groups from other Latin American countries. Even though Peruvian companies could have bid for assets with little fear of competition from 1991 onwards — foreign companies only entered with force in 1994 — their longstanding weakness and the effects of successive crises meant that they were poorly placed to take advantage of the situation. They participated mainly in the purchase of medium-sized operations or as junior partners in foreign-dominated consortia.[1]

Foreign purchases gained impetus with the 1994 acquisition by Telefónica of the telecommunications industry, and the process continued until 2001. Between 1991 and 2000, a total of 150 companies were sold at a value of US$9.2 billion. Of the 35 largest privatised companies up until 2004, 22 were wholly or majority-owned by multinationals or power groups from other Latin American countries; only 13 were acquired by Latin American groups in conjunction with Peruvian investors. Only one Peruvian-owned company features among the 'top 15', whereas five of the last six are. The 'jewels in the crown' thus changed hands, the main beneficiary being the foreign private sector. This has led to increased economic concentration; only in exceptional cases is there a diffuse shareholding (Durand, 2004, p. 29).

Subsequently, the brakes were put on privatisation by the emergence of more assertive social movements, encouraged by the collapse of the Fujimori regime and the return of democracy. The most significant protest was the so-called 'arequipazo', an eruption of social movements in Peru's second city opposed to further privatisation there.

Foreign Investment

The strengthening of market forces also came about through foreign direct investment (FDI), both through the establishment of new companies and the purchase of existing ones. This is particularly the case in sectors like banking, pensions, mining, energy and some media outlets (Channel 4).

1   **Banking**. In the case of banking, eleven of the 13 largest banks in 1995 were Peruvian-owned, accounting for 85 per cent of total deposits. The Banco Continental, one of the largest, was jointly owned by the BBVA from Spain and the Brescia group, and another small bank, the Santander, was foreign-owned. In 2004, after strong foreign penetration and the sale of shareholdings, nine of the banks were controlled by foreign multinationals or power groups from neighbouring countries, while the Banco Continental remained in co-ownership with the Brescia group. Only three banks were Peruvian owned, led by the Banco de Crédito del Perú (BCP), which was part foreign owned. Peruvian banks' share in total deposits had fallen to 37 per cent (mainly

accounted for by the BCP with 35 per cent of the total). The Banco Continental had 27 per cent, while foreign banks accounted for the rest, the most important being the Wiese Sudameris (16 per cent) and Interbanc (nine per cent) (Durand, 2004, p. 22).

2   **Pension funds**. Pension funds (AFPs) were a new investment area opened up by the private sector, whose importance lay in its management of savings and in its investment in leading companies. Founded in 1995, there were seven AFPs of which three were controlled by multinationals and Latin American power groups (Nueva Vida, wholly foreign owned; Integra, where the Wiese group had 29.5 per cent of the shares, and others 19.5 per cent. Of the other five, Horizonte was nationally owned, as was Megafondo (with a 30 per cent Chilean shareholding), El Roble (13 per cent Venezuelan owned) and Unión (19.9 per cent Chilean owned). By 2004, the situation had changed. Several AFPs had merged, leaving only four. Of these, the Unión Vida was 99.97 per cent owned by the Banco Santander Hispano; the Horizonte was 100 per cent foreign-owned (mainly Spanish capital but some Chilean); the Integra was 29.5 per cent owned by the Grupo Wiese and the rest of its capital was foreign; and Profuturo was 42.5 per cent owned by Citibank, the rest Peruvian-owned (BCRP 2005). As a consequence, two AFPs were wholly foreign owned and the other two were majority foreign owned with a minority Peruvian shareholding.

The AFPs are important for other reasons. Through their investment portfolios, the AFPs ended up as one of the main motors of property concentration. In 2005, the four AFPs controlled 41.9 per cent of the shares in Credicorp (the holding company for the BCP); 31.7 per cent of Southern Peru (SPCC); 34.2 per cent of Edegel, 38.8 per cent of Edelnor, 18.7 per cent of Luz del Sur (all three electricity companies); 35 per cent of Alicorp (flagship of Grupo Romero); 12 per cent of Buenaventura (flagship of the Benavides de la Quintana group); 6.4 per cent of Graña y Montero (flagship of the Graña group); 39.9 per cent of Ferreyros (flagship of the Ferreyros group); six per cent of the Banco Continental; 30 per cent of Cementos Lima (flagship of the Rizo Patrón group); 33.6 per cent of Milpo and 6.7 per cent of Atocha (both small mining companies), 26 per cent of the La Pampilla refinery; 21 per cent of Cementos Pacasmayo; 7.9 per cent of Gloria SA (flagship of the Rodríguez group) (*Caretas*, 17 March 2005; BCRP, 2005).

3   **Mining**. In the mining sector, unlike pensions and other sectors, industrial dispersion rather than concentration was the norm, owing to the development of new mines. The only significant presence of national capital is Minera Yanacocha, jointly owned by Newmont Mining and the Benavides de la Quintana group. The rest of the sector is dominated by foreign mining operations, such as Antamina, Barrick, Cerro Verde, Tintaya and others. A number of smaller mining operations belonging to Peruvian power groups, such as SIMSA and Volcan, have been acquired by multinationals. Of the Peruvian power groups, the only significant participants are the Benavides de la Quintana group (with its silver mines led by Buenaventura) and the Brescia group (with Minsur, an important tin producer).

4   **Other sectors**. In the oil industry foreign capital predominates, as it does in the gas sector (Camisea), that of electricity (Luz del Sur and Endesa — both in Lima — with US and Spanish capital respectively). The brewing industry is wholly dominated by Latin American power groups (Colombia's Bavaria and Ambev from Brazil). In other areas, like telecommunications (fixed line and mobile), major stores, hotels, commercial aviation, even pharmacies, ownership is predominantly foreign. In the case of supermarkets and major construction firms, there is a tussle for control between local and foreign firms. Peruvian firms maintain a presence in manufacturing, export agriculture, fishing and are clearly the dominant force among small and medium-sized companies.[2]

Peruvian Business Groups

National capital (state enterprise and domestically-owned economic power groups), has therefore been displaced from its commanding position in the economy. This transformation is still taking place. Although it is the case that many of these have undergone changes involving technological, managerial and even philosophical modernisation (i.e. reconsideration of their business mission, Vásquez 2000), the numbers that have retained their position — or even survived — are relatively few.

Peruvian business groups reached the peak of their power in the mid-1980s as the so-called 'twelve apostles'. Following successive bouts of crisis (including those of 1978, 1984, 1988–90 and 1998) and market opening (initiated in 1990), the situation two decades on for the 20 largest companies was as follows. Those that had vanished or had strongly contracted were the Lanata Piaggio group (brewing); Nicolini (flour); Lucioni (banking and commerce); Arias (mining); Bentín (brewing); and Wiese and Picasso Salinas (banking). Their firms were bought up by multinationals or other power groups. Those that remained in the market, albeit somewhat diminished, included Delgado Parker (radio and TV); Galski (fishing); Graña y Montero and Piazza (both in construction and computers); Raffo (banking and textiles); and Olaechea (wines).

Three groups remain strong. The BCP is still the country's largest bank although it has lost ground among the AFPs. It is controlled by the Romero Group and by Romero (Alicorp, food and textiles). The second is Benavides de la Quintana (mining). The third is Brescia (mining, banking, commerce, hotels, textiles). At an intermediate level there is Ferreyros (sale of heavy machinery), Rodríguez (milk and cement) and Wong (supermarkets). The last two are emerging local power groups that have invested over the last 20 years and have grown in competition with importers and multinationals.

Of those groups that remain, many operate outside Peru and hope to win foreign markets (mainly in neighbouring countries). However, this business projection abroad lacks impetus. While Chilean private groups have invested US$4 billion in Peru, for instance, Peruvians have only invested US$24.7 million in Chile (*La República*, 28 April 2005).

At the middle and lower echelons of the pyramid, there has also been a reconfiguration, and new firms have gradually appeared or existing ones have undergone restructuring. This competitive business world consists mainly of medium-sized companies, and few have managed to constitute themselves as economic power groups or to do business abroad. One of the few is Añaños, the makers of Kola Real, a cheap fizzy drink that has gained a quarter of the Peruvian market and has opened up bottling plants in Venezuela and Mexico. There are a number of successful textile exporters that supply large stores in the United States. They include Topy Top and Nettalco. In the last few years, there have also emerged exporters of flowers, asparagus, mangoes, artichokes and other rural products, mainly concentrated on the coast. These new primary exporters demonstrate a degree of business dynamism, but they are exceptions and are hardly likely to turn into major power groups. Even so, within the new agro-industrial sector, they will still have to compete with established groups (such as Romero, Picasso, Wong) as well as foreign companies.

In 2004 textiles predominated among non-traditional exporters, with exports of US$683 million, followed by agro-industry with US$422 million. All these have been stimulated by a temporary preferential trade treaty with the United States, known as the Andean Trade Preferences and Drug Eradication Act (ATPDEA) and signed as part of the US anti-drug policy. After these came chemicals (US$224 million — mainly exports to the Andean Community countries), with fishing in fourth place (US$171 million) (*La República*, 14 November 2004). This sector of the economy remains fairly small and closely linked to the primary sector, another sign that there has not been (nor is there likely to be) any export-led industrial revolution.

More generally, since 1990, a new business map has taken shape. We can get a brief idea of this from the country's largest firms. Taking the 100 largest firms by sales in 1987, 1994 and 2001, we see that in 1987 there were 28 state companies with 48.5 per cent of total sales; in 1994, there were 14 with 33.4 per cent of sales; and in 2001 there were only 12 with 20.6 per cent of sales. Large Peruvian companies were 43 in number in 1987 with 28.9 per cent of sales; 46 in 1994 (presumably because of their participation in privatisations) with 28.9 per cent of sales; and 30 in 2001 with 23.1 per cent of sales. Foreign companies numbered 25 in 1987 with 20.6 per cent of sales; 30 in 1994 with 48.5 per cent of sales; and 41 with 48.5 per cent of sales in 2001. There is also a category of 'others' consisting of four firms in 1987 with 2.1 per cent of sales; ten in 1994 with 4.6 per cent of sales; and 17 in 2001 with 7.7 per cent of sales (Shimizu, 2004, p. 26).

Strengths and Weaknesses in Civil Society

This new map of economic power has brought important changes in the system of interest representation. So far as business organisation is concerned, there were two major changes.

Firstly, business lobby organisations have become the most organised and best financed component of civil society. The tendency among trade unions and popular organisations (unions, peasant federations and movements of the urban poor) has been the exact opposite. Although some organisations have emerged in defence of new rights (like the Asociación Nacional de Desafiliación de AFPs and some other consumer groups), they are still incipient.

Secondly, there has been a weakening in the standing of largely Peruvian industrial organisations, such as the National Industries Society (Sociedad Nacional de Industrias, SNI) and the Exporters' Association (Asociación de Exportadores, Adex). At the same time, other exporter organisations, notably the National Society for Mining, Oil and Energy (Sociedad Nacional de Minería, Petróleo y Energia, SNMPE), along with those representing banks and AFPs, have grown in strength (Cotler, 1998). These assumed control over the Inter-sectoral Confederation of Private Business (Confederación Intersectoral de las Empresas Privadas, Confiep), the business umbrella organisation. Confiep underwent a period of crisis as of 1998, when the SNI, Adex and the Lima Chamber of Commerce (Cámara de Comercio de Lima) all left to form the Coordinator of Business Organisations (Coordinadora Gremial). Already weakened, Confiep then lost further weight and representativeness. In part, this is because relations between key firms and the state are today conducted directly, or through the specific organisations that represent the newly empowered sectors of business. Three stand out here: the American Chamber of Commerce, the Peruvian-Spanish Chamber of Commerce (Cámara de Comercio Peruano Española), and the North American Peruvian Business Council. None of these operates within the framework of Confiep.

We should also briefly note some changes in the institutional matrix which have given rise to new sources of tension and conflict, previously aimed at the state but now also aimed at the private sector. Neoliberalism has given rise to a mass of consumers and users now linked more strongly through the market to large corporations, whether as purchasers of food, users of airports, people with current accounts, buyers of telephones, pensioners with savings in AFPs or people with insurance policies. The withdrawal of the state has opened up for the first time a space for institutional representation to millions of Peruvians directly with the private sector.

With the strengthening of market economics, leading corporations have assumed 'responsibility', especially in public services. However, they operate in a context in which the state fulfils more of a support function for big business than as defender of the common good, ignoring for the most part the interests of consumer groups. For their part, and with a few exceptions, consumers tend to be disorganised and dispersed, fighting to become pressure groups and occasionally protesting. They fail to articulate their concerns in any systematic way through the media, political parties or congressional commissions, mainly because of the power exercised over all of these by corporate interests and the unwillingness or inability of political leaders to articulate their demands. It is worth pointing out that this has an impact on the crisis of party political representation, since the parties fail to give a voice to these new interests made up of millions of people.

From the employment point of view, the situation is quite distinct from the earlier more 'populist' period, since large scale business is capital intensive and linked up not with small and medium-sized business but with the global economy. With a small state and with capital intensive corporations producing mainly primary products from natural resources, the labour market has become much more precarious both in terms of income and employment. At the beginning of 2005, following four years of continuous growth, wage earners constituted only 37 per cent of the workforce; the rest (63 per cent) were non-wage earners in the informal sector or in rural areas and the unemployed. The average estimated income for rural areas was 100 soles (around US$30) a month and 544 soles in urban areas (*La República*, 1 May 2005). Among the 37 per cent of wage-earners, the level of union membership was low, because changes to labour legislation have made it easier for management to dismiss workers and to take on others on a part-time or seasonal basis. This is what generates the 'de-classing' of political action now typical of Latin America (Roberts, 2002). However, since 2001, unions have regained some of their capacity to mobilise people, raising once again their former banners. Nevertheless, they do not take up the rights of consumers and users, who constitute a new social group and not one strictly of class.

Because wages are predominantly low and forms of taxation regressive (19 per cent sales taxes and taxes on fuel), the underground economy has tended to grow and develop. It supplies cheap contraband products, pirated trademarks and informally-produced goods to the large mass of consumers. In sectors like music, videos, cigarettes, electrical items, clothing and shoes, informal sales have outpaced formal ones. The 'narco' economy also provides a strong gravitational pull in the rural economy, accounting for as many as 150,000 jobs in 2005, distributed across the 13 coca-producing valleys (*El Comercio*, 14 May 2005).

Given the failings of the formal market, the 'narco' sector, contraband, informal production and commerce have together become the most important sources of employment in a parallel, illicit economy which operates by not paying taxes but paying bribes, therefore further undermining the fragile institutionality of the state. Such economies tend not to produce a strong and organised civil society. Those that predominate are those who mediate this market: industrial and commercial (informal or criminal) wholesalers who act strictly in defence of their own narrow economic interests. They use the poor for mobilisation against any attempt by the state to return them to the world of (tax-paying) formality or to combating illegality through the use of sanctions and penalties.

While in the previous period of populism, the state was subject to an overflow of pressure from popular sectors (*desborde popular*) directed by trade unions in a matrix of formal employment, today the overflow is one of informal and illegal commerce. This coexists with sporadic and dispersed outbreaks of union and popular protest that puts pressure on the system but fails to change it. They merge and mix with 'movements' orchestrated by those who manage the channels of informality, contraband and drug trafficking.

Changing Relations between the Private Sector and Civil Society

Large corporations and the private sector are keen to take steps to improve their image, and thereby contribute to institutional consolidation. However, such initiatives are limited in scope. They include new concepts that originate in developed economies: new types of philanthropy (better organised than in the past with more clearly defined objectives, thorough methods and more stringent evaluation) and 'corporate social responsibility' (CSR) (Caravedo, 1998; Portocarrero et al., 2000). Multinationals adopted CSR some time back in response to the sort of criticisms levelled against them in their home countries. Latin American power groups, having restructured and modernised to confront the international competition, have done likewise.

The basic aim here is to give the firm a social face, to present it as being environmentally responsible and sensitive to social problems and so to create a more harmonious and stable relationship between it and the society in which it operates. CSR involves creating good relations within the firm (with workers and their families) and outside it (in the community where it operates, with suppliers, customers, local municipalities, but only where these are considered to be significant 'stakeholders'). Such relations are particularly important for large extractive firms that seek a 'social license' to operate. In other spheres, including public services, the social pressure is less.

Important individually, such activities have limited effects. They vary a good deal between stakeholders. Only a handful of new mines and oil companies, with major exposure to environmental and social milieux, do so in a comprehensive, systematic manner with proper budgets. They do so to acquire a 'social license'. However, they often find themselves under pressure to give more and more, facing demands for ever greater activity. As the state is weak or even non-existent, they turn into a 'state'; yet this does not necessarily diminish levels of protest. The limitations are obvious and are indicative of the problems involved in achieving consolidation of the new matrix. In a number of cases, notably mining activities such as Yanacocha, Barrick, Tintaya and Manhattan, the opposite has been the case, especially in 2005 when there was a wave of mobilisation against mining companies in different parts of the country. Often business and political leaders regard CSR with some suspicion as publicity stunts, pointing to its many limitations (Portocarrero, 2002). Philanthropy is usually fairly tepid and sporadic; few are the companies that make large regular tax-deductible donations. Finally, notwithstanding their discourse about responsibility, large corporations have not made significant collective efforts to understand the rights of users and consumers, particularly when these are not organised. Nor do they demonstrate much fiscal responsibility or sensitivity towards racial or gender discrimination. Overall, their degree of 'civic responsibility' is fairly low, and is likely to remain that way as long as the state remains inept and corrupt and civil society weakly organised.

Changes with Regard to the State[3]

In terms of access to and influence over the state, there have also been some important changes. As the neoliberal reforms got under way, the large corporations achieved a privileged political position. Political decision-making was concentrated in the Ministry of Economy and Finance (MEF), and the MEF was able to exert influence (if not control) over regulatory and tax agencies. Reflecting the new power balance, all the ministers at the MEF from 1990 onwards were businessmen or technical people with close business links: Juan Carlos Hurtado, Carlos Boloña, Jorge Camet, Víctor Joy Way, Efraín Goldenberg, Pedro-Pablo Kuzcynski, Javier Silva Ruete.[4] The same has been the case in other ministries, especially the Ministry of Industry (MI). Similarly, tax and legal advisors, along with the technocratic back-up at the MEF and the MI have been recruited primarily from neoliberal networks and the major legal practices. No other group, particularly unionised workers or peasants, have had anything like the same degree of influence for so long or at such a high level.

Although this level of influence probably peaked during the Fujimori years, it did not change in any fundamental way thereafter. State 'capture' was further advanced by the formation of a special transmission belt between the private corporate sector and the MEF: the Peruvian Economy Institute (Instituto Peruano de Economía, IPE). Established in 1994, it received money from Confiep, local Peruvian business groups, multinationals and the World Bank to provide advice on trade and tax matters to the MEF. It was founded by Roberto Abusada, a one-time top advisor to the MEF. Thereafter he left to run Aeroperú during the period of its privatisation and then re-entered the MEF by the back door. The IPE's board of directors included representatives of the largest Peruvian companies and multinationals, as well as technocrats and lawyers who worked in top positions in the MEF under Fujimori. It also included Jorge Camet, who ran the MEF for five years. After the change of government in 2000, IPE worked slightly more at arms length, but maintained a close rapport with the MEF. It took a rather more open public role in as much as its experts took part with opinion leaders on radio shows, TV and in the written press. The IPE also advises Confiep and writes pro-business articles and reports for the press.

Applying Influence

The influence of this network of interests became evident as soon as Fujimori took power in 1990 and market reforms got under way. It was maintained after Fujimori, although its leeway was reduced as a consequence of democratisation and decentralisation. From 2000 onwards, Congress and public opinion took a more independent line and there was a greater measure of judicial autonomy. This made the exercise of business influence rather more complex, but it did not reduce its extent in any fundamental way. The executive remains the subject of capture, chiefly through the MEF. Influence over the media also continued, and may have grown since the fall of Fujimori because of a decline in revenues from government advertising. Through its various lobby organisations, business managed to maintain its influence over Congress and both regional and local government. The main reason for this influence over the government is to be found in the support that Toledo enjoyed during his election campaign from business groups as leader of the opposition. He rewarded them with key positions in the government and Congress, continuing the practice initiated in 1990 of giving business leaders and their technocratic acolytes important economic posts (Durand 2003, pp. 511–15).

With the process of political change under way, and with foreign capital being invested regularly and local firms either dying or adapting, the transmission belts between the corporate world and the neoliberal state became more firmly established. These were in large measure an inheritance from liberalisation under Fujimori and the corporate privileges conceded which companies came to think of as 'acquired rights'. A number of such rights were defended by the Toledo government. The results varied, but on balance the interests of the private sector were upheld. Some more typical cases follow.

The example of the pensions system is particularly illustrative since this was a new creation that reflected very clearly the new power relations created under Fujimori; indeed it was crafted by the state with no other external pressures than those of the private sector. According to one study, 'in July 1995, the pension system was changed along the lines demanded by the AAFP (Pension Fund Association)'. The study concluded by analysing some other changes: 'the pensions reform was carried out with little or no oversight from Congress, rather it was centralised in the executive with which businessmen were developing close ties' (Arce, 2001, pp. 105–6). Thus it was that a pensions system was crafted with high charges and high profits (among the highest in all of Latin America), but low recognition of pensioners' rights.[5] For example, pensioners were allowed to disaffiliate from the state pension system, but not that of the private AFPs. It was this that gave rise to the establishment of the Association for the Disaffiliation from AFPs (Asociación para la Desafiliación de las AFPs), which launched an unsuccessful campaign in 2005 to change the legal framework.

Tax stability contracts were created to attract foreign capital and investment by freezing the existing tax regime and thereby offering guarantees that the rules of the game would not be changed. This effectively created a differentiated tax regime to the detriment of smaller Peruvian businesses that lacked such contracts. Between 1990 and 2000, the MEF signed 332 contracts, of which 286 were with multinationals. They vary in detail and in duration, aspects in which there was considerable executive discretion. The contracts were negotiated behind closed doors, the lack of transparency encouraging corrupt dealing. Symptomatically, they only came to light when the tax authority (Sunat) and investigating commissions in Congress demanded copies during the Paniagua and Toledo governments (CIDEF, 2002).

The case of tax exonerations is also typical. These mainly came into being when Camet was minister, and were only altered thereafter on an exceptional basis. They enabled corporate taxes to be lowered or sales taxes to be eliminated through a number of mechanisms applied to different sectors of the economy or to different types of transaction (credit card purchases, share dividends, etc.). With the fall of Fujimori, such was the concern for the dwindling tax yield on income tax and sales tax that it was estimated that exonerations cost the Treasury 2.36 billion soles, or 1.34 per cent of GDP. This shows us how the competitive playing ground was tilted, a situation criticised by the IMF (*Gestión*, 27 November 2001). The degree of power and influence of large corporations is indicated by the following figures. In the period between 1995 and 2000, corporate income tax fell from 2.88 per cent of GDP to 2.73

per cent. The fall was proportionately higher the larger the company concerned. The tax yield of the 56 largest companies fell from 1.9 billion soles to 1.2 billion. The yield for small and medium-sized firms went from 1.18 billion soles to 939 million (Durand, 2003, pp. 455–6).

Decree Law 120–94–EF was particularly important, providing tax incentives for corporate mergers and acquisitions, enabling the double depreciation of assets and allowing companies themselves to estimate their market value. The decree was cooked up in secret in the offices of the then minister, Jorge Camet. It involved various advisors from private legal practices, but not specialists from the MEF and Sunat, whose advice was ignored. The law generated a total of more than 1,000 mergers and acquisitions. It is thought to have contributed greatly to the fall in levels of corporate income tax (CIDEF, 2002).

In the case of the four Lima electricity companies and the mining company Barrick Misquichilca, mergers were undertaken with companies in the same group of shareholders, tied to tax stability contracts through legal sophistry.[6] The most extreme example was that of Edelnor (which belongs to the Spanish multinational Endesa) which paid no corporate income tax at all between 1995 and 2000, and which then considered that it should continue to enjoy exoneration until the end of its end of its stability contract in 2005. Firms were thus able to diminish their tax obligations, to the Treasury's detriment. The Paniagua government undertook an audit, and demanded payment of back taxes from 1998 onwards, the date when the contractual exoneration ended. This led to a conflict that revealed the power of the actors and the resilience of the system they sought to defend. It was at this point that the manager of Luz del Sur, Mile Kasic, coined the phrase 'acquired rights'. He said that the [superintendent of Sunat] 'tried to deprive us of our acquired right to the stability contracts', adding that 'this was sending the very worst signal to investors' (*El Comercio*, 16 July 2003).

The cases of the electricity companies received a good deal of public attention because of the response of Sunat and the position taken by the interim Paniagua administration (which came to power without being in hock to business interests) and investigating commissions in Congress. It became particularly notable because only a few days before Toledo took office, Raúl Diez Canseco, a businessman and future industry minister, met with executives of Endesa in Madrid, whence he phoned to make sure that Sunat changed tack. As soon as Toledo took over, the head of Sunat was abruptly removed, presumably at the insistence of the affected companies and in view of the commitments given to them during the campaign. The MEF and Sunat named an arbitration panel that quickly ruled in the company's favour. By May 2005 the case was resolved. It took some time because, apart from the stability contracts, there were oversight problems on a number of other issues (*La República*, 4 March 2005).

Mining royalties are another area of conflict on taxation matters. In spite of the insistence of independent congressmen to include the issue of royalties on the congressional agenda, it was systematically side-stepped. It was for this reason that Congressman Javier Diez Canseco criticised Congress of wilful neglect, threatening to go on hunger strike if the issue was not debated. He criticised the economy and industry ministers and the SNMPE lobby for applying pressure on the legislature 'not to discuss the document' (*La República*, 22 April 2004). While the regional government supported the norm (with backing from the unions), business leaders and lobby organisations argued that the measure would lead to a fall in wages and would deter investment. Meanwhile, the medium-sized mining companies (*minería mediana*) noted that the changes would primarily affect them since they had no tax stability contracts (*La República*, 18 June 2004). The case is illustrative because it shows the playing field to be far from level given the propensities of neoliberal policies. After considerable delay, the Congress did take a decision in March 2005, approving the collection of royalties. The corporations involved, represented by the SNMPE, appealed the decision in the courts. The final decision, taken by the Constitutional Tribunal, was in favour of royalties. The resolution against the business groups was made against the backdrop of mobilisations and protests involving congressmen, regional presidents and mayors, who marched to the Tribunal, amid criticisms by the SNMPE about 'pressures from independent organisations' (*La República*, 9 March, 2005).

Conclusions

One of the main results of applying neoliberal policies in Peru has been that corporations have prevailed over the market economy. They have become a gravitational centre, acquiring the economic power and the capacity decisively to influence the institutional matrix, in other words the state and civil society. Such power and influence is made manifest in the ability of big business to establish a pattern of favourable inter-institutional relations which shows the main political actors how the 'game is played'.

In its relations with the state, corporate power has maintained close ties with political power, especially with the executive which it has penetrated and influenced from within. It has an immediate influence in those key areas of political power where public policy decisions are discussed that affect their economic interests. This pattern came about in the 1990s under an authoritarian government when the powers of the state were concentrated in the executive. In spite of re-democratisation since 2000 and the restoration of greater balance between the branches of the state (with Congress and the judiciary taking a more active role), economic power has managed to defend its interests, thanks primarily to financing electoral campaigns, lobbying in Congress and influence over the media. It has not won all the battles fought, but in many the results have been favourable to its interests. In other spheres, it has successfully delayed measures to cut or reduce those 'acquired rights' won in the 1990s on corporate taxation and other privileges. A constant pressure has been applied to contain social demands to improve worker and consumer rights, as well as measures that would help build a better and more democratic state.

So far as civil society is concerned, there have been a number of important changes. State shrinking and privatisation, alongside massive foreign investment, has helped build up a market relationship with millions of people who have contact with corporations whether as consumers, pensioners, holders of insurance policies and users of services. This has led to new social problems with respect to tariffs charged, the quality of services and those rights created (or which ought to be created) to counterbalance the market power of those that provide services. Given the very limited capacity to represent interests and the inadequacy of the response by political elites to solve such demands (the state is perceived as not being interested or able to defend the public interest), dissent is expressed through protest and direct action.

With respect to labour, the relationship is less important than it used to be because of the economic predominance of the private sector, the capital intensity of the sort of technology used, and the changes made to labour legislation. On the one hand, levels of formal employment and income provided by the private sector are low, whilst on the other the sort of employment that exists is precarious owing to the erosion of labour rights and the resort to temporary or part-time employment or sub-contracting. Whether as workers or consumers, the mass of the population faces a corporate world which is increasingly concentrated and mainly-foreign owned. This maintains better and closer ties with a state that theoretically concerns itself with the common good but in practice fails to do so. At the same time, since workers are unable to insert themselves in the formal economy, the majority is drawn into the informal and/or criminal sectors, a factor which further undermines institutionality. This predicament both for consumers and workers coexists with a reduction in the role of the state, a situation of regulatory weakness and an inability to provide a better social response, whether because of inefficiency and corruption, lack of resources or a lack of orientation.

Given the vacuum created by the withdrawal and shrinking of the state, and the individual response of each corporation to managing its own micro-context in the area where it operates, programmes of social responsibility have gained salience alongside new forms of philanthropy. Such programmes are most in evidence where the presence of the state is weakest, namely in the remote and poor areas which are the new enclaves for export-oriented extractive industry. Such programmes merit reflection, since they are carried out by those that command the new economy, but the experience of recent years shows up the inadequacy of CSR. There have been significant bouts of protest, increasing in scale, which make clear the need for a state presence that cannot be supplanted by individual initiatives in delimited areas.

For the reasons noted above, relations between the corporate world and civil society are distant and increasingly problematic. This is also because the former cuts out the expression of the interests of consumers and workers through its influence over the media. It tends to operate in an authoritarian way and seeks to orchestrate democratic institutions in such a way as to defend its interests.

Faced with bouts of social tension and periodic conflict with unions and consumer groups, businessmen decry this as 'political noise', pointing out the dangers of this 'scaring off investment'. They see the primordial task of the state as being to defend the market and guarantee order above all. Since corporate power upholds a close and stable relation with political power, they argue that economic interests can function in ways that are 'divorced' from politics. Such concerns reveal the growing difficulty that corporations have in managing the context in which they operate, not least with respect to civil society. However, these problems are not just limited to the consequences of asymmetries arising from poverty and the precarious nature of social rights or the inequalities of political access. Analysis of the changes that have taken place within the private sector itself point to the marked concentration of property and wealth and the rapid process of de-nationalisation.

Such systemic risks are largely the product of the extreme and authoritarian way in which neoliberal policies were introduced during the 1990s, a time when traditionally fragile national capital was at its weakest in the wake of successive recessionary and inflationary crises. It was this that generated a new type of economic elite, smaller in number, larger in scale and with scant participation by Peruvian capital. What took place within the business nucleus accentuated the problems of the new institutional matrix, and (together with the factors already mentioned) reduced or eliminated the chances of its consolidation over the longer term and its ultimate stabilisation. The tensions and conflicts arising from the asymmetries we have noted, and the difficulty of the political system in reducing them, point to the presence of permanent areas of uncertainty and social discontent. One way of confronting such problems, among others, is the development of a more efficient, transparent and democratic state. However, the key actor (corporate power) prefers to use the state to its own ends, rejecting institutional change and containing protest, rather than transforming it and advancing towards a resolution of social problems.

Notes

1   Historically, this weakness was more evident than in other Latin American countries, but recurrent periods of crisis (as in Argentina) also explain the rapid pace of multinationalisation of the economy. On neoliberalism and the historic weakness of peripheral countries, see Arrighi, Silver and Brewer (2003).

2   See the sectoral information of Peru Top Publications (2004). In agriculture there is a strong presence of Chilean and Colombian capital, as well as former landowners returning to the sector and new Peruvian investors. These have concentrated on the coast, purchasing shares in the former cooperatives in some of the larger valleys, as well as new land brought under cultivation (Pampa de Villacuri in Ica and Chavimochic in the north). On the few 'new groups', see *El Comercio-Día 1* (14 May 2005). See also Chapter 6 of this volume.

3   This section is based on Durand (2004).

4   For a list of the numerous businesses belonging to the various ministers of economy, see Durand (2003, p. 494).

5   An analagous situation to what happened with banking, with banks charging high rates of interest and demanding large guarantees. Two successful medium-sized business leaders from the provinces in an interview agreed that 'I no longer ask for loans, because I do not wish to work for the banks' (interviews by Hugo Villachica and Fernando Ochoa, Lima, March 2005). Bank loan rates for small-sized enterprises are very high and help generate larger profits than loans to large businesses.

6   Barrick Misquichilca won the case in mid 2005 thanks to a decision made by the MEF that could not be challenged by Sunat. The case generated an open conflict, with the mining company writing a four-page report criticising Humberto Campodónico, a columnist who had questioned the company's behaviour. See *La República* (7 July 2005, p. 5). Part of the problem is that the Ancash regional government and various local organisations there were being mobilised against Barrick for not making significant monetary contributions. The regional government depends on income taxes paid by the company and distributed by the central government.

10

The Regulation of Market Power in a Democratic Transition

José I. Távara

Introduction

A major area of debate in contemporary Peru is the supposed divorce between the economy and politics. Some analysts heap praise on ongoing macroeconomic policies and growth, while complaining about the negative effects on investment that might result from 'political noise' — an ambiguous expression that reflects both a sound reaction against the demagogic and trivial nature of much political discussion, as well as the well-known disdain that Peruvian elites have traditionally shown towards democratic values, which they claim have no validity within the economy. At the same time, much of the literature on democratic transition has steered clear of economic problems, tending to treat the interaction of the economy and politics as if they were clearly defined and separate spheres of activity.

A key area for analysis of the relationship between the economy and politics is the regulation of private companies that provide public services. Peru provides a good case-study for such analysis, given the coincidence of regulatory reform with the process of democratic transition. Although there are various studies on privatisation in the 1990s,[1] little attention has been given to the institutional development in regulation during the post-Fujimori period. A key issue here is whether the transition from an authoritarian regime, noted for corruption and the concentration of decision-making, to one more committed to democratic norms has had any major impact on the way that the institutions of regulation have evolved.

This chapter therefore aims to cast some light on this area. Regulation is taken to mean the adoption and application of a set of rules that constrain or widen the range of transactions allowed in companies providing such services. I focus on institutional design, seeking to identify elements of continuity and change with respect to the previous decade. For reasons of space, I limit this to consideration of the electricity and telecommunications industries. In the following section, I look at the main characteristics of privatisation and its effects. There follows a brief discussion about the main problems and challenges, particularly with respect to the criteria normally adopted in the institutional design of regulatory systems. The next section aims to identify the main attributes of the regulatory system under the Fujimori government, relating these to the discussion in the preceding section. Then I look at the main innovations that have taken place since the fall of Fujimori, first during the transitional Paniagua government and then under the Toledo administration. The penultimate section identifies issues pending in the reform agenda. The chapter ends with some final remarks.

Privatisation and Regulation under an Authoritarian Regime

Privatisation got under way in the 1990s in a context in which public opinion had become highly sensitised to the deficiencies in the management and performance of state companies. As had been the case previously, the García government had used these companies to provide its supporters with employment opportunities. It had also manipulated the tariffs charged by such companies for short-term political ends, resorting to indiscriminate and fiscally unsustainable subsidies. The crisis of hyperinflation in the late-1980s brought with it a contraction in public investment, further accentuating problems in the reach and quality of public services.

The Fujimori government brought in new measures to improve the investment climate and prepare the ground for privatisation. In mid-1991, a decree was issued establishing the principle of equal treatment for domestic and foreign investment. It guaranteed the unrestricted right of foreign investors to acquire property and assets, as well the repatriation of capital, dividends and profits in freely convertible currency. A little later, in November 1991, a new law was promulgated, the Framework Law for Private Sector Growth, which sought to deregulate economic activity and remove barriers to investment. The main chapter headings of this law indicate its content: judicial stability in the administrative and tax treatment of investment, removal of investment restrictions, and the creation of insurance for private investment.

In April 1992 Fujimori staged his coup d'état, concentrating powers of decision, dissolving the Congress and controlling the judicial system. This established the authoritarian system that was to govern Peru for the rest of the decade. International pressure forced the government to call elections for a Constituent Congress to draft a new constitution. The 1993 Constitution included the norms for a new economic regime: freedom for business and freedom to hire and fire; freedom of competition; equal treatment for foreign and local investment in all spheres of activity; freedom to sign stability accords between private investors and the state; guarantees for private property; and national or foreign arbitration on disputes involving the state. The Constitution also established legally-binding contracts under which the state may 'set guarantees or authorise securities', contracts 'which cannot be altered by legislation'. International agreements for protecting foreign investment were also made along the same lines.

The objective of all these measures was to 'buy credibility' among investors. They rested on assumptions about the institutional weakness of the country and especially on the absence of counterweights to executive discretion. The previous expropriations of the military government were invoked to argue the need to provide incentives and guarantees as a quid pro quo to attracting investment.

Privatisation Process

This was the context for the privatisation of state companies, marked by 'its depth and rapid rhythm of implementation' (Ruiz Caro, 2002, p. 9).[2] The assets of public companies were transferred to private consortia. Although most were majority foreign-owned, they involved Peruvian firms as minority shareholders — some of which were very well-connected to the regime.[3]

In terms of the effects on general welfare, privatisation was positive. It led to substantial improvements in efficiency and productivity. The large-scale investment that took place made possible a huge expansion in service networks and brought improvements in both coverage and quality of service (Gallardo, 2000; Torero and Pasco Font, 2001). For this reason, privatisation led to an improvement in living standards for many people, especially those previously denied access to services. It also had an important positive impact on efficiency and productivity. At the same time, in common with other Latin American countries, opinion surveys showed that a high proportion of citizens remained sceptical about the benefits of privatisation. Revealing a degree of candour on this, the Inter-American Development Bank (IDB) has asked itself 'what accounts for this apparent paradox?' (Banco Interamericano de Desarrollo, 2002).[4]

Available evidence shows that the benefits of privatisation in Peru have not been equally shared by all social groups. For instance, of a total of 1,750 local districts, around 1,300 do not have access to fixed telephony. At the same time, those consumers who previously enjoyed access to public services have seen their tariffs rise. One of the core arguments for privatisation was that the state should delegate business activity to the private sector and focus its attention on providing basic welfare services such as health, education and public security. For some analysts, the level of dissatisfaction with the coverage or poor quality of these basic services 'is clear evidence of failure to meet one of the major justifications for privatisation' (Ruiz Caro, 2002, p. 10).

In fact, privatisation formed part of a programme of macroeconomic stabilisation that sought to eliminate the operating deficits of public companies and to generate fiscal income.[5] One of the ways of reducing the deficits was to raise the tariff levels of companies to be privatised. Privatisation therefore involved a prior 'sanitation' of their accounts (including the firing of excess labour) and the 'sinceramiento' of tariffs, a euphemism for the removal of all public subsidies. On the other hand, the state has offered investors generous tax exonerations (thus undercutting tax revenues) and has passed legal norms that allow for the rapid depreciation of assets which helps boost profits and reduce tax income to the state.

A key aspect of privatisation (and one consistent with notions of institutional fragility and the need to 'buy credibility' among investors) was the adoption of concession contracts which became at once rigid and permissive with respect to the abuse of market power to the detriment of competitors, suppliers and consumers (Távara, 2000). Such contracts are legally protected so that they cannot be subsequently changed by legislation. In contrast with the main arguments in the literature on transaction costs and incomplete contracts, these concession contracts seem to be consistent with the quest for a regime that is of 'low intensity' in institutions.[6] Though the rigidity of these contracts may be attractive to investors in the short term, in the longer term they prove counter-productive because of the tensions they generate when the natural evolution of markets (especially very dynamic ones like telecommunications) parts company with the course anticipated in the concession contracts.

   Another point related to the above is the concentration of decision-making power in the hands of technocrats appointed by the executive, without counterparts in other branches of the state. During the 1990s it was considered more effective and efficient to legislate through decrees. Transparency was not considered necessary as opposed to the need to privatise as quickly and expeditiously as possible. Those who criticised were simply ignored or were associated with the 'gradualist' approach, an approach that supposedly failed to heed the dangers of policy reversal. Some privatisations were conducted in ways in which there were flagrant conflicts of interest and whose failure was at the expense of public welfare.[7]

Designing Regulatory Systems

From a normative point of view, the main aim of regulation is to protect consumers — both present and future — by preventing firms from abusing their market power to gain extraordinary profit, for instance, by fixing high tariffs or reducing costs at the expense of quality. From this normative perspective, investment is not an end in itself but a means to facilitate access to public services. However, some authors, such as Levy and Spiller (1996), maintain that regulation should be geared towards protecting investors' interests, since otherwise there would be no investment in the first place. They argue that regulated industries provide services for mass consumption and therefore regulation is highly susceptible to political pressure. Furthermore, a large fraction of capital costs constitute a sunk cost, which means the cost is unrecoverable if the investors decide to exit the market. Investors are thus exposed to opportunistic behaviour on the part of governments.

   By contrast with the consumers who normally are dispersed and disorganised, businesses within an industry have much greater opportunities to exert political influence, especially when there is a high level of concentration in that industry as in many public services. Stigler's central thesis is particularly pessimistic on this point, arguing that '... as a rule, regulation is acquired by the industry and is designed and operated primarily for its benefit' (1971 p. 3).

Regulatory systems ought to provide guarantees to investors, reducing the risks of their investment being expropriated, while also avoiding the dangers of 'capture' by the industry itself. Regulation needs to be credible both to investors and consumers, predictable, based on consistent decisions over time, and legitimate, geared to the higher order values of society. The main characteristics of a good regulatory system are the regulator's independence and accountability, which entails transparency in the regulatory process and clear procedural rules (Jamison et al., 2005).

Among the necessary conditions for independence, a special legal mandate is required that clearly defines all functions and powers. Members of the boards of regulators need to be appointed for fixed terms during which they cannot be removed except in case of gross misconduct and even then respecting due process. Appointments to the boards should be staggered, to avoid the influence of the electoral cycle and ensure greater pluralism in their composition (Smith, 1997). Procedures for selecting board members need to include methods of identifying people with a reputation for independence and ethical behaviour. In some countries, the legislature is involved in the confirming and even appointing of nominees. Autonomy also implies independent sources of funding (usually a percentage levied on the revenues of regulated firms) and enough resources to hire and train qualified personnel. Regulators should have the power and authority to demand and receive the information they require from those they regulate in order to make well-informed decisions. There is a strong consensus about the need to include these characteristics in the institutional design, especially in countries where there is little tradition of independent public management.

But autonomy for its own sake is inadequate, and there need to be checks and balances to make sure that regulators do not deviate from their mission, respond to special interests, or work in an inefficient manner. So measures and procedures are required that encourage greater transparency and force regulators to be accountable for the decisions they make. To this end all concerned parties must have the opportunity to express their views in public hearings and to appeal decisions.

Proposed norms, rulings and decisions should be published in advance so that all parties can express their opinions. It is also essential that ethical codes of conduct are adopted and obeyed, thus avoiding conflicts of interest, including restrictions on the traffic of officials between the regulatory agencies and the firms they regulate. The information that regulators use should be made freely available to all interested parties, except in those cases where the law classifies it as confidential. Regulators also need to be subjected to methods of accountability, such as to a commission or the legislature, and have their performance evaluated by other state entities and by civil society (Smith, 1997).

Regulation under an Authoritarian Regime

To what extent did the systems of regulation introduced under Fujimori have these characteristics? The organisational structures took shape as privatisation moved forward with specialist agencies taking charge of regulation in each sector. Under the old system of state property and management, the setting of tariffs had been the responsibility of commissions working within the ambit of each ministry. At the end of 1993, a few months before privatisation, the Supervisory Organism for Private Investment in Telecommunications (Organismo Supervisor de la Inversión Privada en Telecomunicaciones, OSIPTEL) was set up, replacing the regulatory commission for telecommunications tariffs.

In the case of electricity, privatisation also got under way in 1994. Previously, a new Concessions Law had been approved which had envisaged a new model for electricity tariff regulation. Its implementation came under the Electricity Tariffs Commission (CTE), made up of professional teams under the aegis of the state companies in the sector. However, it was only in 1996 that a law was enacted that gave rise to the system of supervising investment in this sector through the Supervisory Organism for Investment in Energy (Organismo Supervisor de la Inversión en Energía, OSINERG), which became functional a few months later. Regulatory functions were divided between different organisations in the system for most of the decade.[8]

The 1993 Constitution also gave rise to the Ombudsman's Office (Defensoría del Pueblo), whose function was to defend basic and constitutional rights, oversee the workings of public administration and offer public services to the citizenry. The first ombudsman was appointed by Congress in 1997. The Defensoría has the right to submit legislative initiatives to Congress and, as part of its investigatory work, to demand information and assistance from any public office. Also, it has the authority to oversee the activities of non-state entities which exercise public prerogatives or provide public services.

A key characteristic of the political regime of the 1990s was the concentration of decision-making in the hands of Fujimori, who at the outset appointed people he could trust to run the regulatory agencies. The Telecommunications Law established that OSIPTEL came directly under the president, who had the power to appoint its head from a roster presented to him by the prime minister. This norm made no reference whatsoever to the criteria and procedures for appointments which remained at the president's pleasure. Although the members of the managing council were figures from the Ministry of Economy and Finance and the Ministry of Transport and Communications, their appointment was in the hands of the president. When the detailed regulations governing OSIPTEL were approved in August 1994, a period of three years was agreed for members of the management council 'renewable for the same and successive periods'.[9]

The initial design for the electricity sector was similar. Under the Law for Electricity Concessions, the management council of the CTE were nominated by the president by means of a resolution endorsed by the Ministry of Energy and Mines and subject to a vote of approval by the prime minister. Subsequently, when OSINERG was established, the mechanism for appointing the council was slightly amended to give a greater say to ministers.[10] Nevertheless, the normative framework for the sector had some major gaps, including procedures for the appointment and removal of members and the extent of their terms of office. Tacitly, it was assumed that these could be removed willy-nilly at the behest of the president. Similarly, the regulations of the law establish for OSINERG that dismissal is a prerogative of the minister, making no reference whatsoever to the causes or principles of due process.[11] In other words, the members of the managing councils were under the thumb of the president or the minister, and as such were vulnerable to the influence that the economic groups they regulated could wield over political actors.

Staggered appointment of board members was not considered in any sector. Nor did the legislature play any role whatsoever in appointing or confirming the proposed directors, and this is still the case. Up to 1998 these boards of directors included representatives of the firms that were regulated, and in the case of OSIPTEL the board also included a consumer representative. In that year, a law was enacted that removed from the boards the representatives of both the firms and consumers. Since then, the boards have been made up exclusively of public sector representatives.[12]

Another key aspect that impinges upon regulators' independence is their control over an autonomous budget and reliable sources of funding. In the electricity sector, the rules establish that those with concessions 'are obliged to contribute to sustaining normative, regulatory and oversight entities through contributions established by the Ministry of Energy and Mines, which in no circumstances may exceed one per cent of their annual revenues'. Similarly, in the telecommunications sector, operating companies should pay for the regulatory services provided by OSIPTEL a sum equivalent to five per thousand of their revenues net of tax.

In view of the rapid expansion of these industries during the 1990s, the sums paid by the industry were sufficient to pay for the activities of the regulators. Furthermore, the regulators came under a special labour regime, akin to that of the private sector, and for this reason they were able to attract professionally qualified personnel, which is not the case for the public sector as a whole. However, at the same time there were a number of austerity measures imposed by the central government that affected the regulators and limited their effective autonomy.

Finally, regulatory institutions need to operate in a legal framework that allows them to have access, when they need it, to relevant information concerning the companies they supervise. In the case of telecommunications, the concession contracts with the main operating company establish that 'OSIPTEL will have the right to inspect or to instruct authorised accountants to revise the files, archives and other information of the concessionaire to ensure compliance with the terms of the concession'. In practice, however, and according to OSIPTEL's own reports, the company failed to comply with these provisions. Only on 27 July 2000, the day before Fujimori inaugurated his ill-fated third term, did he enact a new law that gave greater powers to OSIPTEL in this area. This made it possible to set time limits and conditions for access to information from the companies, including confidential commercial information (under the understanding that this would be kept secret), to carry out inspections without prior notice, and to resort where necessary to police backing.

Little was done during the 1990s with respect to transparency, citizen participation and accountability.[13] There was a 'culture of secrecy' during these years which facilitated corruption on a truly massive scale. As seen above, there were various normative loopholes that limited the regulators' capacity to supervise companies adequately. At the same time, taking arguments about commercial secrecy to absurd lengths, the regulators routinely labelled information as secret or confidential, depriving consumers and consumer associations of the chance of being informed or of taking a more active role in the setting of tariffs.

Organisations such as the Defensoría began to play a very active role in this sphere, carrying out systematic campaigns to promote more transparent procedures and to make both the public and authorities aware of the constitutional right to access information in the hands of different state institutions. As we shall see, these activities — combined with similar initiatives by the Peruvian Press Council and the NGO Transparencia amongst others — led to substantial legal reforms during the Paniagua transitional government. However, it should also be noted that some of the regulators, like OSIPTEL and the CTE, began to publish their norms and rulings beforehand in order to receive feedback. They also called meetings and public hearings with a view to disseminating relevant information and encouraging greater participation by the representatives of both companies and consumer associations.[14] In July 1999 the managing council of OSIPTEL approved arrangements for greater transparency, including the posting of the agendas and minutes of its meetings on its website, along with decisions reached and agreements made. It also included on the website (amid other relevant information) the agendas of meetings of its officials with those of companies and consumer associations.

Such initiatives were clearly positive moves, particularly given the nature of the regime and the political situation at the time. However, they also revealed important limitations. Taking the case of OSIPTEL, transparency in its own operations depended on discretional decisions adopted on a case-by-case basis. For instance, with regard to public hearings it established that 'OSIPTEL will order the calling of a public hearing, when it deems it necessary so to do, in order to encourage the pluralistic participation of interested parties and to receive feedback from them'. On the other hand, the adoption of measures to disseminate and encourage access to relevant information was hindered as a result of OSIPTEL's tendency to classify most of the information as confidential.[15]

Summing up, any norms of transparency adopted in this period were the consequence of self-regulatory decisions on the part of these supervisory entities, and with rare exceptions did not result from the adoption of a normative framework that was general and obligatory. The central government took no initiatives in this respect. Furthermore, the public hearings held occasionally by the likes of OSIPTEL did very little to encourage public participation. Indeed, the government manipulated the term, giving it a very narrow interpretation which really subverted its true meaning. The phrase *participación ciudadana* was appropriated to mean the sale of state shares in privatised companies to the public — a limited version of popular capitalism or democratic ownership, which linked citizen participation to property rights. The great majority of citizens and consumers of public services who did not buy shares found themselves excluded from this sort of 'citizen participation'. It is also important to point out the lack of any mechanisms for supervising or ensuring accountability of the regulators. Leaving aside the auditing function carried out by the Office of the Comptroller, little was done in this respect. The Congress of the Republic stood out both for its passivity and subordination to the Executive. With a few notable exceptions, it provided no counterweight whatsoever.

A controversial issue in the 1990s was the large number of officials who worked in the regulatory agencies (particularly in telecommunications and energy) who retired and then immediately went to work for the firms they had previously regulated. There were also similar instances of employees of the Privatisation Commission moving to the investment banks. A report by a local consultancy considered that this was never seen as a source of concern by the Fujimori administration and that 'these transfers took place most frequently at times when the economy was expanding fast and when there was a shortage of top-rank professionals. The public administration was a shop window for the best known ones.' It also stated that 'it was never clear whether private companies took these officials as a reward for favours received or because they needed high-level people with experience and contacts' (Apoyo, 2001, p. 6).

Such behaviour was tolerated for the best part of a decade and there were no norms put in place to prohibit it. It was only in 1999 that a general law was passed which restricted such practices by prohibiting officials or executives of a regulator working for a regulated company until at least a year had passed from the submission of their resignation.[16]

Finally, it is worth noting that the Framework Law for Regulatory Organisations, passed in the final days of the Fujimori regime, effected no changes whatsoever with respect to the problems I have highlighted, particularly the autonomy of the regulators and their transparency. It simply legally confirmed the status quo in certain sectors, established common rules for the managing councils and appeals tribunals, and defined some specific requisites and incompatibilities with respect to selecting their members.[17]

Change of Regime and Regulatory Reforms

During his eight-month period of office, Valentín Paniagua sought to create the basis for a democratic transition. The economic situation he inherited was deteriorating, and there was a slump in investment and growth. It was in this context that the new government issued a decree to 'strengthen the existing level of autonomy and independence of the regulatory agencies' in order to encourage 'the development of mechanisms that will permit better oversight over their performance'. The decree embodied new ideas about the design of regulatory systems and the impact of such reforms on the development of the industries subject to regulation. The decree posited that 'the autonomy and independence of the regulatory agencies in the exercise of their functions constitutes, among other things, a guarantee for the consumers of these public services as well as for the companies that operate and invest in those sectors'. It therefore obliged the regulatory agencies to 'establish mechanisms that permit (i) citizens to have access to the information administered or produced by them, and (ii) the participation of citizens in decision-making and in evaluating the performance of such agencies'. Among the new requirements was the duty to publish draft norms and resolutions along with their justification, correspondence with the companies and other sectoral organisations, and a report on the advances towards these objectives.

The new rules also included for the first time a system of sequential and staggered appointments for members of managing councils, under which each year one member is replaced.[18] With respect to the appointments procedure, the rules stipulate that details of the candidates' links to interested parties are published and disseminated. With respect to strengthening institutional autonomy, restrictions were introduced for the removal of senior authorities. Such dismissals 'can only take place in cases of gross dereliction, both proven and justified, and after an investigation in which at least ten days is given to present evidence for the defence'.

Toledo was sworn in as the new president in July 2001, and five months later the government issued a decree with the stated purpose of 'establishing additional transparency mechanisms', based on the argument that 'application of these mechanisms will help enhance the legitimacy and predictability of decisions made by regulatory agencies'. Firstly, the rules obliged the regulators to establish and disseminate procedures for setting regulated prices. These included: a list of the relevant organisations; the nature of their legal responsibility; the length of time over which each organisation should publish its judgements; the appeals that the companies can submit and the time limits for doing so. Secondly, the rules established that 'the companies providing services, the consumers and their representative associations have a right of access to the reports, studies, judgements or economic models that provide the basis for resolutions that set regulated prices, except when such information is expressly classified as confidential by the regulatory agency because the information impinges on the interests of one of the parties involved in the procedure'. In this case the declaration that such information is 'confidential' had to be justified with specific criteria through a public resolution by the board of directors of the regulatory agency.

On the other hand, the decree recognised the right of regulated companies and representative consumer associations to 'request and obtain hearings with officials of the regulatory agencies in order to exchange views about the process for setting regulated prices'. The decree made it incumbent on the agencies to publish on their websites the minutes of such meetings. Finally, the decree established that 'the regulatory agencies have a duty, prior to publishing a resolution setting regulated prices, to hold a public hearing in which it makes clear the criteria, methodologies, studies, reports, economic models or judgements that it has used to base its decision for the setting of a regulated price'. It also stated that non-compliance with these duties would be considered a gross dereliction, punishable by dismissal, as well as subject to criminal charges.

Such norms constitute a landmark in bringing principles of transparency and citizen participation to bear in procedures to set regulated prices. They were subsequently raised to the status of a law when, in October 2002, the Law of Transparency and Simplification of Regulatory Tariff Procedures was promulgated.[19] It is worthwhile also mentioning a more recent law that reinforces the autonomy of regulatory institutions and establishes new mechanisms for removal of members of the board. The new law allows board members facing removal a longer period (15 days) to present evidence in their defence. More importantly, the law states that 'in cases of removal, the prime minister will inform within ten working days the Permanent Commission of the Congress of the Republic the reasons for this decision'.[20]

At the same time, the law establishes that 'the regulatory agencies will have one or more Consumer Councils whose purpose is to become channels for participation for agents interested in regulatory activity in each of the sectors involved'. These councils are charged with voicing their opinion regarding the performance of the regulator, participating in public hearings, organising academic events about problems in the sector, receiving and presenting consultations with consumers, and making policy proposals. Finally, the law stipulates that every regulatory agency 'will establish the method by which the Consumer Councils are funded, and to that end they may channel a percentage of the fines imposed by the regulatory agency'.

It will be seen, therefore, that this law raises the requirements that need to be met to remove members from the boards of directors, involving for the first time the legislative branch. Another important innovation, that contrasts with the doctrine upheld under Fujimori, is the establishment of consumer councils with funding from the regulatory agency. This may give rise to problems of dependency on the regulator, raising the risk of them being neutralised in the way they work. It may have been preferable to have adopted a different model.[21] However, in view of the lack of policies or mechanisms in the 1990s for strengthening the involvement of consumers, it was a step in the right direction.

It is now clear that during the transition Paniagua government and subsequently under Toledo, a number of substantive reforms were implemented in the regulation of public services. What factors explain these reforms? First, there was the emergence onto the political scene of new actors and new ideas. While it is difficult to draw a clear distinction between the forces of change associated with the diffusion of new ideas and economic interests, it is clear that intellectual conceptions, ideologies and public opinion (particularly with respect to government control of companies providing public services) have played a critical role in the history of regulation (Baldwin and Cave, 1999, p. 26; MacCraw, 1984).

Second, while one cannot be certain, it is reasonable to argue that the distrust shown by certain sectors towards the privatisation discourse of the 1990s, and more specifically the abusive behaviour of certain companies, has increased public awareness, especially among public officials and political leaders, about the importance of strengthening regulatory systems. It can also be argued that a current of opinion led by groups of professionals, NGOs and sectors of the Church may have had an effect, albeit indirect. These protagonists in political reform have stressed the importance of citizen participation in decision-making, as well as the need for transparency and accountability in public affairs. They have been engaged in activities around the National Accord (Acuerdo Nacional) and the participatory dialogue (*mesas de concertación*) over poverty reduction.

Both at the national and local level, these groups have stressed the need for active public participation in the formulation of budgets, as well as campaigns against corruption and in defence of human rights. In addition, the press and other media have become more active advocates since the end of the Fujimori regime. They have denounced malpractice and on occasions have stood up for the rights of consumers, thereby helping to disseminate new ideas. Television stations have changed hands since the 'Vladivideos' showed their former owners receiving money from Montesinos. Also much of the 'yellow' press failed to survive the Montesinos era.

An important actor has, without a doubt, been Congress. Not only was it responsible for the laws promulgated that are described above, but it also took an active role in providing oversight. Unlike the Congress under Fujimori, the Congress elected in 2001 maintained a consistent interest in the regulation of public services. One of the first decisions in this regard was the creation, in the first legislature, of a Commission for Consumer Defence and for Regulatory Agencies of Public Services. This commission followed the regulatory process with a keen eye, frequently inviting the presidents and officials of the regulatory agencies to account for their actions and explain the basis for their decisions. It also often questioned company representatives, those of consumer associations and officials from the Defensoría. Even though not all the initiatives taken by the Commission have been successful, it is important to note that the experience in regulation is very recent in Peru, and only gradually have we been advancing towards a political culture in tune with the regulatory best practices that can be seen in other countries. Here, as in many other spheres, the political class is in a process of learning and development.

It is also important to acknowledge organisations that under Fujimori were active in the defence of consumer rights and those of citizens more generally: the Peruvian Association of Consumers and Users (Asociación Peruana de Consumidores y Usuarios, ASPEC) and the Defensoría respectively.[22] With the fall of Fujimori, the legitimacy of such organisations was strengthened. Their ideas about the importance of protecting regulatory autonomy, ensuring transparency and promoting citizen participation have encountered growing acceptance among political actors.[23] Last, but by no means least, the regulatory agencies themselves were important actors in the reform process. As noted above, some regulators under Fujimori took steps independently to raise the standard of regulatory transparency. The few spaces for relative autonomy were well used to appoint highly qualified professionals, encourage training and to strengthen team work. As a result, a cooperative sentiment imbued with an ethical spirit developed, in marked contrast to the bureaucratic culture that has traditionally pervaded Peruvian state institutions.

The Pending Agenda

In spite of the advances made in the last few years, there continue to be limitations that reduce the autonomy of regulatory agencies and hamper their performance. First and foremost, there are budgetary constraints. As we have seen, the agencies are financed from contributions from the companies that are regulated, as a percentage of their income.

However, the regulators are subject to austerity measures that, for instance, make it impossible for officials to travel to other countries to consult with their peers or to attend international meetings and events to discuss common problems. Given the dynamism of the regulated industries, participation in such events is of real importance; it would allow them to share information and experiences in decision-making, incorporate the lessons learnt from the experience of others, and improve coordination so as to adopt similar approaches in areas of common concern. Unfortunately, in Peru it is only possible for officials to attend such meetings if they manage to secure external financing for that purpose.

At the same time, while progress has been made in strengthening the autonomy of regulators, there is room for improving the selection procedures for members of the boards of directors, so as to make these procedures more transparent and open to citizen scrutiny. Just as the presidents of these boards are chosen through open competition, the same system could be used to chose all members.[24] A greater degree of involvement by the legislature in their selection should also be commendable, for instance in ratifying the individuals proposed by the executive. The amendment to the Framework Law mentioned above — the duty of the prime minister to inform the Permanent Commission of the Congress about the reasons for removals of board members — is inconsistent with the lack of involvement of the legislature in the procedure for appointments.

On the other hand, it is necessary to be aware that the changes suggested here would make selection procedures more cumbersome, and for this reason such changes might weaken the mechanism of staggered appointments each year now in place by delaying appointments. Even without involving Congress in appointments, there have been delays in replacing those whose terms of office have expired.[25]

Similarly, it is important to bear in mind that participation by congressmen is subject to limitations. On occasions, they have presented legislative proposals on specific or complex technical problems, ignoring the special competences of the regulatory agencies.[26] This points to the need to define with greater precision what the role of Congress should be in regulation. Congress is best qualified to approve generic laws, exercise oversight and control over the various organisations involved. For example, what is required here is approval of laws that have been postponed for many years, such as a law to limit concentration of business ownership. Among the countries that have adopted competition policies, Peru is alone in not adopting a framework for preventing excessive concentration of market power (Távara and Diez Canseco, 2003). The main opposition to such a law came from those running the Peruvian competition agency in the 1990s and from the lawyers of large private companies.[27]

It is also important to establish and strengthen organisational mechanisms for the defence of citizen rights, both within civil society and the state. During the Paniagua government, some questioned the role of the Defensoría in defending consumer rights under the Fujimori regime. They argued that 'it is dangerous and ambitious for the Defensoría del Pueblo to convert itself into the guardian of economic rights, whose defence is in the hands of trade unions and civil society organisations that should emerge with greater strength'. They also expressed concern over the activities of the Defensoría in the sense that it risked 'invading the areas of competence of (regulatory) organisations ... or to interfere arbitrarily in the free play of supply and demand'. In light of this, 'the Defensoría del Pueblo should maintain fluid and close coordination with state entities and a range of economic agents, fulfilling a role of oversight, mediation and promotion rather than one of denunciation'.[28] In response to the above, it is worth pointing out that during the last years of the Fujimori regime, Defensoría officials found themselves obliged to criticise publicly some of the activities of the authorities. They did so by resorting to the few independent media outlets, in order to highlight repeated violations of citizen rights generally, and specifically those of the consumers of public services. This was after seeking and failing to persuade the relevant authorities.[29] Furthermore, it makes little sense trying to exclude the institutions of the state responsible for the defence of citizen rights. The Constitution itself lays down that 'the state defends the interests of consumers and users', and this is quite consistent with strengthening organisations in civil society. It should also be pointed out that, with few exceptions such as the ASPEC case, consumer organisations in Peru are very weak. They have played a secondary role in regulatory activities, even though most of their leaders were disposed to participate when called upon to do so. In most cases, they lack the resources to ensure more effective participation, especially in undertaking studies and hiring outside consultants. The extent of their specialised knowledge is also limited.[30]

Some analysts say that the reforms to date have 'concentrated only on the availability of information and (have done) little to develop the capacities that civil society requires to process that information' (Gallardo and Pérez-Reyes, 2004). As we have seen above, a law has been adopted that amends the Framework Law for Regulatory Agencies, creating consumers' councils in each area. This establishes that each regulatory agency will define how these councils will be financed, providing the potential for developing such capacities. In this context, it is probably worth giving priority to 'help in kind', for instance by assigning resources to hire independent consultants and to hold training and dissemination events to strengthen citizen participation in public hearings and other sorts of consultation. Resources would come from a fund to be allocated on the basis of public competition. As argued above, the design used for the consumers' councils may easily give rise to relations of dependency on the regulator, and this should be avoided. This may be one of the main areas of tension in regulatory activity over the next few years.

Finally, the lack of definition in the sphere of decentralisation of regulatory activity must be overcome. The current legislation upholds that regulatory agencies are decentralised public entities that perform a range of functions.[31] Unfortunately, the Framework Law for Decentralisation, enacted in 2001, gave rise to a number of ambiguities by including shared jurisdictions between national and regional governments with respect to 'promoting, managing and regulating economic and productive activities within each sphere and at each level'.

This lack of precision may give rise to unnecessary conflict in the future.[32] It is important to make explicit certain criteria for revising the normative framework and the process of decentralisation itself. Among these criteria the development of institutional capacities stands out, as does the need for coordination between different levels of government and questions of cost-benefit (such as the generation of economies of scale associated with the centralisation of some functions). In the absence of economies of scale, it is always preferable to assign functions to local government in line with the principle of subsidiarity. For instance, it is clearly the case that the functions of supervision, oversight, conflict resolution and attention to complaints can and should be performed in a decentralised way. Obviously, decentralisation requires the adoption of mechanisms and procedures aimed at facilitating local accountability and citizen participation.

Final Remarks

The main conclusion is that the transition to democracy in Peru has seen significant changes in the normative framework that regulates the provision of public services. In general terms, these changes have enhanced the autonomy of the regulatory agencies and have contributed to promoting transparency and citizen participation. These changes are recent, and there is insufficient evidence so far to show whether or not they have had significant impact on the conduct of economic agents, the development of the regulated industries and on the quality of life.

At the same time, there are a number of issues on the reform agenda that require immediate attention. It would be naïve to think that it is enough simply to promulgate new rules of the game in order to change the reality of things. What make the difference are not the rules of the game adopted but rather the values and democratic processes by which such rules are both designed and implemented (Palast et al., 2003). It is important, finally, to emphasise that the changes in the normative framework I have examined in this chapter took place within a democratic transition that has yet to end in the consolidation of institutions that are able to neutralise and control the exercise of monopoly power.

Nevertheless, it is important to value these changes in so far as they contribute to creating public spaces for debate, civic engagement and accountability. The extent to which these changes impact on people's quality of life will depend on our ability to impart democratic values to these regulatory structures. This chapter has attempted to highlight these changes and to promote further discussion about how to build a legacy of regulatory reform in Peru.

Notes

1   See Gallardo (2000); Torero and Pasco-Font (2001); and Ruiz-Caro (2002).

2   In terms of fiscal income, privatisation brought in US$9.5 billion. The
     figure for committed investment was in excess of US$11 billion. Of the
     total, 84 per cent of receipts were in the following sectors: telecommu-
     nications (38 per cent), electricity (23 per cent), mining (13 per cent) and
     hydrocarbons (ten per cent).

3   In the case of telecommunications, the winning consortium — led by
     Telefónica Internacional — involved the Banco Wiese and the construc-
     tion firm Graña y Montero, with five per cent each. In the energy sector,
     the privatisation of the distributor Edelnor (which supplies half of the
     Lima market) involved participation by the Romero Group and another
     construction firm Cosapi, with 13.9 per cent and 1.1 per cent apiece. In
     the case of Edegel, an electricity generator in the Lima region, Wiese
     Inversiones and Graña y Montero became minority shareholders.

4   A number of sometimes ingenious replies have been made to this para-
     dox. Some allege that insufficient effort went into propagating informa-
     tion as to the benefits. It has also been suggested that the sentiment of
     anti-privatisation in Latin America is due to a failure to grasp the
     achievements and a tendency to forget the performance record of state
     companies. Another explanation is that the benefits of privatisation have
     been obscured by poor performance records in macroeconomics. More
     recently, the argument has gained currency that attitudes reflect the poor
     performance of the regulators.

5   The resources generated by privatisation were explicitly included in the
     Letters of Intent signed by Peru with the IMF. The structure of incentives
     during privatisation also explains the primacy given to this objective.
     Indeed, the consultants and investment banks involved in the contracts
     had a direct interest in the companies being sold at the highest price pos-
     sible in order to maximise their own honorariums and commissions.

6   I borrow this phrase from Santiago Urbiztondo. An example includes
     the concession contracts for fixed telephony in 1994. These established
     a timetable for tariff adjustment for a five-year period, during which the
     functions of the regulator were limited mainly to supervising the fulfil-
     ment of this timetable.

7   The privatisation of Aeroperu, the national flag carrier, falls into this
     category.

8   Up until the enactment of this law, normative functions with respect to
     oversight of quality and safety came under the General Electricity

Controller (Dirección General de Electricidad, DGE) of the Ministry of Energy and Mines. Oversight functions were then transferred to OSINERG, and afterwards the CTE came to form part of OSINERG as the Joint Management of Tariff Regulation (Gerencia Adjunta de Regulación de Tarifas). Normative functions still come under the Ministry.

9   When this was approved in August 1994 (DS 092) a norm was included which, to some extent, limited the possibilities of arbitrary dismissal of members. Indeed, Article 50 established as a cause for dismissal (to be declared by the president of the republic) 'in cases of negligence, incompetence or immorality duly verified'. This formula was partially retained under a subsequent law that modified the makeup of the management councils of OSINERG and the CTE (Law 27010 of 10 December 1998), which left out a specific enumeration of causes of dismissal.

10   Article 8 of Law 26734 established that members of the managing council of OSINERG are nominated by the president through a resolution endorsed by the energy minister, who has the power to propose two council members. For his part, the prime minister proposes a slate from which two council members are chosen. The last one is chosen from the slate presented by the finance minister.

11   Supreme Decree No. 005–97–MEM, Article 10.

12   In the case of the CTE, two of the five members were chosen from slates proposed by the electricity distribution and generating concessionaires, respectively. The other three were chosen by the president. In OSIPTEL, the management council had six members. Three were appointed by the president, two were representatives of the firms, and one was chosen by the consumers.

13   See, for example, the 'Country Report of the National Integrity System', carried out by the Grupo Apoyo for Transparency International, as well as the report of the Iniciativa Nacional Anticorrupción (2001).

14   OSINERG, by contrast, was noted for its opacity during these years. On several occasions, it refused to respond to requests for information by the Defensoría. On one occasion, its president even decided that it would refuse to receive correspondence from the Defensoría.

15   According to its transparency regulations, 'The directors, officials and employees of OSIPTEL, either on active service or not, are obliged not to transmit to third parties, whether in part or in full, any information

they have in their possession or have had knowledge of in the carrying out of their duties, except where such information is public knowledge or where a judicial resolution requires them to divulge it.'

16   Supreme Decree (DS) 023–PCM. According to the Apoyo report quoted here 'the restriction of a year imposed in 1999 was a result of Fujimori's displeasure when informed that a person had been a member of an INDE-COPI commission who had also been contracted as a consultant for a private firm in a case taken up by another regulator' (Apoyo, 2001, p. 6).

17   Law 27332, promulgated on 27 July 2000. This established that members of managing councils had to fulfil certain requirements, namely: (i) to be a professional with no less than five years experience; and (ii) to have the requisite professional qualifications and standing. Among the incompatibilities, it mentioned holding more than one per cent of the shares of the regulated company; being a director, advisor, official, consultant or employee of such a company; being legally barred by a judicial disposition; or being a director or representative of a bankrupt company.

18   So as to implement the staggered reappointment of council members, the decree established, exceptionally, new periods of office for those then in office. This was one year for the presidents of the managing council, as of the date of their nomination. In practice, this meant the removal of those who had occupied this position under the previous government. The transitional government initiated the selection process of new presidents by means of an open recruitment process, and this process was concluded during the Toledo government.

19   Law 27838, promulgated 3 October 2002.

20   Law 28337, promulgated in August 2004. It amends the Framework Law for Regulatory Agencies promulgated at the tail end of the Fujimori regime, and incorporates all the norms contained in Supreme Decree (DS) 032–PCM, approved under Paniagua, improving on some of these.

21   Consideration should be given to the establishment of independent user councils so that these can provide more effective oversight.

22   For a summary of ASPEC and its activities, see its website: www.aspec.org.pe.

23   Under Fujimori, the Defensoría encountered many limitations in taking part in activities geared to the regulation of public services. Under the new regime, this situation changed dramatically. The Defensoría was invited to provide an analysis of the regulation of public services to the first session of the congressional commission.

24   Some ministries have taken the initiative of organising public competitions
        in order to select their representatives on the managing councils. Still, there
        is no evidence to show that all public bodies are complying with DS
        032–2001 in using 'a procedure that guarantees at least the possibility that
        interested parties become acquainted with existing candidacies'.

25   Such delays apparently are due to political entanglements within the
        executive, and these impact negatively on the operations of the boards
        of directors. These have had to operate with four or even three mem-
        bers for prolonged periods of time, instead of the five full members
        specified in the legislation.

26   An illustrative example was a bill, based on no technical criteria what-
        soever, to establish interconnection charges for mobile telephony. In
        some instances, the presence of television cameras in Congress has led
        congressmen to indulge in a demagogic behaviour.

27   Opposition to regulating mergers has been strong also within regulators
        like OSIPTEL, whose board of directors chose to ignore a draft bill in
        this area in early 2003. These predated the acquisition by Telefónica of
        the assets of BellSouth in various Latin American countries.

28   See the Road Map developed in 2001 by a team led by Richard Webb,
        Gabriel Ortiz de Zevallos, Juan Julio Wicht and Jaime de Althaus.

29   See the various reports by the Defensoría to Congress. These are avail-
        able at www.ombudsman.gob.pe.

30   As one ASPEC leader has noted, most of their affiliates only join to
        resolve personal problems, and once these are resolved they cease to
        belong.

31   Among these are the functions of supervision (ensure compliance with
        legal norms), regulation (set tariffs), establishing norms, oversight and
        punishment (impose penalties for infraction of norms and contractual
        obligations), conflict resolution (between firms and between firms and
        users) and resolution of user complaints.

32   Article 36 of Law 27783. The Regional Government Law gives to region-
        al governments a series of duties linked to policies of infrastructure devel-
        opment. In the case of telecommunications, it establishes that one of the
        functions of regional governments is 'to formulate, approve, execute, eval-
        uate, direct, control and administer plans and policies with respect to the
        telecommunications of the region, in line with national policies and
        regional plans'.

11

Financing Institutional Development in Peru

Richard Webb

The 1990s, above all the years 1992–95, saw a wave of institutional innovation in Peru. Looking back to earlier decades, however, one finds a continual process of institutional change, from grass-roots initiatives to constitutional reforms. Many of those changes contributed to political, economic and social development. Although development took place, it was not sustained. Failure in this respect was blamed on previous reforms, prompting new changes, described as 'institutional development'. However, as the record shows, change has not always meant development. The Peruvian experience, in the end, consists of a great variety of institutional forms so that, in a way, continuous change has become an institution in itself, and, at the risk of slight exaggeration, it could be said that the one institution that Peru has not experienced is institutional stability.

The question for this chapter concerns the relationship between institutional change and financing. Two years ago, when asked whether he planned to carry out a reform of the state, Peru's then minister of economy and finance, Jaime Quijandría, replied, 'We don't have the funds for that now,' an odd reply in view of the wastefulness of government activity. The idea that institutional improvement requires up-front funding is widely shared, but this chapter suggests that it is questionable.

The link between institutional development and money is complex. Money is sometimes provided by an external agent in exchange for institutional change, as in structural adjustment loans that carry conditionalities. In other cases it serves to enable the costs of change, usually in the form of technical assistance or small loans for training and equipment. Funding also serves to empower agents of change, as when funds for social expenditures are channelled through the finance ministry, whose hand is thereby strengthened vis-à-vis other ministries. A different sort of relationship exists when an institution is strengthened by being assigned earmarked revenues or authorised to generate its own revenues. But often it is not the availability, rather the lack of funds, that drives change, whether it is a fiscal crisis that pushes a government into improving tax administration or to reform pension schemes, or a recession that stimulates families to create self-help communal kitchens.

'Institutions' and 'development' are loosely defined concepts, open moreover to definitional disagreement. This discussion will focus mostly on efforts to improve the rules and organisational structures that govern the actions of the state and the market economy, whether or not the result is a sustained improvement. Changes in social institutions, such as those related to family, justice and religion are not examined.

This chapter reviews institutional development in Peru in a historical perspective, from the 1960s until to the 1990s, seeking to examine the interaction of funding and change. What emerges from this historical account is a mixture of continuous fiddling with the organisational structures of government, continuous though pendular evolution with respect to the institutions that govern the economy, and occasional bursts of institutional activism. The period under review divides into four parts.

The 1962 Junta and the First Belaunde Administration (1962–68)

The year 1962 marked one such burst of activism, when a military junta seized and held power for 12 months. Most notably, the junta created a planning institute, thereby developing a broader framework of economic and social planning, and established the legal foundations for agrarian reform and for state ownership of the oil industry. The planning office and agrarian reform initiatives were designed and carried out with external technical assistance, with the United Nations Economic Commission for Latin America (ECLA) playing the main role. In the area of finance, the junta created a state housing bank to provide support for the expansion of a newly-created system of savings and loan associations. These institutions were highly successful, but the entire system of housing bank and *mutuales* was wiped out by hyperinflation in the late 1980s. For the most part, the junta's initiatives required little additional expenditure, so that financing did not play a significant role.

The succeeding, democratic government, led by Fernando Belaunde (1963–68), focused more on an ambitious programme of infrastructure and social spending than on institutions or organisational issues. For most of his term, Belaunde's institutional initiatives were evolutionary. He continued the steady creation of new semi-autonomous government spending agencies, particularly regional development corporations (Cordes), financed by earmarked tax revenues. One innovation was Cooperación Popular, a developmental programme targeted at small communities that encouraged self-help by offering technical assistance and the use of construction equipment to communities that embarked on small-scale public works. This was accompanied by a Peruvian version of the US Peace Corps, whereby youths volunteered to spend time working in rural communities. Belaunde's most radical and profound institutional move was political: in 1963 and 1966 he called municipal elections to re-establish elected local governments, reversing four decades of appointed mayors and extreme government centralisation.

In his last few months in government, however, between June and August 1968, there was a sudden burst of major, reformist legislation on fiscal and financial matters. This uncharacteristic development was a response to the fiscal and balance of payments crisis that had brought about a devaluation of the currency in 1967, along with a jump in inflation. A political agreement broke a congressional deadlock and led to the 'Special Powers Act', under which Congress delegated legislative authority to the executive for a period of 60 days (Philip, 1978). During that period, the cabinet under Prime Minister Manuel Ulloa raised taxes and decreed nine major laws (*leyes orgánicas*) that reformed the central bank, other state banks, and other key financial and corporate laws. Most of these laws remained in effect during the subsequent Revolutionary Government of the Armed Forces and the governments of Belaunde and Alan García in the 1980s (Kuczynski, 1977).

The Military Government 1968–1980

The leftist military coup of October 1968 opened the way for another round of institutional innovation. The new government, headed by General Juan Velasco, was strongly predisposed to reforms, by ideology and by managerial culture. Though Peru had experienced military dictatorships in the past, the Velasco regime was the first 'institutional' military government in the sense that it involved a corporate commitment by the armed forces as a whole. The military moved into government wholesale, staffing almost all top level and many middle-level government positions, and during its first two to three years in office produced a new burst of innovation touching on a wide range of social, economic, political and administrative institutions.

Financing, whether internal or external, seems to have had very little to do with any of those changes. The economy was doing well at the time, and the foreign aid community was largely sympathetic to the overall thrust of Velasco's policies. Oil nationalisation was a significant exception to that agreement, but it was not seen as connected to other initiatives. The foreign aid community at the time was not pressing an agenda of institutional change, other than the World Bank's longstanding insistence on planning which, in this case, did not need to be pushed since the role of state planning was immediately upgraded by the military. The government's institutional agenda required little financing. It consisted largely of administrative re-engineering, involving an increased role of government and worker cooperatives in key productive sectors established through legislation and expropriation. It also included political changes that did involve new organisations, but which entailed relatively small budgets within the overall structure of government.[1] Perhaps the most successful reform in terms of its developmental effects was the least political, least noticed and probably the least costly in terms of implementation, namely new government personnel management procedures. The core institution for those procedural changes was a relatively small but powerful office, the National Institute of Personnel Administration (Instituto Nacional de Administración de Personal, INAP), and many of its new managerial procedures have since remained in effect.

Institutional change returned to the agenda during the final years of the military government, particularly between 1978 and July 1980. Its most significant manifestation was a Constituent Assembly, elected in 1978 and which approved a new Constitution in 1979, but also the stabilisation package adopted to deal with a financial and inflationary crisis. The need for emergency financing opened the door to international financial institutions, and these were able to thrust their agenda into national policy-making. That agenda, however, was almost entirely focused on policy, and involved little by way of institutional measures. The important institutional changes of the moment were those introduced through political bargaining in the Constituent Assembly, including a return to a subsidiary role for the state in direct economic activity, central bank autonomy, the enhancement of executive powers and the extension of the franchise to illiterates. Financing was not required to carry out these institutional decisions. It is particularly interesting that the constitutional decision in favour of central bank autonomy was entirely absent from the IMF's agenda, and instead the decision was largely a one-man initiative by a senior central bank official.[2]

One institutional innovation of the late 1970s that had positive and lasting effects — the creation of communal kitchens (*comedores populares*) — resulted, not from the availability of money, but rather its absence. It was during those years of recession and inflation in the late 1970s that communal kitchens began to appear in the urban marginal areas of Lima and other large cities, entirely at the initiative of the settlers.[3] The kitchens were only noticed later by politicians, who began to provide them with subsidies and thereby seek their cooptation.

The Second Belaunde and García Governments (1980–1990)

The 1980s was a relatively quiet decade for institutional development. A possible explanation for this is that both the Belaunde government (1980–85) and that of Alan García (1985–90) were overwhelmed by stabilisation and internal security problems (in addition to a sharp bout of El Niño in 1983) though crises have produced institutional responses in other regimes. The agendas of the Washington-based international financial institutions were highly influential during the Belaunde period, but institutional development was not yet part of the pre-Washington Consensus agenda. Neither president had the ideological leanings that might have resulted in new institutions, or in institutional re-engineeering. Under both, the governmental tool kit was limited to policies and spending, perhaps because both were unwilling or unable to focus on medium-term and even less on long-term objectives. One can speculate that, in García's case, his dominant personality ran counter to the delegation that is inherent to institutions, in which rules and organisational systems replace individual discretion.[4] This anti-institutional bias was reinforced by the highly clientelistic nature of the APRA government.

In the private sector, too, there was more institutional continuity than creativity, despite a major innovation represented by the creation of an umbrella business sector organisation, the Confederación Nacional de Instituciones Empresariales Privadas (Confiep) in 1983.

Nonetheless, four initiatives by the García government bear mentioning. One was a make-work programme, the Programa de Apoyo de Ingreso Temporal (PAIT), which operated at a significant scale during only two years, between 1986 and 1988. Treasury funds were crucial to this initiative, first to make PAIT possible during the boom years 1986–87 and, with the onset of a fiscal crisis in 1998, their absence helped bring about its demise. What is noteworthy in the case of PAIT is that the concept of make-work programmes was almost universally frowned upon at the time, by both left and right, despite the success of a similar scheme in Chile, the Programa de Empleo Temporal, in cushioning the impact of that country's severe stabilisation and adjustment programmes in the mid-1970s and early 1980s. A second and also unorthodox initiative was an inexpensive programme of public dialogues between *campesino* leaders and government officials, the so-called *rimanacuy*. Once again, the programme was short-lived, run as a series of personal events by García rather than as a fully institutionalised programme. The third institutional initiative was the failed and politically damaging effort to nationalise banks in 1987. Public reaction proved surprisingly negative to this, and García was forced to backtrack. And fourth, in 1988 García finally gave the green light to the long-postponed decentralisation process mandated by the 1979 Constitution. However, soon after the election of regional assemblies under García, the process was interrupted by the new regime of Alberto Fujimori, who suspended the transfer of authority to the elected regional governments. García's steps, however, had kindled regional demands, and when government changed hands again in 2000, regionalisation was finally allowed to proceed.

However, the deliberate institutional change of the 1980s was less significant than the unintended institutional destruction that resulted from wrong-headed policies, severe recession with hyperinflation, and cumulative corruption over the decade. The extent of the damage is hard to measure, but the indications of institutional regression are many. Patronage and clientelism ran rampant, destroying what there had been of merit-based personnel recruitment, promotion and management procedures. The hiring of teachers, a standard device for clientelism, expanded at the phenomenal rate of 7.4 per cent per annum over the decade, doubling the total number of teachers. Though this could be seen as positive from a social standpoint, the methods used for hiring neglected all existing recruitment standards and requirements. At the start of the decade, 80 per cent of all teachers held teaching degrees, but only 19 per cent of those hired between 1980 and 1990 had degrees. Most of the personnel records disappeared from the Education Ministry. This destructive administrative style was common throughout the public sector. Even the central bank saw an 80 per cent increase in the number of employees, as well as a lowering of hiring and promotion standards. Worse, the introduction of multiple exchange rates and import controls in 1986 brought corruption into the institution.[5] The overall degradation of existing institutions because of large-scale, undisciplined hiring was, of course, made possible by the availability of funding.

Unintended institutional destruction took on a new form between 1988 and 1991 as a consequence of the economic crisis that affected both government and private institutions. During that brief period, many of the institutions of government were brought to their knees. With the collapse of funding, institutions lost their authority and administrative capacity. Government spending fell 30 per cent in real terms between 1987 and 1990. From 1991 the Fujimori government authorised large-scale dismissals of employees, which added to a mass voluntary emigration from the public sector, much of it going to other countries. As usual, leavers included many of the best. During this period, the private sector also lost institutional capacity as a result of emigration, collapse in investment and the impoverishment of the universities. Self-help organisations, however, continued to develop. It could be argued that the indirect effect of the 1980s policy disaster and financial crisis was to downsize the state and legitimise private economic and civic activity, thereby contributing to institutional reform.

The Fujimori Period (1990–2000)

As noted above, Peru experienced a new burst of institutional initiative between 1991 and the mid-1990s. In the first moments, the overriding goals of the new government were economic stabilisation and the fight against terrorism, but these were soon followed up and reinforced by a coherent package of policies and institutional innovations. The centre-piece was a new constitution, approved in 1993. Executive attention to institutional development increased as stabilisation was consolidated, terrorism checked and Congress shut down. The closure of Congress, in itself an institutional setback, gave the executive a freer hand to proceed with the large-scale dismissals of government personnel that were prerequisites for several major reforms, such as that carried out in the tax collecting agencies. The main thrust of the policy and institutional package was to formalise the de facto reduction in state powers through deregulation and privatisation, and to create institutions that would regulate and promote competitive markets. The package had two other major objectives: to reinforce financial control within the state and to create a strong anti-poverty programme.

These changes enjoyed substantial legitimacy in the media and among political groups, to a large extent because they appeared as the inevitable and necessary alternative to policies that had produced disaster during the 1980s. Professional opinion came to be dominated by younger professionals, many trained abroad. They were predisposed towards markets and open economies, ideas given further legitimacy by the example of other developing countries. At the same time, however, the general thrust of the reforms was strongly encouraged and even pushed by the foreign aid community. Even before he assumed office, Alberto Fujimori appeared to have decided to accept the quid pro quo offered by the international financial community: a settlement of the external debt plus new financing, conditioned on an IMF agreement and close adherence to the policies recommended by the international financial institutions. By the early 1990s this 'Washington' agenda had evolved with the addition of 'second generation' reforms, seen as a necessary complement to the structural reforms of the 1980s. Many of these second generation reforms were institutional in nature. Fujimori empowered Peruvian technocrats who believed strongly in such reforms, and they in turn worked comfortably with the donors. Thus, the need to settle Peru's external financial situation and re-open access to external capital worked hand-in-hand with the turn in domestic opinion in favour of a more open and market-oriented economy.[6]

To varying degrees, specific institutional initiatives were supported by external financing, but no one reform seems to have been wholly dependent on that backing. Institutional changes were largely low-cost items. However, outside finance was decisive in cases where reforms were obstructed not so much by lack of funding but because procedures for the use of government funds for hiring, promoting, spending, accounting and auditing were cumbersome and slow. In a context where political windows of opportunity are short-lived, the availability of more flexible outside funding acquired a premium in achieving reform goals.

Notable institutional reforms of this period include two tax collecting agencies, the National Superintendency for Tax Administration (Superintendencia Nacional de Administración Tributaria, Sunat) and the customs office; the creation of the National Institute for the Defence of Competition and Protection of Intellectual Property (Instituto Nacional de Defensa de la Competencia y de la Protección de la Propriedad Intelectual, Indecopi) to regulate foreign and domestic competition; the shackling of the central bank (forbidden by the 1993 Constitution to lend to the government and severely restricted in its capacity to lend to banks); and the reinforcement of financial sector control through a new banking law. Also, special agencies were created to carry out privatisation, the umbrella entity the Commission for the Promotion of Private Investment (Comisión de Promoción de la Inversión Privada, Copri) and sectoral agencies called Special Commissions for the Promotion of Private Investment (Comisiones Especiales para la Promoción de la Inversión Privadas, Cepris).

The internal reform achieved by Sunat and the customs administration (Aduanas), and the institutionalisation of Indecopi were all facilitated by the substantial financial autonomy enjoyed by each agency. The initial Sunat reform was made possible by the 'free' use of a team of central bank officials, and was sustained later by the earmarking of a fraction of tax revenues for its expenses (Durand and Thorp, 1998). The customs service is largely financed by a similar earmarking of a share of its revenues. And about 80 per cent of Indecopi's budget is financed by revenues generated by fees. A related common feature of these institutional developments was the high degree of administrative autonomy enjoyed by the new or reformed agencies. In the case of Indecopi, the agency enjoys considerable administrative and policy autonomy, but in addition, it serves as an umbrella organisation for seven commissions, each charged with a regulatory task, and each manned by an autonomous board recruited from the private sector. Under this highly novel arrangement, separate and autonomous commissions regulate consumer protection, unfair competition, market access, dumping and subsidies by foreign countries, free competition, technical regulations and bankruptcy procedures.

A more detailed view of the customs reform is provided in the box below.

Box 1. The Customs Reform

The customs office in Peru (Aduanas) was transformed over the course of the 1990s. Once a byword for corruption and inefficiency, it became an internationally admired model of modern public administration. Revenues grew twice as fast as exports and imports, even though tariff levels were cut to a fraction of previous levels. Goods that once sat for weeks, even months, awaiting clearance and completion of interminable red tape, were dispatched in under 24 hours.[7] Business activity in Peru now suffers less insecurity because assessed import charges and taxes are no longer wildly unpredictable. In 1990 the Aduanas became the first public institution in Peru to obtain an ISO 9000 rating,[8] and indeed, the second customs office in the world to do so.[9] International organisations have pointed to the Peruvian customs office as a model of reform, and the office has provided technical assistance to other countries.

Most of the changes took place over about four years, from late 1990 to 1994. The reform consisted of a sequence of legislative and administrative initiatives, each adding cumulatively to the process. Significant steps continued even after 1994: the present General Customs Law, which made significant modifications to the previous legislation, dates from January 1997. In fact, one of the major achievements of the Aduanas has been to create a capacity for continuous on-going change.

The reform was forcefully opposed and obstructed, particularly in its early stages, by Congress. Customs officials mobilised to protect their jobs and perks. Business lobbies also objected, since they feared that facilitating imports would, in effect, reduce their import protection and eliminate the basis for special treatment that favoured only a few. Reform had no public support, and would have been stymied had Fujimori not personally and continuously supported the superintendent, Carmen Higaonna. He met with her frequently in the first years and screened her from pressure to use the Aduanas payroll for political patronage. Congressional opposition disappeared when Congress itself was closed by Fujimori in April 1992.

How autonomous was the customs office? By law, it is a 'decentralised public institution under the Ministry of Economy and Finance that enjoys administrative, economic, budgetary, financial and technical autonomy'.[10] As noted above, however, the superintendent is nominated by the economy minister, selected by the president and appointed by a cabinet resolution. The superintendent, in turn, can hire and fire all other Aduanas officials. In other words, the office enjoys administrative and policy autonomy to the extent that its actions are meeting with presidential approval. The Aduanas, likewise, is formally under the aegis of the Ministry of Economy and Finance and reports to it on a monthly and annual basis.

Its budgetary autonomy, moreover, is equally contingent on governmental decision. By law, it is assigned three per cent of import revenues, and can charge fees for its services, but those rights can be modified by a simple majority in Congress at the executive's request. More easily, in periods of financial stringency, the Aduanas can be persuaded to share in general cost-cutting, and hand over part of its three per cent to the Treasury, as occurred in 1999. Until then the customs had neither received nor returned funds to the Treasury. It must be noted, however, that financial independence was tolerated during a period of rapidly rising import revenues, when larger customs revenues helped legitimate a large and expanding Aduanas budget. The growth of its budget greatly facilitated its investment in personnel and in equipment, infrastructure, and training. It is not certain whether, in a situation of fiscal constraint, that it would be allowed to retain the same share of customs revenues.

Two other major institutional innovations during the Fujimori period require mention. One was the creation of the Fund for Development and Social Compensation (Fondo de Desarrollo y Compensación Social, Foncodes) in 1991 to carry out social spending targeted at the rural poor. It was strongly motivated by the war against terrorism, and received substantial budgetary support from the World Bank, the Inter-American Development Bank (IDB) and other external aid agencies. This financial support was undoubtedly crucial during the early stages of Foncodes, between 1991 and 1993 in particular, when the government spending remained constrained by high inflation rates and recession. However, later in the decade, though such support continued, it is unlikely that the programme would have suffered any major reduction without such backing. One reason for this is that the subversive threat that had given rise to the programme had not disappeared entirely, but a more important reason may have been that the programme acquired a political function during Fujimori's electoral campaigns: during the constitutional referendum in 1993, his re-election campaigns of 1995 and 2000, and in municipal elections. One of the contributions of Foncodes that should be highlighted was the establishment of poverty-targeting as a widely used procedure in Peru. Before 1990, the term poverty was not part of the government's operational discourse or procedures; but by the late 1990s it had become routine and obligatory. Foncodes introduced both the explicit rhetoric and the statistical apparatus of income measurement of poverty-alleviation, replacing vague and inaccurate concepts such as 'social objectives', 'social justice' and 'employment generation', which had been reference points previously for government discourse and in justifying public spending. A second innovation was a land titling programme run by the Commission for the Formalisation of Property (Comisión de Formalización de la Propiedad, Cofopri), created in 1996, though the legal procedures for mass titling had begun in the late 1980s. Cofopri was supported by World Bank funds, but was a small item in the overall budget and could easily have been financed directly by the government.

This impressive list of successful innovations, most of which survived the change of government in 2000, stands in sharp contrast to Fujimori's failure to improve core government institutions, especially education, health, security and justice. In each of those sectors, efforts were mounted to initiate institutional reforms, with substantial external financial and technical assistance, but to little effect. Education reform was given major financial support by the World Bank, the IDB and bilateral agencies, with special emphasis paid to improving teaching quality, teaching methods and the curriculum; increasing parental and community participation; and to raising the priority afforded to rural education. End-of-decade evaluations of those efforts all concluded that the change achieved had been minimal, in spite of the large financial outlays involved in each case.

This failure cannot be attributed to a lack of appreciation by Fujimori of the importance of either education or of public administration. In 1992 he published three major decrees to reform educational administration. He also launched the Communal Education Councils (Consejos Comunales de Educación, Comuned), a programme to create community participation in school management, starting in 10,200 schools. However, in May 1993 he reversed this policy, saying that he had changed his mind. It seems likely that this was to avoid confrontation with Sutep, the radical teachers union, which was believed to have links to the terrorist movement. At the same time, he may have seen the political value of the enormous resources of the education budget for the purposes of patronage. A similar failure to follow through with judicial reform brought Fujimori into open confrontation with the World Bank, which publicly cancelled its loan for that reform.

The story in health was somewhat different. Primary and rural health received top priority and unprecedented financial support from both external and domestic sources. Institutionally, health establishments were given greater autonomy and authority to achieve self-financing, and the management of many primary health posts was delegated to local communities through the Local Council for the Administration of Health (Consejo Local de Administración de Salud, CLAS) programme. Much of this advance in the field of health survived the Fujimori period, though bureaucrats and politicians who lost authority and opportunities for patronage have been steadily trying to erode local autonomy. Meanwhile, delegation based on financial autonomy has worked against the original anti-poor objective. Public sector health personnel and their establishments have in effect become quasi-private, funding themselves by charging patients and seeking a higher income level clientele. In the end, it could be argued that health reforms contained an internal contradiction brought about by an unwillingness to meet the full financial cost of a public health service for the poor.

There was a larger paradox in Fujimori's efforts at institutional reform. In several areas of government, notably in education and health, but also in justice and in many smaller units of the civil service, the administrative solution to bureaucratic and legal obstacles was to ignore them. Quick fixes were therefore adopted as answers. The most striking example is that of the short-term labour contracts used to circumvent the job stability and benefits enjoyed by civil servants. A large expansion of primary health establishments was staffed in this way, by hiring an army of doctors, nurses and technicians, originally on three-month, but later six- and twelve-month contracts that carried none of the normal civil service benefits such as pensions, health insurance and vacation entitlements. This finessed the law in a way that was possible under an authoritarian government and with the political legitimacy given by the economic crisis and terrorist insurgency, but which in the long run was to prove unsustainable under a weak democratic regime. Since 2000 this army of *contratados* in the health and education sectors has pressed successfully for full, tenured appointment with the social benefits provided by labour legislation. Though the immediate cost is financial, at a deeper level there is an institutional cost in the form of a failure to reform the civil service career.[11] Indeed, partly in response to the abuse implicit in the short-term contract, civil service unions with public support have been winning even more favourable benefits, especially in tenure. Ultimately, these are financially unviable and worsen root problems within the civil service, the lack of motivation and discipline.

Self-financing by government institutions, through the introduction of fees and other charges for services, became an accepted practice as a way to survive the fiscal crisis of the early 1990s, and it was given legitimacy by the concept of 'cost recovery'. The indirect effect, however, was to privatise much of the government's public goods function. In the Ministry of Health, for instance, the share in total spending funded by fees and other own income of health establishments rose from 6.7 per cent in 1980 to 13.0 per cent in 2003. And, by 2001, the National Institute of Statistics and Informatics (INEI) was devoting at least half its staff time to servicing the needs of private clients who had paid for special studies or statistical data

bases. Other examples could be mentioned whereby the real purpose of
government agencies was distorted by self-financing.

An analogous 'quick fix' that offers an attractive institutional innovation is the land titling programme administered by Cofopri, and
designed to sidestep the impossible formalities that put regular titling
out of reach for the poor. However, Cofopri land titles are granted by
skipping search and registration procedures, and do not carry the same
degree of security as regular titles. While the Cofopri solution might be
seen as better than no title — just as the rural teacher or doctor under
contract is better than none — the underlying institutional problem of
unrealistic, impractical and financially unsustainable legal requirements
has not been resolved and may have actually become worse. In such
cases, the obstacle to lasting institutional improvement has not been a
lack of funding; rather the political inability (or unwillingness) to challenge special interests.

The Paniagua and Toledo Governments (2000–05)

The Paniagua and Toledo administrations showed little concern for
institutional change, with the significant exception of political and
administrative decentralisation through the creation of a tier of regional governments. Indeed, the indirect effect of many government practices has been institutional erosion.

One of Toledo's first acts as president was to call elections to regional governments, initially on the basis of existing departments but with
the possibility that — subject to local referendums — larger regions
would be created through the merger of existing departments. At the
same time, the National Decentralisation Council (Consejo Nacional de
Descentralización, CND) came into existence. This was an executive
instrument charged with the progressive transfer of responsibilities
from central to regional government, on the basis of the proven capacity of the latter to assume them. A third step towards decentralisation
during this period was the substantial increase in the budgets of local,
district and provincial government; their share of total public spending
rose from 4.3 per cent in 2002 to 7.4 per cent in 2005. This was a rather
more dramatic increase than that of regional government, which
increased from 12.5 per cent in 2002 to 15.9 per cent in 2005.[12]

Although the legal framework contained numerous gaps and internal contradictions, and although the process of transfer was in some cases based more on de facto decisions than on the written norms (for example, the appointment of regional government managers), there is little doubt that decentralisation is now irreversible.

The financial implications of this process have been controversial. Most forecasts were that decentralisation would be an inevitable source of additional government spending, if only because many functions and staff positions end up being duplicated. But in addition, decentralisation is expected to weaken the centralised system of fiscal control. However, there is little evidence that, under Toledo at least, decentralisation has actually resulted in major fiscal costs, or that there has been a build-up in prohibited forms of regional indebtedness. Despite the duplication of functions, the cost of regionalisation does not appear to have been a major obstacle to its gradual advance towards consolidation as a historic change in the way in which Peru is governed.

The negative side of the institutional balance sheet since 2000 has been an erosion in technical autonomy and in meritocratic procedures in many government offices. Backsliding is evident in several of the institutions that were created or reformed during the 1990s, such as the regulatory institutions and those that administer social programmes, as well as many of the older and more centralised agencies, such as the judiciary and the Ministries of Health and Education. For the most part, the erosion of institutions has been a consequence of increased political interference in day-to-day management and of increased clientelism and corruption. It is paradoxical that in almost all cases, this institutional erosion has happened despite on-going reform and modernisation programmes, some inherited from the previous government and others of more recent origin.

Indecopi, for instance, suffered from continual resignations by members of its various autonomous commissions. The standing of the Ombudsman's Office (Defensoría del Pueblo) was undermined by the political failure to designate a new ombudsman. Politically-motivated nominations at the central bank had a similar effect, with excessive rotation of jobs and the inability of the bank president to appoint officials. The modernised customs administration was integrated into the tax administration (Sunat) for political purposes, and ended up losing some of those efficiency gains. Foncodes was colonised by political appointees. The deterioration in public education standards, manifest in previous decades, was exacerbated by an excessive rotation of posts, political appointments and weakness in not standing up to union pressures. As we have seen in other chapters, reforms in the internal security apparatus and in the judiciary were paralysed because of political and bureaucratic interference. In none of these instances was the erosion in institutions a product of lack of finance. Indeed, the pattern of causation may have been the exact opposite: the appetite for political interference and corruption was heightened by the fact that finance was available over different areas of government.

Conclusions

From this brief survey of recent Peruvian institutional history, it is clear that the process of institutional change has been almost permanent and highly variable, but that in few instances has there been much correlation between change and the availability of finance. Indeed, where finance has played an important role, the pattern of causation has been precisely the opposite: it was those periods of fiscal crisis that drove the most dramatic instances of institutional innovation. The Toledo government appears to confirm this thesis. The lack of interest and concern for institutional development during this period has been associated with a relative fiscal bonanza which has reduced the concern for more effective spending.

Notes

1   Public external debt rose rapidly during the 1970s, but as a consequence of purchases of military equipment and of borrowing for large infrastructure and industrial projects unrelated to institutional changes.

2   Alonso Polar, then general manager of the central bank, had been introduced to the concept of autonomy in central banking when he first joined the bank in the late 1960s. In 1978 Polar grasped the opportunity afforded by the proposed constitutional reform, sought audiences with the Banking and Constitutional committees of the Assembly for his idea, and was successful in persuading them in favour of the idea. By happy coinci-

dence, his father was then a key senator and president of the Congressional Banking Committee.

3   Real per capita GDP fell six per cent between 1976 and 1979, while modern sector wages in Lima, in manufacturing, commerce, construction, banking and non-government services declined from an index of 100 in 1973 to 65 in 1979. Wage figures are from Weeks (1985) and Webb and Fernández Baca (1990).

4   See Graham (1992). Also Crabtree (1992). Graham says, 'The way in which programs such as PAIT and Rimanacuy were implemented — always from above and with no respect for existing organizations — limited their potential' (p. 131).

5   Parallel official and market exchange rates existed in the early 1980s, but with a small differential. The gap was two per cent in December 1984. Subsequently it rose to 24 per cent in December 1985 and then jumped to 641 per cent in December 1987 as an effect of tighter controls.

6   However, institutions created for social redistribution, especially Foncodes, soon began to lose their strict technical and social character and to be used for political purposes.

7   According to the annual report of the Aduanas (Servicio de Aduanas, 1995, p. 10), the average delay for dispatch of imports in 1990 was 28 days.

8   ISO 9000 certification, provided by the International Organization for Standardization, is based on measures of quality in management.

9   El Salvador's customs service also qualified for ISO 9000, though for a smaller proportion of its overall transactions.

10   Article 1 of Decree Law 26020, General Law of the National Superintendency of Customs.

11   Richard Webb and Sofía Valencia, Human Resources in Public Health and Education in Peru, World Bank and Centro de Investigación de la Universidad San Martin de Porres (draft report), August 2005.

12   See Consejo Nacional de Descentralización (2005).

Conclusions

John Crabtree

The Weight of History

One of the purposes of this volume has been to draw attention to the way in which institutions and institutional practices form part of an historical process with roots deep in the past. Discussion of institutional reform therefore needs to pay due attention to the past; to ignore the weight of history is often to expect too much of what can be achieved by way of reform. All too often discussion of institutional change fails to identify and grapple with long-term underlying trends. All too often, the remedies offered fail to respond to the deeper cultural context in which proffered reforms are supposed to fit. In talking about institutions and institutional development in Peru, therefore, we have sought to relate these to the underlying trends. Institutions may 'matter', but what matters more is the way in which they relate to the political and social dynamics which they seek to affect. We have also tried to emphasise the various layers that exist, and the distinction between the formal or informal rules of the game and the players.

In his opening chapter, Paulo Drinot quotes North and the distinction he draws between 'institutions' and 'organisations'. This is helpful in drawing our attention to understanding the full social, cultural and even racial context in which institutional reforms take place. It helps explain some of the ambiguities inherent in reform — why some things change and others do not and why some areas of reform repeatedly disappoint. How far can we go in reforming institutions if the underlying rules of the game — values, culture and even property relations — remain unchanged? Clearly, these more structural characteristics place real obstacles to any process of reform, embedded as they are in the cultural substratum that is not susceptible to administrative fiat or to speedy transformation. When talking about reform, it is therefore important to bear in mind not just the institutions as narrowly defined but to understand why it is that these have evolved in the way that they have. As Drinot shows, this can sometimes mean confronting uncomfortable truths.

In each of the areas of reform analysed here, what might be called '*los problemas de siempre*' re-emerge in new forms to limit what can actually be done. The story of the last 50 years in Peru is full of episodes in which attempts were made to break free from the shackles of the past and to build anew. Looking back at these with the advantages of hindsight, it is easy to see why high expectations have given way to feelings of frustration and disillusion. Probably the classic example of this is the experience of the Velasco government, which set out to break many of Peru's traditional institutions, but whose bold reforms largely failed to resolve the problems they set out to resolve. So too, the García government set out to spearhead a number of changes to achieve a '*Perú diferente*' but ended changing little, at least for the better. Another opportunity was lost (Crabtree, 1992). The Fujimori administration also brought to the table an agenda of institutional reforms, mainly in the field of economic liberalisation, but this reformist energy ended in spectacular disarray. Likewise, the Toledo administration — the focus of much of the discussion in this book — came into office on a wave of reformist optimism, but this spirit of confidence was swiftly dashed; like its predecessors, his term ended in a mood of frustration and disillusion.

The values, customs and attitudes to which Drinot draws our attention are not things that are static or fixed in time. However, they tend to change slowly and often in ways that are hard to discern with any great clarity until well after the event. Nor are they uniform across society. Still, there are clearly moments that are more propitious to change than others. Periods of crisis, for example, may see values and behaviour patterns shift quite radically, opening the way to doing things that were previously impossible. For example, the economic, political and security crisis of the late 1980s brought a point of rupture that facilitated new approaches. Fujimori was adept in recognising this, taking advantage of the new situation to engineer institutional reforms that would not have been possible previously. These led to major shifts in the patterns of asset ownership and economic power. Part of the skill of reformers is therefore to recognise the ways in which changes in people's values open up new opportunities.

Even with the aid of opinion polls across a wide range of problems and pointers to the public mood, it is not altogether clear whether today's politicians are much better at perceiving the opportunities than their forebears. Often opinion polls tell only part of the story, and they are only as good as the questions that go into them. Part also has to do with the ability to respond effectively. Reforms themselves can be important in changing social values, therefore encouraging further change. Virtuous circles can be created. But identifying these in advance is not so easy, and all too often the results of reform are far from what their architects originally had in mind.

Structural Constraints

Looking back over the history of institutional change over the last two decades in Peru, two key trends stand out. The first of these is the persistence of high levels of inequality, particularly with respect to the ownership of assets. In Chapter 10, Francisco Durand underscores the scale of this transformation caused largely (but not entirely) by the extent of privatisation in Peru. A similar picture is painted on a narrower canvas by Fernando Eguren, who charts the growing breach in land tenure between traditional highland peasants and relatively few successful agricultural entrepreneurs aiming (mainly) at export niches. The second key trend is the attempt to construct a more democratic, more participative and less centralised system of government. This began to a certain extent in the early 1980s, but gained momentum in reaction against the authoritarianism and centralism of the Fujimori years. In terms of the locus of power, these two trends can be seen as pulling in opposite directions.

Durand's chapter describes the scale of the transformation in ownership in the Peruvian economy. The state has largely bowed out of the productive sphere, relinquishing asset ownership to the private sector. Most of these assets have been transferred to foreign owners, at least those in the most dynamic sectors of the economy. He also shows how local entrepreneurs have been squeezed, and how only relatively few of Alan García's 'twelve apostles' have managed to survive into the new economic dispensation. The liberal economic reforms, of course, sought to reduce the scale of state intervention, reversing the drift of the Velasco reforms, a transformation that owed much to the fiscal crisis of the state in the 1980s and the pressures imposed on Peru by the international financial community. It altered profoundly the whole relationship between the public and private sector, greatly increasing the ability of the latter to influence decisions and decision-making.

More research is required on the ways in which private interests influence public decision-making (it is all too obviously a 'cloudy' area), but Durand suggests that today these are less 'institutional' in that they are conducted in ways that privilege informal arenas that link leading businessmen and the top echelons of government. More institution-alised brokers, like Confiep, therefore find themselves bypassed. This in part explains the growing insulation between economic management and the 'noise' emanating from the world of politics; businesses pursue their own agendas, unperturbed by developments in the world of politics. However, 'business as usual' implies that this separation is respected and politics does not begin to intrude in any decisive way to challenge the basic ground-rules of the liberal economy.

Within the political sphere, though, the Toledo government found itself embarked on a project with different horizons. Here the accent was on restoring the legitimacy of government by increasing levels of participation and enabling popular pressures to find institutional channels through which to express themselves. As we have seen, the priority was to enhance public confidence in government, badly shaken by the 'Vladivideos' and the negative image they had projected about how and in whose interests government actually worked during the Fujimori period. But the concern also went deeper than this. In order to make Peruvian democracy more meaningful, a new relationship had to be forged between the state and civil society, between the government and electors, and between Lima and the rest of the country.

As others have argued (Tanaka, 2004), the military reformism of the mid-1970s effectively destroyed the 'oligarchic state' without creating in its place a 'democratic state'. This is a task that is still pending, and one which was clearly an objective among the new generation of reformers (some of whom have authored this study) that gained prominence in public policy management after Fujimori's fall. They sought to pursue the goal of democratic reform, increasing the influence of society in the political process and widening arenas for decision-making. This was certainly the case of those who advocated reform of the political parties (Chapter 2) as institutions performing their unique role in providing bridges between government and people. In the following chapter on decentralisation, Carlos Monge complemented this by looking in detail at the efforts (unprecedented) in seeking to create both a less centralised political structure but a more participatory one in which those previously excluded from the political system found a voice. In both cases, it became evident that such reforms were incipient and that the real challenge lay not so much in reforming institutions as such but ensuring that such reforms had a real impact in reshaping the political system.

Bringing together the goals of economic and political liberalisation in a mutually supporting process was one of the broader ambitions of the so-called Washington Consensus and its sequels. Democratisation, it hoped, would help legitimise the new economic order, while the economic dynamism that resulted from export-led growth would make it easier to consolidate the new democracy by creating new interest groups with a strong material interest in its preservation. In this context the 'second generation' of institutional reforms played a key role in building a more business-friendly environment and consolidating democratic institutions. Experience in Latin America as a whole over the last decade would seem to question this thesis, or at least make it seem that the relationship between affirmation of the primacy of the market economy and that of deepening democracy was a great deal more complicated than the original Consensus would have us believe. Peru, as well as some of its Andean neighbours, highlights these difficulties, and our enquiry into institutional development raises questions that are central to all political analysis: how are decisions made, by whom and for whom?

The experiences of institutional reform and the frustrations and tensions generated therefore need to be seen in this light: there are clear limitations to processes of democratisation (understood as sharing power among the many) and an economic model which concentrates real decision-making (especially the most strategic and important decisions) in the hands of the very few. Ultimately, voters need to have a conviction that their vote makes some difference, otherwise their confidence in democratic institutions (however weak and incomplete) will dissipate and those who wish to see their will prevail will choose other methods, possibly violent ones, which they perceive as being more effective. The recent history of Bolivia is perhaps instructive here: waves of public protest have proven effective in forcing political and economic elites to heed their voice, in a situation where faith in political parties as representative intermediaries is at a low ebb. In Peru, the strength of such protest is by no means as effective in forcing elites to heed public demands, but it likewise runs the risk of escaping from the hands of professional political intermediaries. During the Toledo government there were many instances of local political conflict that revealed the inefficacy (or at times non-existence) of state institutions at the local level, hardly a situation that would provide confidence among asset holders as to the virtues of legal security.

Reform Variables

However, it is important not to be too determinist. Despite a situation in which the logic of democratisation and that of economic concentration appear to pull in opposite directions, the experience of recent years in Peru provides some useful clues as to some of the more important variables that can make a difference in deciding whether reforms prosper or, alternatively, wither on the vine. The experience of the various reforms undertaken in Peru since 2001 are not all the same, and the foregoing chapters, many written by those closely involved, provide important testimony and insights into what it is that makes the difference.

First, reform requires leadership from the top. In a polity where political institutions are weakly constituted and where there has long been a strong tradition of presidentialism, presidential determination to press ahead makes a huge difference. This is a conclusion made clear repeatedly in Peru since the 1970s. Presidents begin with the authority born of political legitimacy, but the reforming impetus declines as that authority diminishes. The story told by Fernando Rospigliosi in Chapter 4 here is illustrative in this regard. Rospigliosi, a key actor in the very process he is analysing, claims that a serious attempt to 'modernise' the security forces was in the end undermined by the government's (especially the president's) lack of concern about the need for a thorough transformation. It demanded political will on the president's part to sustain a policy that naturally clashed with vested interests, especially when these recovered their poise and regrouped following the debacle of 2000–01. This account, however, is paralleled by others — for example Dargent's story of judicial reform (Chapter 7) — and it is hard to avoid the general conclusion that Toledo's loss of political authority in the years that followed and his increasing preoccupation with survival in office weakened the reform dynamic across the board, increasing the ability of opponents to dilute or even sabotage reform.

Second, reform requires a clear blueprint and the ability to carry policy through. The functions of state planning and the managerial/administrative capacities to put plans into practice have never been strong in Peru, despite pretensions sometimes to the contrary. Institutions like the National Planning Institute (Instituto Nacional de Planificación, INP), always a highly bureaucratic entity, did not survive the neoliberal purge of the early 1990s. The very notion of state planning was discredited. Private-sector planning remained primarily concerned with the immediate business preoccupations rather than wider social goals, and exercises in 'corporate social responsibility' have been isolated and ultimately self-interested. As Pedro Francke shows in Chapter 5, institutions like Foncodes, brought in by Fujimori to mastermind social policy, became clientelistic machines, and the temptations of clientelism were just as strong for Toledo as they had been for Fujimori. The second generation reforms brought in 'islands' of state efficiency, such as the tax collection agency, Sunat, and helped improve levels of competence and honesty in previously corrupt departments, like the customs administration. But as Távara (Chapter 10) shows, the record of the regulatory institutions brought in to supervise privatised service provision is patchy, and he concludes that their consolidation is far from complete. Meanwhile, the main areas of government charged with the delivery of social provision to the country as a whole — such as the Ministries of Education and Health — remained very limited and the quality of the services they provide desperately poor. Other ministries, severely cut back under Fujimori in terms of resources and responsibilities, were unable to meet the expectations placed upon them. Eguren's account of the Ministry of Agriculture is symptomatic.

Third, reform is more likely to succeed where the beneficiaries gain political power at the expense of those that stand in its way. The way in which the neoliberal reforms of the Fujimori era were able to advance owed much to the access to power granted to the business sector, and the privileged relationship it enjoyed with the Finance Ministry, as Durand shows. It also was due to the decline in the power of organisations to stand in its way, like the trade unions, already critically weakened by hyperinflation and the collapse of the left in the late 1980s. Similarly, in the period after 2001, the ability to pursue policies such as decentral-isation were limited by the weak capacity of authorities and society more generally at the regional, provincial and local levels to drive the process forwards. Reversing the historical tendency towards centralisa-tion would always be difficult in a country where demographics and industrial concentration continue to reaffirm the primacy of Lima, thus further weakening the political ability of the *provincias* to reverse these longstanding trends. The issue of 'empowerment' of the excluded through the defence of rights, a notion taken very seriously by many NGOs and development specialists (DFID, 2005), is clearly oriented towards changing power relations at the local level, but how to achieve these changes within a society where the power structure remains intact is easier said than done. It would seem that the capacity to defend and advance social rights in a country like Peru depends a great deal on the stance adopted by the state. Without committed support from the state, it is unlikely to go very far.

Fourth, another factor that is important in advancing or retarding reform is the attitude adopted by the mass media. In Peru, as elsewhere, the media play an important role in shaping public attitudes towards social or economic problems. Indeed, politics are crucially influenced by the editorial positions adopted by key media outlets, and public support for reform is clearly affected by the way it is treated in the media. The Peruvian media are, of course, not homogenous or entirely lacking in competition, but they have emerged in recent years as spaces in which editorial positions are often subsumed by business interests and elite infighting. The lack of a chapter in this volume on the media is perhaps a shortcoming. The way in which Fujimori and Montesinos manipulat-ed the media is now well-known, but the corporate interests of media groups continued to affect coverage under Toledo, often seemingly defending those involved in the corrupt and murky world that he had started promising to sweep away.

Fifth, reform is facilitated where there are effective lobbies in socie-ty, beyond the confines of government, which manage to keep reform issues firmly in the public debate and which interact with state actors in such ways as to influence the way decisions are made. A prominent example, and one highlighted in this book, is the story of the Coordinadora de Derechos Humanos, as recounted by Coletta

Youngers. Here we have an institution that effectively managed to har-
ness the efforts of local organisations across the country, developed an
institutional profile that enabled it to deal head-on with those in government (even under Fujimori), and reinforced this through the build-up of
a credibility at the international level so that even President Bill Clinton
saw it as a key reference point in his policy towards Peru. The
Coordinadora is, of course, not alone. The country has fairly dense networks of NGOs which influence policy across the board, but particularly on social issues. Many have built up their own capacity for providing informed comment on policy design, influencing government decisions in sometimes crucial ways. It was from these circles that many of
the reformers were recruited following the fall of Fujimori in 2000.
Some of those that have contributed to this volume have long been
involved in such agencies. CEPES, directed by Fernando Eguren, has a
long track record in agrarian policy issues, and Propuesta Ciudadana,
where Carlos Monge works, has become a strong protagonist in the
push for more vigorous decentralisation.

A final point — of a more negative than positive nature — is that
successful reform is not primarily a question of money. In his chapter,
Richard Webb identifies some instances of institution building over the
last two decades. Though foreign funding may be helpful at points (in the
shape of World Bank or IDB loans, for instance), it is not the determinant
factor, and can be detrimental to sustainability. Some of the more successful institutional reforms of the Fujimori period involved building institutions with the capacity for budgetary autonomy. External foreign support
often becomes a mechanism of disguised bribery. Indeed, Webb argues
that lack of money is generally more a trigger to institutional change than
its availability. The same principle may indeed be applied to the Toledo
administration, whose paucity in terms of lasting institutional development does not reflect the absence of funds; rather the opposite: the economic growth of these years generated a much more healthy fiscal situation than had been the case for much of the previous 20 years.

Obstacles to Reform

Summing up, clearly some conjunctures are more propitious for change
than others, and the fall of Fujimori at the end of 2000 represented a

particularly promising moment. However, in spite of the number of proposals for institutional reform and the energy with which some of these were put into practice, the lasting effects were disappointing. This is not the first time in recent Peruvian history that reformist zeal has been dissipated and the opportunities largely squandered. Bouts of reform have repeatedly failed to meet the expectations vested in them. This therefore invites some reflection on why the process of institutional change is so difficult in a country like Peru. An important part of the answer lies in the nature of the country's political economy, particularly the extremely unequal distribution of economic and political power. In such circumstances it is hard to forge the sort of basic consensus required for institutional development. Those patterns of inequality appear to have become more pronounced in recent years, not less. This makes it harder to build a society in which democratic rights are heeded and where real citizenship is a reality.

However, pressure for change will not stop. A new government, elected in 2006, will have another opportunity to grapple with some of these problems inherited from the past. A new democratic mandate may provide new opportunities, and there are important lessons to be learned from history. It is to be hoped that Peru's future leaders will ponder on these, reflecting on the way in which previous efforts have failed to meet the expectations placed on them. At the very least, the issues involved need to be widely discussed at all levels of society. It is hoped that this book will help in this endeavour.

Bibliography

Abusada, R et al. (2000) *La reforma incomplete*, 2 vols. (Lima: Centro de Investigaciones de la Universidad del Pacífico).

Adelman, J. (2001) 'Institutions, Property, and Economic Development in Latin America,' in M.A. Centeno and F. López-Alves (eds.), *The Other Mirror: Grand Theory through the Lens of Latin America* (Princeton and Oxford: Princeton University Press).

Alvarado, J. (1996) *Los contratos de tierras y crédito en la pequeña agricultura. Un análisis institucional* (Lima: CEPES).

Ames, R. et al. (February 1988) *Informe al Congreso sobre los sucesos de los penales* (Lima, Peru: The Peruvian Congress).

Amnesty International (1989) *Caught Between Two Fires* (New York, N.Y.)

Amnesty International (May 1992) *Human Rights During the Government of Alberto Fujimori* (Washington, DC).

Angell, A. (2004) 'Party Change in Chile in Comparative Perspective,' paper delivered at the 2004 LASA Conference, Las Vegas.

Apaclla, R., Eguren, F., Figueroa, A. and Oré, T. (1993) 'Las políticas de riego en el Perú,' in Grupo Permanente de Estudios sobre Riego, *Gestión del agua y crisis institucional. Un análisis multidisciplinario del riego en el Perú* (Lima: Grupo Permanente de Estudios sobre Riego, ITDG-Servicio Holandés de Cooperación Técnica).

Aparicio, M. (2004) 'Formación de precios y abuso de poder de mercado en la intermediación del maíz amarillo duro,' en *Debate Agrario*, no. 37 (Lima).

Apoyo (2001) *Country Report on the National Integrity System*, report for Transparency International (Lima: Apoyo SA).

Appelbaum, N.P., Macpherson, A.S. and Rosemblatt, K.A. (eds.) (2003) *Race and Nation in Modern Latin America* (Chapel Hill and London: University of North Carolina Press).

Arce, M. (2001) 'The Politics of Pension Reform in Peru,' *Studies in Comparative International Development* (Fall), vol. 36, no. 3, pp. 90–115.

Arrighi, G., Silver, B.J. and Brewer, B.D. (2003) 'Industrial Convergence, Globalization and the Persistence of the North-South Divide,' *Studies in Comparative International Development* (Spring), vol. 38, no. 1, pp. 3–31.

Arroyo, J and Irigoyen, M. (2004) *Desafíos de la democracia participativa local en la descentralización: una lectura a partir de doce experiencias* (Lima: DFID-UNFPA).

Baer, W. (2002) 'El neoliberalismo en América Latina: ¿Un regreso al pasado?' in C. Contreras and M. Glave (eds.), *Estado y mercado en la historia del Perú* (Lima: Pontificia Universidad Católica del Perú), pp. 25–33.

Baldwin, R., and Cave, M. (1999) *Understanding Regulation. Theory, Strategy and Practice* (Oxford: Oxford University Press).

Ballón, E. (2003) 'Participación ciudadana en espacios locales: un balance necesario,' *Cuaderno Descentralista*, no. 10 (Lima: Grupo Propuesta Ciudadana).

Banco Interamericano de Desarrollo (2002) 'La paradoja de la privatización,' *América Latina Políticas Económicas*, vol. 18 (2002), pp. 1–8.

Barraclough, S. and Collarte, J. (1972) *El hombre y la tierra en América Latina. Resumen de los informes CIDA sobre tenencia de la tierra en Argentina, Brasil, Colombia, Chile, Ecuador, Guatemala, Perú* (Santiago: Editorial Universitaria).

Basadre, J. (1931) *Perú: problema y posibilidad* (Lima: E. Rosay).

Basombrío, C. (1998) 'Sendero Luminoso and Human Rights: A Perverse Logic that Captured the Country,' in Steve Stern (ed.), *Shining and Other Paths* (Durham, NC: Duke University Press).

Basombrío, C. et al. (2004) *Manejo y gestión de la seguridad. De la reforma al inmovilismo* (Lima: Instituto de Defensa Legal).

BCRP (2005) 'Grupos vinculados y la inversión en acciones de las AFP' (Lima: BCRP), unpublished paper.

Belaunde, V.A. (1930) *La realidad nacional* (Lima).

Bernales, E. et al. (no date) *Violencia y pacificación en 1991* (Lima: The Peruvian Congress).

Boesten, J. (2004) 'Negotiating Womanhood, Reproducing Inequality: Women and Social Policy in Peru,' Doctoral dissertation, University of Amsterdam.

Boesten, J. and Drinot, P. (2004) 'The Allure of Eugenics: Peru and the History Without People'. Paper presented at the 'Crime, Justice and Violence' Seminar; ESRC Seminar Series: Social Policy, Stability and Exclusion in Latin America, Institute of Latin American Studies, London.

Booth, D. and Sorj, B. (ed.) (1983) *Military Reformism and Social Classes: The Peruvian Experience, 1968–1980* (London: Palgrave).

Bowen, S. (2000) *The Fujimori Files* (Lima: The Peru Monitor).

Burt, J.M. (1998) 'Shining Path and the "Decisive Battle" in Lima's *Barriadas*: The Case of Villa El Salvador,' in S. Stern (ed.), *Shining and Other Paths* (Durham, NC: Duke University Press).

Caballero, V. (2004) 'Problemas y retos de la transferencia de los programas sociales alimentarios de lucha contra la pobreza,' in *Allpanchis*, no. 63 (Instituto de Pastoral Andina).

Callirgos, J.C. (1993) *El racismo: la cuestión del otro (y de uno)* (Lima: Desco).

Caravedo, B. (1998) *Perú: empresas responsables* (Lima: SASE y Comité Perú 2021).

Carrión, F. (2004) 'La inseguridad ciudadana en la región andina,' in L. Dammert (ed.), *Seguridad ciudadana, experiencias y desafíos* (Valparaíso: Municipalidad de Valparaíso).

CEPES (2002) (Cooperation Programme with FAO and the World Bank) *Estudio de la rentabilidad de la agricultura de la costa peruana y las inversiones para el mejoramiento del riego* (Lima: CEPES, www.cepes.org.pe).

Chambers, S.C. (1999) *From Subjects to Citizens: Honor, Gender, and Politics in Arequipa, Peru, 1780–1854* (University Park: Pennsylvania State University Press).

Chang, H-J. (2002) *Kicking Away the Ladder. Development Strategy in Historical Perspective* (London: Anthem Press).

Chang, H-J. (2003) 'Rethinking Development Economics: An Introduction,' in H-J. Chang (ed.), *Rethinking Development Economics* (London: Anthem Press), pp. 1–18.

Chaquilla, O. (1990) 'El mercado de tierras agrícolas,' in *Debate Agrario*, vol. 8 (January–March).

Chocano, M. (1987) 'Ucronía y frustración en la conciencia histórica peruana,' in *Márgenes* II, pp. 43–60.

Comisión Andina de Juristas (2000) *La reforma judicial en la región andina: ¿Qué se ha hecho, dónde estamos, adónde vamos?* (Lima: Comisión Andina de Juristas).

Comisión Andina de Juristas (2003) *Currupción judicial: mecanismos de control y vigilancia ciudadana* (Lima: Comisión Andina de Juristas).

Comisión de la Verdad y Reconciliación (2003) *Informe Final* (Lima: Comisión de la Verdad y Reconciliación, www.cverdad.org.pe).

Comisión de la Verdad y Reconciliación (2004) *Hatun Willakuy: Versión Abreviada del Informe Final de la Comisión de la Verdad y Reconciliación* (Lima).

Comisión Investigadora de los Delitos Económicos y Financieros– CIDEF (2002) 'Informe final de investigación' (Lima: Congreso de la República).

Consejo Nacional de Descentralizacón (CND) (2005) 'Informe al Congreso' (Lima: Consejo Nacional de Descentralización).

Contreras, C. (2004a) '¿Inmigración o autogenia?: La política de población en el Perú, 1876–1940,' in C. Contreras, *El aprendizaje del capitalismo: Estudios de historia económica y social del Perú republicano* (Lima: Instituto de Estudios Peruanos), pp. 173–213.

Contreras, C. (2004b) 'Maestros, mistis y campesinos en el Perú rural del siglo XX,' in C. Contreras, *El aprendizaje del capitalismo: Estudios de historia económica y social del Perú republicano* (Lima: Instituto de Estudios Peruanos), pp. 214–73.

Contreras, C. (2005) 'El centralismo peruano en su perspectiva histórica,' Documento de trabajo no. 127 (Lima: Instituto de Estudios Peruanos (IEP)).

Conveagro (2004) *Memoria 2003-2004* (Lima: Conveagro).

Coordinadora Nacional de Derechos Humanos (1993) *Informe sobre la situación de los derechos humanos en el Perú en 1992* (Lima).

Cortez, R. (2001) 'El gasto social y sus efectos en la nutrición infantil' (Lima: Centro de Investigación de la Universidad del Pacífico), Working Paper 38.

Cotler, J. (1998) 'La articulación y los mecanismos de representación de las organizaciones empresariales' (Lima: Instituto de Estudios Peruanos), Working Paper no. 97.

Crabtree, J. (1992) *Peru under García: An Opportunity Lost* (London: Macmillan and Pittsburgh: University of Pittsburgh Press).

Crabtree, J. (1994) 'La crisis del sistema partidario peruano (1985–95)' *Apuntes*, no. 35.

Dargent, E. (2000) 'Hijos de un dios menor: cifras, súbditos e inocentes,' in E. Dargent and A. Vergara, *La batalla de los días primeros* (Lima: El Virrey).

De Belaunde, J. (1998) 'Justice, Legality and Judicial Reform,' in J. Crabtree and J. Thomas (eds.), *Fujimori's Peru: The Political Economy* (London: Institute of Latin American Studies).

De Janvry, A. (1981) *The Agrarian Question and Reformism in Latin America* (Baltimore: the Johns Hopkins University Press).

de la Cadena, M. (2000) *Indigenous Mestizos: The Politics of Race and Culture in Cuzco, Peru, 1919–1991* (Durham, NC: Duke University Press).

De la Jara B., E. (2001) *Memoria y batallas en nombre de los inocentes (Perú 1992–2001)* (Lima: Instituto de Defensa Legal).

Deere, C. (1992) *Familia y relaciones de clase. El campesinado y los terratenientes en la sierra norte del Perú, 1900–1980* (Lima: IEP).

Defensoría del Pueblo (2000) *La desaparición forzada de personas en el Perú (1980 a 1996)* (Lima: Defensoría del Pueblo).

Del Aguila, L and Monge, C. (2005) 'Voces agregadas' (working paper) in Banco Mundial-Grupo Propuesta Ciudadana, *Voces de los pobres* (Lima: BM-GPC).

del Pino, P. (2003) 'Uchuraccay: Memoria y representación de la violencia política en los Andes,' in P. del Pino and E. Jelin (eds.), *Luchas locales, comunidades e identidades* (Madrid: Siglo XXI), pp. 11–62.

Denegri, F. (2003) 'Distopía poscolonial y racismo en la narrative del XIX peruano,' in S. O'Phelan et al., *Familia y vida cotidiana en América Latina, Siglos XVIII–XX* (Lima: Pontificia Universidad Católica del Perú), pp. 117–35.

Department for International Development (DFID) (2005) *Alliances against Poverty: DFID's experience in Peru 2000–05* (Lima: DFID).

Dietz, H. (1998) *Urban Poverty, Political Participation and the State: Lima 1970–1990* (Pittsburgh: Pittsburgh University Press).

Domingo, P. and Sieder, R. (2001) *Rule of Law in Latin America: The International Promotion of Judicial Reform* (London: Institute of Latin American Studies, University of London).

Drzewieniecki, J. (2004) 'Peruvian Youth and Racsim: The Category of "Race" remains Strong'. Paper Presented at the Meeting of the Latin American Studies Association, Las Vegas, Nevada, 7–9 October.

Dubois, F. (2005) *Programas sociales, salud y educación en el Perú: un balance de las políticas sociales* (Lima: Instituto Peruano de Economía Social de Mercado).

Durand, F. (2003)*Riqueza económica y pobreza política. Reflexiones sobre las elites del poder en un país inestable* (Lima: Pontificia Universidad Católica del Perú).

Durand, F. (2004) 'Fuego y humo: reconfiguración de la clase empresarial y cambios políticos en la globalización' (Lima: Fundación Friesdirch Ebert), Avances de Investigación no. 11.

Durand, F. and Thorp, R. (1998) 'Tax Reform: the SUNAT Experience,' in J. Crabtree and J. Thomas (eds.), *Fujimori's Peru: the Political Economy* (London: ILAS).

Durand, F. and Thorp, R. (1998a) 'Reforming the State: A Study of the Peruvian Tax Reform,' *Oxford Development Studies*, vol. 26, no. 2, pp. 133–151.

Eguiguren Praeli, F. (1990) *Los retos de una democracia insuficiente: diez años de regimen constitucional en el Perú* (Lima: Comisión Andina de Juristas).

Eguren, F. (1988) 'Revisión y balance de los estudios sobre reestructuración de empresas agrarias asociativas,' in F. Eguren, R. Hopkins, B. Kervyn and R. Montoya (eds.), *Perú: El problema agrario en debate. SEPIA II* (Lima: SEPIA-Universidad Nacional San Cristóbal de Huamanga).

Eguren, F. (1989) 'Los nuevos grupos dominantes en la agricultura peruana,' *Debate Agrario* 7, July–December (Lima: CEPES).

Eguren, F. (2002) 'Sector agrario, pequeños agricultures y campesinos: una vision sucinta,' *Socialismo y Participación*, no. 94.

Escobal, J. and Ágreda, V. (1994) 'La comercialización de arroz en la costa norte del Perú. El caso de los productores de Ferreñafe,' in J. Escobal (ed.), *Comercialización agrícola en el Perú* (Lima: GRADE-AID).

Flores Galindo, A. (1988) 'La imagen y el espejo: la historiografía peruana 1910-1986,' in *Márgenes* IV, pp. 55–83.

Gallardo, J. (2000) 'Privatización de los monopolios naturales en el Perú: economía política, análisis institucional y desempeño,' CISEPA Documento de Trabajo 188.

Gallardo, J. and Pérez-Reyes, R. (2004) 'Diseño institucional y desconcentración de funciones de OSINERG,' Documento de Trabajo no. 9, Oficina de Estudios Económicos del OSINERG, Lima.

Gonzalez Cueva, E. (2000) 'Conscription and Violence in Peru,' in *Latin American Perspectives*, vol. 27, no. 3, pp. 88–102.

Gootenberg, P. (1993) *Imagining Development: Economic Ideas in Peru's 'Fictitious Prosperity' of Guano, 1840–1880* (Berkeley: University of California Press).

Gorriti, G. (1999) *The Shining Path: A History of the Millenarian War in Peru* (Chapel Hill, NC: The University of North Carolina Press).

Gorriti, J. (2003) '¿Rentabilidad o supervivencia? La agricultura de la costa peruana,' *Debate Agrario*, vol. 35.

Graham, C. (1992) *Peru's APRA, Parties, Politics and the Elusive Quest for Democracy* (London: Lynne Rienner).

Grompone, R. (2001) 'Tradiciones liberales y autonomías personales en el Perú. Una aproximación desde la cultura,' in S. López Maguina, G. Portcarrero, R. Silva Santisteban and V. Vich (eds.), *Estudios culturales: Discursos, poderes, pulsiones* (Lima: Red para el Desarrollo de las Ciencias Sociales en el Perú), pp. 491–514.

Grupo Propuesta Ciudadana and Ministerio de la Mujer y el Desarrollo Social (2004) *Suplemento Participa Perú*, vol. 21, in www.participaperu.org.pe/publicaciones.

Hammergren, L. (1998) *The Politics of Justice and Justice Reform in Latin America* (Boulder, CO: Westview).

Hammergren, L. (2004) 'La experiencia peruana en reforma judicial: tres décadas de grandes cambios con pocas mejoras,' in L. Pásara (ed.), *En busca de una justicia distinta* (Lima: Consorcio Justicia Viva).

Harris, J., Hunter, J. and Lewis, C.M. (1995) 'Introduction: Development and Significance of NIE,' in J. Harris, J. Hunter and C.M. Lewis (eds.), *The New Institutional Economics and Third World Development* (London: Routledge).

Hayner, P.B. (2001) *Unspeakable Truths: Confronting State Terror and Atrocity* (New York, NY: Routledge).

Heinz, W. and Pedraglio, S. (1997) *Informe de la Evaluación de la Coordinadora Nacional de Derechos Humanos: 1992–1997* (Lima, internal document).

Henríquez, N. (2000) 'Imaginarios nacionales, mestizaje e identidades de genero: Aproximación comparativa sobre México y Perú,' in N. Henríquez (ed.), *El hechizo de las imágenes: Estatus social, género, y etnicidad en la historia peruana* (Lima: Pontificia Universidad Católica del Perú), pp. 317–88.

Herrera, J. (2004) *La pobreza en el Perú, 2003* (Lima: INEI).

Hunefeldt, C. (2000) *Liberalism in the Bedroom: Quarrelling Spouses in Nineteenth Century Lima* (University Park: Pennsylvania University Press).

Iniciativa Nacional Anticorrupción (2001) *Un Perú sin corrupción. El secreto de la ética pública es la transparencia*, two parts (Lima, July), pp. 1–98.

Jamison, M., Berg, S., Gasmi, F. and Távara, J. (2005) *The Regulation of Utility Infrastructure and Services. An Annotated Reading List* (Washington, DC: The World Bank).

Jiménez, F. (2002) 'Estado, mercado, crisis y restauración liberal en el Perú,' in C. Contreras and M. Glave (eds.), *Estado y mercado en la historia del Perú* (Lima: Pontificia Universidad Católica del Perú), pp. 415–37.

Justicia Viva (2004a) *Plan de reforma de la administración de justicia de la Ceiajus: el acuerdo por la justicia que debemos respetar* (Lima: Justicia Viva).

Justicia Viva (2004b) *La reforma del sistema de justicia: ¿Qué reforma?. 2004–2005* (Lima: Justicia Viva).

Justino, P., Litchfield, J. and Whitehead, L. (2003) 'The Impact of Inequality in Latin America,' Working Paper no. 21, Poverty Research Unit at Sussex.

Karl, T.L. (2003) 'The Vicious Cycle of Inequality in Latin America,' in S.E. Eckstein and T.P. Wickham Crowley (eds.), *What Justice? Whose Justice: Fighting for Fairness in Latin America* (Berkeley: University of California Press).

Knight, A. (1999) 'Britain and Latin America,' in R. Louis and J. Brown (eds.), *Oxford History of the British Empire, Vol IV The Twentieth Century* (Oxford: Oxford University Press).

Kristal, E. (1991) *Una visión urbana de los Andes: Génesis y desarrollo del indigenismo en el Perú 1848-1930* (Lima: Instituto de Apoyo Agrario).

Kuczynski, P.P. (1977) *Peruvian Democracy under Stress: An Account of the Belaunde Administration 1963–68* (Princeton: Princeton University Press).

Latinobarómetro (2005) *Latinobarómetro 2005: una década de mediciones* (Santiago de Chile: Latinobarómetro), www.latinobarómetro.org.

León, G. (2003) 'El uso político del gasto social: economía política del fondo de inversion social en el Perú durante el fijimorato,' mimeo (Lima: Pontificia Universidad Católica del Perú).

Levy, B. and Spiller, P. (1996) 'A Framework for Resolving the Regulatory Problem,' in B. Levy and P. Spiller (eds.), *Regulations, Institutions, and Commitment: Comparative Studies in Telecommunications* (Cambridge: Cambridge University Press).

López Jiménez, S. (1997) *Ciudadanos reales e imaginarios* (Lima: Instituto de Diálogo y Propuestas).

López Lenci, Y. (2005) 'Sacralidad e identidad en tiempos de globalización,' in *Identidades: Reflexión, Arte y Cultura*, no. 81 (March 2005), pp. 4-7.

López Maguina, S. (2003) 'Arqueología de una mirada criolla: el informa de la matanza de Uchuraccay,' in M. Hamann, S. López Maguina, G. Portocarrero and V. Vich, *Batallas por la memoria: Antagonismos de la promesa peruana* (Lima: Red para el desarrollo de las ciencias socials en el Perú), pp. 257–74.

López Ricci, J. and Wiener, E. (2005) 'Planeamientos y presupuesto participativo regional 2004–2005,' in *Cuaderno Descentralista*, vol. 11 (Lima: GPC).

López, C. (2005) 'La gobernabilidad en distritos rurales: Santo Domingo camino al desarrollo,' in Ayuda en Acción, *La nueva ruralidad. Desafíos y Propuestas* (Lima: Ayuda en Acción).

López, S. (1997) *Ciudadanos reales e imaginarios: concepciones, desarrollo y mapa de la ciudadanía en el Perú* (Lima: Instituto de Diálogo y Propuestas).

Lowenthal, A.F. (ed.) (1975) *The Peruvian Experiment: Continuity and Change Under Military Rule* (Princeton: Princeton University Press).

MacCraw, T. (1984) *Prophets of Regulation* (Cambridge, MA: The Belknap Press of Harvard University).

Magaloni, B. (2003) 'Authoritarianism, Democracy and the Supreme Court: Horizontal Exchange and the Rule of Law,' in S.

Mainwaring and C. Welna (eds.), *Democratic Accountability in Latin America* (Oxford: OUP).

Mainwaring, S. (2005) 'State Failure, Party Competition and the Crisis of Trust in Representative Democratic Institutions in the Andes,' in A-M. Bejarano, E. Pizarro and S. Mainwaring (eds.), *Crisis of Democratic Representation in the Andeas* (Palo Alto: Stanford University Press).

Mainwaring, S. and Scully, T. (1995) *Building Democratic Institutions: Party Systems in Latin America* (Stanford: Stanford University Press).

Mallon, F. (1994) *Peasant and Nation: The Making of Postcolonial Mexico and Peru* (Berkeley: University of California Press).

Manrique, N. (1993) *Vinieron los sarracenos: el universo mental de la conquista de América* (Lima: Desco).

Manrique, N. (1999) *La piel y la pluma: escritos sobre literatura, etnicidad y racismo* (Lima: CIDIAG/SUR).

Marcone, M. (1995) 'Indígenas e inmigrantes durante la República Aristocrática: Población e Ideología Civilista,' *Histórica*, vol. XIX, no. 1 (July), pp. 73–93.

Mariátegui, J.C. (1928) *Siete ensayos de interpretación de la realidad peruana* (Lima: Amauta).

Matos Mar, J. (1984) *Desborde popular y crisis del estado: El nuevo rostro del Perú* (Lima: Instituto de Estudios Peruanos).

Matos Mar, J. and Mejía, M. (1980) *La reforma agraria en el Perú* (Lima: Instituto de Estudios Peruanos).

Maxwell, S. (2005) 'The Washington Consensus is Dead! Long Live the Meta-narrative!' Working Paper 243, Overseas Development Institute.

Mayer, E. (1991) 'Peru in Deep Trouble: Mario Vargas Llosa's "Inquest in the Andes" Reexamined,' in *Cultural Anthropology*, vol. 6, no. 4, pp. 466–504.

McClintock, C. (1998) *Should the Authoritarian Regime Label be Revived? The Case of Fujimori's Peru, 1995–1998*, paper presented at the Latin American Studies Association meeting, 24–26 September 1998.

McClintock, C. and Lowenthal, A.F. (eds.) (1983) *The Peruvian Experiment Reconsidered* (Princeton: Princeton University Press).

Méndez, C. (1996) '*Incas sí, indios no:* note on Peruvian Creole nationalism and its contemporary crisis,' in *Journal of Latin American Studies*, vol. 28, no. 1, pp. 197–225.

Ministerio de Agricultura (2002) 'Lineamientos de política agraria para el Perú. Documento de trabajo para una agenda concertada' (Lima: Ministerio de Agricultura).

Monge, C. (1989) 'Las demandas de los gremios campesinos en los ochenta,' in *Debate Agrario*, no. 5 (CEPES: Lima).

Monge, C. (2003) 'Participación concertación, inclusion y gobernabilidad en el Perú rural. Y después de la violencia ?Qué?' *Cuaderno Descentralista*, no. 10 (Lima: Grupo Propuesta Ciudadana).

Moore, B. (1973 [1966]) *Social Origins of Dictatorship and Democracy. Lord and Peasant in the Making of the Modern World* (London: Penguin Books).

Moore, M. (1997) 'Societies, Politics and Capitalists in Developing Countries: A Literature Survey,' *Journal of Development Studies*, vol. 33, no. 3 (February), pp. 287–363.

Morón, E. and Sanborn, C. (2004) 'The Pitfalls of Policymaking in Peru: Actors, Institutions and Rules of the Game,' unpublished paper.

North, D. (Undated) 'Where Have We Been and Where Are We Going'. http://ssrn.com/abstract=1494.

Oliart, P. (1999) 'Leer y escribir en un mundo sin letras. Reflexiones sobre la globalización y la educación en la Sierra rural,' in C.I. Degregori and G. Portocarrero (eds.), *Cultura y globalización* (Lima: Red para el Desarrollo de las Ciencias Sociales en el Perú), pp. 203–24.

Oliart, P. (2004) 'Los desafíos políticos, sociales y científicos de la megadiversidad,' in P. Oliart, M. Remy and F. Eguren (eds.), *SEPIA X: Peru — el problema agrario en debate* (Lima: SEPIA).

Palast, G., Oppenheim, J. and MacGregor, T. (2003) *Democracy and Regulation — How the Public Can Govern Privatised Essential Services* (London: Pluto Press).

Parthasarathi, P. (2002) 'Review Article: The Great Divergence,' *Past and Present*, vol. 176, pp. 275—93.

Pásara, L. (2004a) 'Introducción,' in L. Pásara (ed.), *En busca de una justicia distinta* (Lima: Justicia Viva).

Pásara, L. (2004b) 'Lecciones aprendidas o por aprender?' in L. Pásara (ed.), *En busca de una justicia distinta* (Lima: Justicia Viva).

Pásara, L. (2004c) 'La enseñanza del derecho en el Perú: su impacto sobre la administración de justicia,' Ministerio de Justicia, www.minjus.gob.pe.

Payne, J. et al. (2002) *Democracies in Development* (Washington, DC: IDB/IDEA).

Pease, H. (2003) *La autocracia fujimorista* (Lima: PUCP).

Peru Top Publications (2004) *Peru: The Top 10,000 Companies* (Lima: Peru Top Publications).

Philip, G. (1978) *The Rise and Fall of the Peruvian Military Radicals, 1968–76* (London: London University Press).

Piqueras Luna, M. et al. (October 1989) *Comisión Investigadora de los Asesinatos de los Señores Diputados Eriberto Arroyo Mío y Pablo Norberto Li Ormeño, así como de las Actividades Desarrolladas por el Grupo Terrorista que Desarrolla Acciones Criminales Incompatibles con la Vida Democrática del País y que Indebidamente Utiliza el Nombre de un Mártir* (Lima: The Peruvian Congress).

Pisconte J. and Villavicencio, L. (2005) '*Formación y funcionamiento de los Consejos de Coordinación Local. Los casos de Abancay, Santo Domingo de Morropón, San Marcos y Calzado. Su articulación con otros espacios de participación. Análisis y propuesta de modificaciones a la Ley Orgánica de municipalidades y propuesta de ordenanza y guía*' (Lima: CND).

Planas, P. (1999) *El Fujimorato: estudio político-constitucional* (Lima: unpublished).

Pomeranz, K. (2000) *The Great Divergence: China, Europe, and the Making of the World Economy* (Princeton: Princeton University Press).

Poole, D. (1997) *Vision, Race, and Modernity: A Visual Economy of the Andean Image World* (Princeton: Princeton University Press).

Poole, D. (2004) 'Between Threat and Guarantee: Justice and Community in the Margins of the Peruvian State,' in V. Das and D. Poole (eds.), *Anthropology in the Margins of the State* (Sante fe and Oxford: School of American Research Press/James Currey), pp. 35–65.

Portocarrero, F. (2002) 'La opinión pública y los grupos de poder económico en el Perú: una aproximación cualitativa sobre ética, valores y responsabilidad social' (Lima: Centro de Investigaciones de la Universidad del Pacífico, March).

Portocarrero, F. et al. (1998) *Economía y política de los programas de apoyo alimentario en el Perú* (Lima: Centro de Investigación de la Universidad del Pacífico).

Portocarrero, F et al. (2000) *Empresas, fundaciones y medios: la responsabilidad social en el Perú* (Lima: Centro de Investigaciones de la Universidad del Pacífico).

Portocarrero, G. (1993) *Racismo y mestizaje* (Lima: SUR).

Portocarrero, G. (2003) 'Memorias del Velasquismo,' in M. Hamann, S. López Maguina, G. Portocarrero and V. Vich, *Batallas por la memoria: Antagonismos de la promesa peruana* (Lima: Red para el desarrollo de las Ciencias Sociales en el Perú), pp. 229–55.

Portocarrero, G. (2005) 'Las relaciones Estado-sociedad en el Perú: un examen bibliográfico,' in P. Zárate (ed.), *¿Hay lugar para los pobres en el Perú? Las relaciones estado-sociedad y el rol de la cooperación internacional* (Lima: Department for International Development (DFID)).

Programa de Naciones Unidas de Desarrollo (PNUD — United Nations Development Program) (2005) *Informe sobre desarrollo human.* (Lima: PNUD).

Quijano, A. (2000) 'Colonialidad del poder y clasificación social,' in *Journal of World-Systems Research*, vol. VI, no. 2, pp. 342–86.

Quijano, A. (2003) 'Notas sobre "raza" y democracia en los países andinos,' in *Revista Venezolana de Economía y Ciencias Sociales*, vol. 9, no. 1, pp. 53–9.

Roberts, K. (2002) 'Social Inequalities without Class Cleavages in Latin America's Neoliberal Era,' *Studies in Comparative International Development* (Winter), vol. 36. no. 4, pp. 3–33.

Rubio, M. (1999) *Quítate la venda para mirarte mejor: la reforma judicial en el Perú* (Lima: DESCO).

Ruiz Caro, A. (2002) 'El proceso de privatizaciones en el Perú durante el período 1991–2002' (Santiago de Chile: ILPES-CEPAL), Serie Gestión Pública 22.

Santa Cruz, F. (1999) 'La nueva institucionalidad rural: el caso del Perú,' in FAO–CEPES. www.rlc.fao.org/prior/desrural/reforma/estudios/peru.pdf.

Sartori, G. (1976) *Parties and Party Systems: A Framework of Analysis* (Cambridge: Cambridge University Press).

Schady, N. (1999) *Seeking Votes: The Political Economy of Expenditures by the Peruvian Social Fund (FONCODES), 1991–95* (Washington, DC: The World Bank Poverty Division, Poverty Reduction and Economic Management Network).

Servicio de Aduanas (1995) *Memoria 1991–94* (Lima: Servicio de Aduanas).

Sheahan, J. (1999) *Searching for a Better Society: The Peruvian Economy from 1950* (University Park: Pennsylvania State University Press).

Shimizu, T. (2004) 'Family Business in Peru: Survival and Expansion After the Liberalization' (Tokyo: IDE–JETRO), Discussion Paper no. 7.

Silverblatt, I. (2004) *Modern Inquisitions: Peru and the Colonial Origins of the Civilized World* (London and Durham: Duke University Press).

Skidmore, T. and Smith, P. (2000) *Modern Latin America* (Oxford: OUP).

Smith, W. (1997) 'Utility Regulators: The Independence Debate, Roles and Responsibilities,' in *The Private Sector in Infrastructure. Strategy, Regulation and Risk* (Washington, DC: The World Bank Group).

Sokoloff, K.L. and Engerman, S.L. (2000) 'History Lessons: Institutions, Factor Endowments, and Paths of Development in the New World,' *The Journal of Economic Perspectives*, vol. 14, no. 3, pp. 217-32.

Stein, S. and Monge, C. (1988) *La crisis del estado patrimonial en el Perú* (Lima: Instituto de Estudios Peruanos (IEP) and University of Miami).

Stepan, N.L. (1991) *The Hour of Eugenics: Race, Gender, and Nation in Latin America* (Ithaca and London: Cornell University Press).

Stern, S. (ed.) (1998) *Shining and Other Paths* (Durham, NC: Duke University Press).

Stewart, F. (2002) 'Horizontal Inequalities: A Neglected Dimension of Development,' Working Paper no. 1, Centre for Research on Inequality, Human Security, and Ethnicity, Queen Elizabeth House, University of Oxford.

Stigler, G. (1970) 'The Theory of Economic Regulation,' *Bell Journal of Economics and Management Science*, vol. 2 (Spring), pp. 3–21.

Stokes, S. (1995) *Cultures in Conflict: Social Movements and the State* (Berkeley: University of California Press).

Tanaka, M. (2002) 'Las relaciones entre estado y sociedad en el Perú: destructuración sin reestructuración,' paper written for the UK Department for International Development.

Tanaka, M. (2004) 'Situación y perspectives de los partidos en la Región Andina: el caso peruano,' in International IDEA/Transparencia, *Partidos politicos en la region andina: entre la crisis y el cambio* (Lima: International Idea, Transparencia).

Tanaka, M. (2005) 'Las relaciones entre Estado y sociedad en el Perú: desestructuración sin reestructuración,' in P. Zárate (ed.) *¿Hay lugar para los pobres en el Perú? Las relaciones estado-sociedad y el rol de la cooperación internacional* (Lima: Department for International Development (DFID)).

Távara, J. (2000) 'Privatización y regulación en el sector eléctrico y las telecomunicaciones. Lecciones de la experiencia peruana,' in D. Sulmont and E. Vásquez (eds.), *Modernización empresarial en el Perú* (Lima: Red para el Desarrollo de las Ciencias Sociales en el Perú).

Távara, J. and Diez-Canseco, L. (2003) 'Estabilizando el péndulo: control de fusiones y concentraciones en el Perú,' *Themis Revista de Derecho*, vol. 47 (December), pp. 159–73.

Thorp, R. and Bertram, G. (1978) *Peru, 1890–1977: Growth and Policy in an Open Economy* (London: Macmillan).

Thorp, R. and Zevallos, G. (2002) 'The Economic Policies of the Fujimori Years: A Return to the Past?' Queen Elizabeth House Working Paper no. 83, University of Oxford.

Thurner, M. (1997) *From Two Republics to One Divided: Contradictions of Postcolonial Nationmaking in Andean Peru* (Durham and London: Duke University Press).

Torero, M. and Pascó-Font, A. (2001) 'El impacto social de la privatización y de la regulación de los servicios públicos en el Perú,' Documento de Trabajo no. 35 (Lima: GRADE).

Trivelli, C. and Abler, D. (1997) 'El impacto de la desregulación en el Mercado de tierras,' in E. Gonzalez de Olarte et al., *Perú: el problema agrario en debate. SEPIA IV* (Lima, CEPES-CIES-CIPCA-COINCIDE-CONCYTEC-Embajada Real de los Países Bajos-Ideas-Solidaridad).

Ugaz, F. (1997) 'Dinámica del mercado de tierras y transformaciones en el agro costeño. Los casos de Piura y Huaral,' in E. Gonzales de Olarte, B. Revesz, M. Tapia (eds.), *Perú: el problema agrario en debate. SEPIA VI* (Lima, CEPES-CIES-CIPCA-COINCIDE-CONCYTEC-Embajada Real de los Países Bajos-Ideas-Solidaridad).

UNDP (United Nations Development Program /Programa de Naciones Unidas de Desarrollo) (2004) 'La democracia en América Latina. Hacia una democracia de ciudadanos y ciudadanas' (Buenos Aires: PNUD. www.undp.org).

Unger, M. (2004) 'Human Rights in the Andes: The *Defensoría del Pueblo*,' in J-M. Burt and P. Mauceri (eds.), *Politics in the Andes: Identity, Conflict and Reform* (Pittsburgh, PA: University of Pittsburgh Press).

Valdivia, M., and Ágreda, V. (1994) 'El sistema de comercialización de frutas: los casos del limón, el maracuyá y el mango en el norte del Perú,' in J. Escobal (ed.), *Comercialización agrícola en el Perú* (Lima: GRADE-AID).

Vásquez Huamán, E. (2000) *Estrategias de poder. Grupos económicos en el Perú* (Lima: Centro de Investigación de la Universidad del Pacífico).

Vásquez, E., and Mendizábal, E. (2004) *Los niños ¿primero?* (Lima: Universidad del Pacífico).

Vich, V. (2002) *El caníbal es el Otro: Violencia y cultura en el Perú contemporaneo* (Lima: Instituto de Estudios Peruanos).

Walker, C. (1999) *Smoldering Ashes: Cuzco and the Creation of Republican Peru, 1780-1840* (Durham: Duke University Press).

Washington Office on Latin America (9 September 1991) *Human Rights Determination for Peru* (Washington, DC).

Webb, R. and Fernández Baca, G. (1990) *Perú en números 1990* (Lima: Ed. Cuánto).

Weeks, J. (1985) *Limits to Capitalist Development: The Industrialization of Peru, 1950–80* (Boulder: Westview Press).

World Bank (1998). *Beyond the Washington Consensus: Institutions Matter* (Washington, DC: The World Bank).

Youngers, C. (1994) *After the Autogolpe: Human Rights in Peru and the U.S. Response* (Washington, DC: The Washington Office on Latin America).

Youngers, C. (2000) *Deconstructing Democracy: Peru Under President Alberto Fujimori* (Washington, DC: The Washington Office on Latin America).

Youngers, C.A. (2003) *Violencia política y sociedad civil en el Perú: Historia de la Coordinadora Nacional de Derechos Humanos* (Lima: Instituto de Estudios Peruanos).

Youngers, C.A. and Peacock, S.C. (2002) *Peru's Coordinadora Nacional de Derechos Humanos: A Case Study of Coalition Building* (Washington, DC: The Washington Office on Latin America).

Zas Fritz, J. (2001) 'El sueño obsecado. La descentralización en América Latina' (Lima: Fondo Editorial del Congreso).

Zas Fritz, J. (2004) 'La insistencia de la voluntad. El actual proceso de descentralización y sus antecedents inmediatos' (Lima: Defensoría del Pueblo).

Zegarra Méndez, E. (1999) *El mercado de tierras rurales en el Perú.* Volume I, 'Análisis institucional'. Volume II, 'Análisis económico' (Santiago de Chile: CEPAL-GTZ).

Zizek, S. (2002) *Welcome to the Desert of the Real* (London and New York: Verso).

Index

Printed in the United Kingdom
by Lightning Source UK Ltd.
110434UKS00001B/151-171